LIVING IN
ITALY

Yve Menzies was born in England, but spent most of
her time living and working abroad before settling in
Liguria sixteen years ago. Trained as an interpreter/
translator, she later became a copywriter and
journalist and has had her work published in
England, the United States and the Far East. Author
of *The Complete Book of Starters* (also published by
Robert Hale), she is married to an international
lawyer and has two adult children.

By the same author

The Complete Book of Starters

LIVING IN
ITALY

*The Essential Guide for Property
Purchasers and Residents*

Yve Menzies

ROBERT HALE · LONDON

© Y.M. Muir-Menzies 1987, 1989, 1990, 1991, 1999
First published in Great Britain 1987
Second edition 1989
Third edition 1990
Fourth edition 1991
Paperback edition 1999

ISBN 0 7090 6311 3

Robert Hale Limited
Clerkenwell House
Clerkenwell Green
London EC1R 0HT

2 4 6 8 10 9 7 5 3 1

Typeset in North Wales by
Derek Doyle & Associates, Mold, Flintshire.
Printed in Great Britain by
St Edmundsbury Press Limited, Bury St Edmunds.
Bound by WBC Book Manufacturers Limited, Bridgend.

Contents

Acknowledgements

No one person can be an expert on all aspects of life in Italy and I have certainly benefited from the advice of many people and their specialized knowledge.

I am most grateful to the following people: Signora Bruna Borgogno, dott. Mario Collivecchi, dott. George Pazzi-Axworthy of London, dott. commercialistà Eugenio Prette, geom. Renato Maccario and dott. Renato Viale as well as countless others who have often been a mine of information on rather recondite matters.

If there are any inaccuracies, and I hope there are not, they are entirely my own.

Y.M.M.

Introduction

Since the last edition of this book over seven years ago, Italy has been convulsed by the most notorious political upheaval since the end of the Second World War. As history shows, Italy always comes through such convulsions and settles down to a period of political calm and increased prosperity. However, if one looks deeper into the latest upheaval one sees that, for a brief moment, the Italians were admitting to the world at large that theirs was one of the most corrupt countries in Europe and this admission affected every person who lived in Italy.

Corruption is part and parcel of life in Italy and although the grosser examples are no longer seen, their everyday counterparts are still well entrenched. Italy still has two economies – a white (national) and a black – which costs the European Union a fortune in lost Value Added Tax. At the Maastricht meeting Italy somehow managed to persuade the other members that her black economy should be taken into account when considering the criteria for her entry into the single European currency. Even so it looks as though she will not be able to make the grade. There are those who consider Italy a tremendous supporter of a single currency for Europe, actually looking forward to an outside force controlling her banks and bankers and perhaps even her national economy. Signora Bonino in Brussels certainly gives that impression though whether her daily histrionics are going to do the trick remains to be seen.

Italy's way of ensuring the country's entry is to impose a 'once-and-for-all tax' on the already over-burdened taxpayer. The country has had one of these taxes before when the Government took 0.6 per cent off all credit balances at the bank. One thing is certain – a lot of people will manage not to pay it in exactly the same way they avoided paying the time before.

Italy is a beautiful country with people to match and yet, sooner or later, all foreigners begin to realize that there is another less attractive side to the country and its inhabitants such as the charming neighbour who has no qualms about denouncing you to the local authority for some minor, or even major, building anomaly.

Most shocking of all to the British is their attitude to animals. Many Italians will happily abandon a dog simply because they don't want it on holiday or it has grown too big for their apartment. '*Non hanno anima*' was how one woman explained it away to me.

Almost as shocking is their inability to pay income tax which makes Italy one of the most expensive countries in Europe, although visitors often have the advantage of a favourable rate of exchange. No Italian can understand that the Government must get its money from somewhere and this is why Italian petrol and diesel are among the most expensive in Europe, why every demand to a government authority has to be made on *carta bollata* or 'stamped paper' which at the time of the last edition of this book was a mere 5,000 lire and is now 20,000 (a million lire equalling approximately £350). Taxes for clearing rubbish, for getting building permits, for having an insurance policy (except on your life) and for virtually any contract have gone up four or five hundred per cent since 1991. Many kinds of transaction must be carried out through a *notaio*, occasionally called a *notaro*. He is a public servant whose first duty is to the Government and thereafter to you. Notaries' fees have gone up though they probably earn little more – it's the Government who get the increase. Anything reported to the *carabinieri* or the police, such as the loss of a wallet and/or credit cards, involves using *carta bollata* at 20,000 lire a time. And yet the Italians still don't understand they have brought this form of heavy taxation upon themselves.

Italy has almost fifty per cent of the world's art, much of it poorly looked after, poorly managed and often, as has been seen by the London auction houses' scandals, much of it illegally exported. There is a tendency to think of all Italians as artistic connoisseurs, which is rather stupid when one sees everyday some of the most hideous modern buildings in Europe to say nothing of the sort of glass and ceramics available in many Italian shops. Italian souvenirs are no worse than those of most countries but they are certainly no better. Venice, the home of some of the most beautiful glass in the world, produces a great deal which is positively nasty. There are shops which deal in nothing but 'favours' for baptisms, weddings and the like where most of the items are made of coloured tulle, plastic dolls, silver paper and ribbon and cost a fortune. The only thing of solid worth in these shops is the sugared almonds. The sort of art one sees at Carneval time, if art it can be called, is far more typical of Italy, at any time in her history, than the work of Piero della Francesca or Bellini. To be a museum curator requires a long, hard academic slog and the pay is not brilliant. To work as a guard in a museum, however, requires no qualifications at all, and many Italians who work as guards during the day are employed as waiters in the evening; the first job pays extremely poorly but gives social security and pension rights, while the second job is often not 'declared' and its small salary is supplemented by unlimited tips.

The Italians do not fork out easily to repair or keep up their national monuments or art treasures. The artistic treasure houses of Rome, Florence or Venice have to look abroad for sustenance. Commercial interests are the greatest pollution threat to Venice and yet the Venetians appear to do little to counteract this threat. Their committees are a little different from the average Italian city committee in that the odd foreigner serves on them. This is only a case of paying lip-service to the foreigners who finance so much of the repair work. Too often Italians become resentful of interfering foreigners and complain they know nothing of Italian life or their way of doing things. I know of one very famous monument left to the Italian State which until recently had slowly gone downhill. When the family concerned tried to intervene and when British organizations offered money and help they were not exactly welcomed. Only international pressure has forced the State to put its pride in its pocket and admit that others may know better.

Family still counts for a lot in Italy. Even a brother-in-law or a cousin will get help when in trouble. Very often this help is entirely material; because of the lack of a welfare state, particularly in the south, it can be a question of family solidarity when a person goes to hospital or has trouble with the authorities.

Although everyone is equal before the law there is, nevertheless, one law for foreigners and another for Italians. This is almost entirely due to the fact that Italians can talk themselves out of situations and they can negotiate their way out of paying fines. Most foreigners find their normally fluent, or perhaps not so fluent, Italian deserts them in such circumstances and they feel at a disadvantage. Italy is a land of fines, the *multa*. If you come from a country where the only fine you pay is for a traffic offence you will be surprised at what the Italians have dreamt up. Fines are all codified and there are state police (who rarely impose fines), municipal police (the most common source of parking fines), the *carabinieri* (the most common source of traffic fines) and the provincial police (the most common source of building fines). The local authority can impose building fines as well as other sorts, ENEL or other electricity companies can, Telecom Italia can, so can the companies which supply water. Many of the people who impose these fines work on a percentage basis so it pays him (or her) to drive around looking for trouble. Building sites are a wonderful place for such work. An innocent owner of land on which he employs workmen to build a house can find he has run up fines of millions of lire without knowing the cause. This is where being Italian comes in useful, since no Italian will pay such fines without an enormous fight. I was fined almost a million lire because ENEL's wire giving electricity to my building site had fallen onto a Telecom Italia wire. We were all innocent and I most of all since I had nothing to do with the wiring. Eventually after a great deal of shouting and threats on both sides they let the matter drop. Righteous indignation and a fast Highland temper carried the day.

By and large, the Italians are eminently likeable and very forgivable; it is difficult to be angry with them for long. They have no rancour and will rarely hold your bad behaviour or quick temper against you. This likeability is their trump card and, in a sense, their undoing. There is a tendency not to take them seriously and to label them romantics. Nothing could be further from the truth. They are extremely realistic and usually very hard workers, particularly when working for their own account. Their gaiety often covers a core of sadness but in spite of this they appear to be eternal optimists. It is the northern Europeans who are the romantics, particularly when, fuddled with too much sun and far too much wine, they do not see Italy or the Italians in their true and rather more complex light.

Italians should be recognized as the most human of human beings – the ideal type, if you like – and much respected for being so. Compared with most other countries in Europe, mostly because of its people, Italy is probably the nearest you will get to an ideal place in Europe.

1
An Identity Card of Italy

Geographical

Italy is a long country – the distance from the most northerly border with Switzerland to the toe is about 1500 km in a car, rather less for a bird. Strangely Italy has a similar population to Great Britain, 55 million and more or less the same area, 260,000 sq.km. However, there the similarity ends. Most of the country is given over to mountains – Italy shares Mont Blanc and the Matterhorn with her neighbours – and there are only three really flat plains in the whole country. The most important is the Po Plain which covers a large part of northern Italy and contains much of her important agricultural land along with a large percentage of her industry. Milan can be said to be its capital. The other two plains, the Maremma on the seaside of Tuscany and Lazio (near Rome), and the flat lands of Apulia in the heel of Italy are both agricultural, except for the several important Apulian ports such as Taranto, Bari and Brindisi. Mountainous areas are also a major geographical feature: the Apennines divide the country into east and west (and are irritatingly difficult to cross unless you are very lucky in your destination), and there are the Dolomites, the Alps which separate Italy from France, Switzerland, Austria and what was Yugoslavia but is now Slovenia. There are important volcanoes in both Campania, especially Vesuvius near Naples and Mount Etna in Sicily. The Ligurian Alps along the Riviera act as a protective barrier to what otherwise would be a north European climate. On the Ligurian coast it rarely freezes, even in mid-winter, but ten miles back into the mountains the weather can be horribly different.

One other geographical oddity should be mentioned. The famous Italian lakes such as Maggiore, Garda and Como are formed from Alpine waters which cannot reach the sea. Even in high summer they make for very cool bathing. The scenery is

11

extremely beautiful and this part of Italy has long been famous for tourism. The downside is that in winter it is extremely foggy, damp and cold, though there are those who find this rather romantic.

Italy has thousands of kilometres of coastline, alas, not all of it particularly attractive. This is more to do with geography than with an inability to maximize sandy beaches. The most famous parts of Italy for seaside holidays are Liguria, the area around Amalfi and Sorrento, parts of Lazio (for those in Rome) around Ancona, Rimini and the Gargano Peninsula. There are famous resorts such as Lido di Jesolo near Venice, Porto Ercole and Portofino but mostly the seaside can be disappointing.

Recently, perhaps as a result of the sheer length of coastline and the impossibility of guarding it efficiently, Italy has become notorious for drug running from both North Africa and the Eastern Mediterranean. Liguria is one of the European centres for this criminal trade with concomitant interest from the *carabinieri* and the drug police. Every customs crossing has its sniffer dogs, as does every port and yachting marina. It is a fallacy to believe that you can have soft drugs in small quantity for your own use. There is no stipulation as to how little is considered a small quantity, and no way of proving that it is for personal use and not for sale. If you are taking certain drugs for medical reasons you should have a letter from your doctor saying so. It is far better not to tangle with the law in a strange country where you do not have a perfect knowledge of their language.

Skiing and winter sports are well catered for and each year the resorts improve. The two most chic resorts are Courmayeur in the Aosta region and Cortina d'Ampezzo in the Dolomites, near Belluno. There are hundreds of others dotted all over the mountainous areas of the country. No short cuts are taken so far as safety is concerned since the insurance companies would refuse to pay if ski-lifts and the like were not kept up to scratch. However, emergency procedures can vary from one skiing resort to another and it pays to investigate before going on holiday to any particular place. Good medical insurance is absolutely essential when skiing in Italy and should be bought in your own country since Italian ski insurance is based on what social security does not pay for.

Political

Italy is a republic and a modern democracy. It was an early member of the European Union and considers itself the fifth most important industrial power in the world. Most who live in Italy find this difficult to believe given that they can only provide householders throughout the country with a mere 3 kilowatts of electricity each. This deficiency has been put down to a lack of raw materials: Italy has neither oil nor coal and is anti-nuclear power. Therefore, most electricity is bought from France and Switzerland. Then there is the question of water supply which, in the country districts, is poor and not always drinkable. This is mainly due to lack of investment in filtration plants and filters at delivery points. In the towns this is less of a problem. Sewage is dealt with in nineteenth-century fashion in many parts of the country and although they may brag about their clean beaches (mostly true) the sewage goes elsewhere, inland, to be treated in a very unmodern way.

Italy's world position figure has been arrived at by accounting for their black economy as well as the legal one, an option apparently not open to the other industrial powers. It is this same black economy which is being used to fulfil the Maastricht criteria for joining the single European currency.

In 1948, the Italian Constitution gave the country a President every seven years, along with a Chamber of Deputies (Parliament) and a Senate who both sit for a maximum of five years. This time limit has not proved a problem for Italy – the country has had some fifty or so prime ministers in fifty or so years.

All Italians have the vote at 21, but must be 25 to vote for the Senate. A Member of Parliament must be 25 years old before he can be elected, and a Senator must be 40.

The President is elected *not* by universal suffrage but by a Joint Session of Senators, Deputies and regional representatives. In the past, the election of the President was often the stage for vaunting ambition and much in-fighting. After the election of the very gentle and honest Sardinian, Signor Cossiga, some years ago, who was elected in record time, Presidential elections have become somehow quieter and more gentlemanly. Most Italians would be hard put to tell you the name of the current President.

On a local level Italy is divided into regions, provinces, cities and municipalities or *comuni*. There are 21 regions divided into 104 provinces as below.

Regions	Provinces
Abruzzo	l'Aquila, Chieti, Pescara
Basilicata	Teramo, Matera, Potenza
Calabria	Catanzaro, Cosenza, Crotone, Reggio Calabria, Vibo Valentia

Campania	Avellino, Benevento, Caserta, Napoli, Salerno
Emilia-Romagna	Bologna, Ferrara, Forlî, Modena, Piacenza, Parma, Ravenna, Reggio Emilia, Rimini
Friuli-Venezia-Giulia	Gorizia, Pordenone, Trieste, Udine
Lazio	Frosinone, Latina, Rieti, Roma, Viterbo
Liguria	Genova, Imperia, La Spezia, Savona
Lombardia (Lombardy)	Bergamo, Brescia, Como, Cremona, Lecco, Lodi, Mantova, Milano, Pavia, Sondrio, Varese
Marche (The Marches)	Ancona, Ascoli Piceno, Macerata, Pesaro e Urbino
Molise	Campobasso, Isernia
Piemonte (Piedmont)	Alessandria, Asti, Biella, Cuneo, Novara, Torino, Verbano-Cusio-Ossola, Vercelli
Puglia (Apulia)	Bari, Brindisi, Foggia, Lecce, Taranto
Sardegna (Sardinia)	Cagliari, Nuoro, Oristano, Sassari
Sicilia (Sicily)	Agrigento, Caltanissetta, Catania, Enna, Messina, Palermo, Ragusa, Siracusa, Trapani
Toscana (Tuscany)	Arezzo, Firenze (Florence), Grosseto, Livorno, Lucca, Massa Carrara, Pisa, Pistoia, Prato, Siena
Trentino-Alto Adige	Bolzano, Trento
Umbria	Perugia, Terni
Val d'Aosta	Aosta
Veneto	Belluno, Padova (Padua), Rovigo, Treviso, Venezia (Venice), Verona, Vicenza

Motor vehicles no longer carry provincial letters as in the past. Vehicle registration has been centralized and so it is no longer necessary to change the number of a Milan-registered car to that of the new owner's province. It is necessary to change only the name and address. However, for postal purposes, it is still necessary to use the right letters for the various provinces preceded by the *codice postale* known as C.A.P. in Italian. For a full list of these abbreviations, see Appendix J.

2
Italy Past and Present

It is by no means essential to have a profound knowledge of Italian history to enjoy living there but it is certainly a help to have some acquaintance with her past, if only to understand the country and its people today. In any event, for the average visitor or foreign resident, 'history', after the fall of the Roman Empire, begins around 1200 or 1300 with the Guelph and Ghibelline Wars which devastated the whole area.

By 1250 the whole Italian peninsula and in particular what is today central Italy, was divided into Guelph or Ghibelline factions. The Guelphs were the party of the Pope and supported strict religious observance and the increasingly wealthy middle class in the City States such as Venice, Amalfi, Pisa and Genoa. The Ghibellines were supported by the minor nobility who in turn supported the Emperor of the day and his state machine. They were far more tolerant both intellectually and of other religions. So far as their wars were concerned, there was nothing to choose between them. There are still people today who consider the Tuscans very quarrelsome as a result of these endless disputes. Boiling oil, death by the sword and total destruction of everything by the winning side were the order of the day. The Guelph castle of the Ricasoli family (of Chianti fame) was systematically dismantled stone by stone by the Sienese Ghibellines only to be rebuilt systematically stone by stone a few years later. As all guides will tell you, the Guelph castles have standard square crenellations whereas the Ghibelline castles are decorated with a swallow-tail balustrade.

Although the country areas suffered greatly as a result of these wars the City States were much less affected. During this time, Venice acquired the beginnings of her overseas Empire, in her own phrase, 'a half and one quarter of the Roman Empire', and Genoa became a decided threat to La Serenissimma having destroyed Pisa as an independent republic. It was to be almost a hundred years before Venice was able to annihilate her rival once and for all. In the country areas and the smaller towns the situation was different and the populace was war weary. The Church stepped in, promising permanent peace and were gladly accepted; the Papal State was born. This survived for almost five hundred years, by which time the inhabitants had become extremely disillusioned. Emilia-Romagna remains, to this day, one of the most anti-clerical areas of Italy. The Marche also belonged to the Pope and its people acted as his tax gatherers. As a result, it is architecturally one of the most beautiful parts of Italy, most of its assets having been built on the inhabitants' 'percentage'.

Surprisingly, the Great Plague in 1347 did not halt the general prosperity of the Italian peninsula. There were one third fewer mouths to feed, fewer peasants to live off the same area of land. People and states were still able to go to war and they fought mostly against each other, until a real enemy appeared in the form of Spain, and stayed for centuries.

One does not have to be a student of history to see that the Italians are far better at being merchants, artists, sailors, scientists, anything other than soldiers. Yet they still waged war for hundreds of years against each other, or together against the French, the Turks, the Spaniards who ruled in Naples and the South, and finally the Austrians who came into Lombardy and its capital, Milan, as well as Tuscany and later the Trentino. No wonder they felt desperate. Enter Napoleon Bonaparte to administer the *coup de grâce*.

Napoleon as King of Italy divided the country among his relations and settled down to pillaging and reforming. Much of Italy's greatest art was removed to the Louvre in Paris. The Pope was taken to Fontainbleau as a prisoner and Rome was divested of some of her finest statues and pictures. University libraries were removed wholesale to France and never returned.

The Venetian Republic and what remained of her Empire was dissolved and St. Mark's Horses, among much other art, were carted off to Paris. A lot of Italians joined Napoleon's victorious armies; at the beginning, they did so voluntarily, but in the end they were conscripted and sent to Poland and Russia where they died in the retreat from Moscow in 1812. History, as we all know, has a nasty habit of repeating itself and Italians died in their thousands in Russia during the Second World War. As luck would have it, when Napoleon was beaten at Waterloo, another oppressor, already well known in other parts of Italy, came to rule what had been Venice and her Empire on the mainland. Austria hung on to parts of Italy until as late as 1918.

The *Risorgimento* and the unification of Italy is taught as one of the glories of Italian history. However, in Italy, nothing is quite what

it appears. Since the Congress of Vienna in 1815, numerous factions
in Italy had been conspiring to build a United Italy under the House
of Savoy, which was the oldest reigning house in Europe. No one
was happy at the clock being turned back as though Napoleon and
his marshals had never existed. The revolution of 1848 which fired
most of Europe, started in Naples in January of that year, as a result
of which the Bourbon King was forced to grant a constitution to his
subjects. By 1850 the Kingdom of Piedmont which included
Sardinia, Savoy and Liguria was one of the most advanced states in
Europe. Count Camillo Cavour became Prime Minister in 1853 and
from that date commenced the true unification of Italy. He openly
quarrelled with the Austrians, reproaching them for their harsh rule
in Lombardy which had started years before with the Austrian
General, Haynau, whipping the women in the streets of Brescia. He
also opened Piedmont to over thirty thousand exiles and, as a result,
much of northern Italy wished to collaborate with him.

Cavour's greatest coup was to get Napoleon III of France to help
oust the Austrians from northern Italy. During the ensuing
campaign Napoleon came to believe that Cavour also intended to
include the Papal States in his unification scheme. This was not the
case. As a result of his devout Catholicism and also of his fear of a
too-powerful neighbour, he called for an armistice shortly after the
Austrian defeat at the battle of Solferino. It was here that Henri
Dunant, a Swiss onlooker, appalled at the carnage, decided to found
an organization to alleviate the suffering of soldiers and civilians
alike in time of war. He called it The Red Cross, taking its name
from the reversed colours of the Swiss flag.

After this short but deadly war, only half the territory had been
won. Venetia and the Papal States remained untouched. Of their own
volition, much of Tuscany voted to join Piedmont. In 1860 Cavour
offered Nice and the Savoy to Napoleon III in return for this annexation and in March 1860 the treaty was signed. The Kingdom of
Piedmont, soon to be Italy, had doubled in size overnight.

Foreigners are often unaware that Cavour's plans for the unification of Italy did not extend to the southern part of the peninsula.
The Kingdom of Naples, sometimes known as the Kingdom of the
Two Sicilies, made up of today's Naples, Campania, Apulia,
Basilicata, Calabria and Sicily, was taken by Garibaldi against the
express wishes of Cavour. Born in Nice when it was Italian,
Garibaldi had been a sailor and an adventurer in South America
during the wars of independence there. However, the amazing
success of Garibaldi's soldiers made the Prime Minister change his
mind and send royal troops to consolidate the victory. Although
Venice together with her hinterland and Rome remained to be

conquered, Victor Emmanuel was proclaimed by an Italian Parliament in Turin 'King of Italy, by the Grace of God and by the Will of the People'. It is true that whenever there was a performance of a Verdi opera anywhere in Italy, but particularly in Austrian held territory, the audience would always call for the composer, VERDI, a code for Vittorio Emanuele, Re d'Italia.

Complete reunification came five years later when Italy, realizing that Austria and Prussia were certain to go to war over the Schleswig-Holstein question, signed an alliance with the Prussians. Austria, forced to fight on two fronts, one against Prussia and one against Italy, signed Venetia over to France's Napoleon III. In the event Austria was defeated at Sadowa and the Italians, who had taken advantage of Austria's vulnerability and declared war against her, were defeated by them at Custozza. Nevertheless, peace was restored and Venice and all Venetia went to the Kingdom of Italy.

Rome was won in 1870 when, as a result of the defeat of France in the Franco-Prussian War, the French withdrew their garrison protecting the Pope. The King of Italy issued an ultimatum, smartly followed by an army at the gates of Rome. Token resistance was offered before Rome gave in. Thereafter, a plebiscite confirmed the annexation to the Kingdom by 133,000 out of 160,000 votes.

This last victory of the new Kingdom of Italy engendered the opprobrium of all Catholic Europe. Italy had stipulated that the Pope was to retain both his sovereign status and the Vatican, and was to receive an annual income to compensate for the loss of the Papal states. The Pope, who considered himself a prisoner in his palace, refused outright to acknowledge the loss of the Papal States and would have nothing to do with the usurpers. Thus, until well after the First World War, Italy was divided into two conflicting groups, one faithful to the Church and its Pope, the other liberal and occasionally anti-clerical.

The Pope had many followers, for at the time Italy was far from being a politically sophisticated country. Every election had more abstainers than voters. This was due not to ignorance but to the lack of a political past; at the time, men had to be 25 years old, literate and have a moderate income before they were entitled to vote. For more or less the same reason, the absence of a parliamentary precedent, the government displayed a distinct lack of zeal. There were notable exceptions, of course, such as Francesco Crispi who ruled over Italy's politics for some twenty years, and Giovanni Giolitti who was in parliament from 1882 until 1924 and who, at 82, publicly protested against the methods of the Fascist regime then new to power.

Italy was a member of the Triple Alliance with Austria and

Prussia when the First World War broke out. She remained neutral for a time but, as a result of overtures and promises from the British and the French to help her recover the Trentino, Dalmatia and Istria, she declared war on Austria. She soon found she was fighting Germany, a far more serious enemy, as well as Turkey and Bulgaria.

The Great War for Italy was a long and bitter one, fought over extremely difficult mountainous terrain with many defeats and much loss of life. There were a dozen battles on the River Isonzo alone. The rout at Caporetto in 1917 was almost the end. Reinforcements were brought in, Generals were changed and Italy went on the defensive, repelling an Austrian attack on the River Piave. From this time onwards the tide turned in their favour and an armistice was signed on the 4th November 1918 at Vittorio Veneto. Badly organized, badly supplied, often badly led, the Italian soldier was at his bravest and most heroic in these alpine battles.

A year later, under the Treaty of Trianon, Italy got most of the provinces for which she had fought for so long. Peace, however, was a bitter deception for the soldier, who came straight from the battlefield to unemployment, inflation and social unrest.

Many Italians will tell you today that at the beginning of the 1920s there was a straight choice between communism and fascism and that the latter seemed the better of the two at the time. Although, like so many inventions, fascism originated in Italy, it was the German variety that the world came to know better.

Benito Mussolini started off as a socialist journalist and in 1919 founded in Milan the *Fasci di Combattimento* (The Fighting Group) whose members were known as Fascists. With clever presentation and much publicity he managed for some time to persuade Italy that things were going well and would get even better. The conquest of Ethiopia proved this for some, though for others it was a hollow victory over people unable to fight back.

More as a matter of political expediency than for reasons of faith, Mussolini had his children baptized into the Catholic Church in 1923 and shortly after re-married his wife in a religious ceremony. None of this stopped him having a mistress.

Nevertheless, it was the beginning of his and Italy's *rapprochement* with the Pope. Over the next five years negotiations took place reconciling the Church and State. As compensation for the loss of the Papal States, the Church received a lump sum and the Vatican came into being as a sovereign state. Roman Catholicism became the state religion of Italy, and the Italian government (i.e. Mussolini) was to approve the appointment of all bishops and cardinals. To all intents and purposes, the Catholic church in Italy had become, if not Fascist, then at least pro-Fascist.

Foolishly, Mussolini took Italy to war once more for no other reasons than his own self-importance and to please Hitler. Earlier, in 1938, the Italians had become disgusted with the anti-Semitic measures their leader had taken, again to please his German ally. A naturally tolerant people, they disliked the break with the centuries-old tradition of a haven in Italy for Jews, particularly in Piedmont. Many Italians disregarded the new racial laws, often to their own disadvantage or even their life. Italian Jews, in any event, were probably the most assimilated in all Europe.

The Italians and Germans were strange bedfellows. Mussolini constantly told the people he was 'always right', exhorting them to live dangerously, never to stop, and to share his conviction that one day as a wolf was worth a lifetime as a sheep. The Italians, however, were not interested enough in Rome's imperial past to want to emulate it. They are not natural soldiers and do not fight without a motive. Mussolini gave neither motive nor armament. Once again, woefully supplied and woefully led, they suffered defeat after defeat and finally Sicily was invaded by the Allies.

On the night of the 25th July 1943, King Victor Emmanuel (the same King as in the First World War) issued orders for the arrest of Mussolini and 800 of his closest associates. Marshal Pietro Badoglio was put in charge of the government. On the 27th the Fascist hierarchy dissolved the party and Fascism died quietly overnight.

Although 'liberated' Italy changed sides and became a co-belligerent of the Allies, the country suffered appallingly at the hands of the retreating army and/or occupying Germans. No one, it would seem, had bothered to work out the consequences of changing sides so suddenly. The Germans were insensate with fury and took it out on the civilian population with extreme brutality.

Mussolini was 'kidnapped' by Nazi gliders from his hotel prison in the Gran Sasso National Park in the Abruzzi mountains and founded, again under Hitler's aegis, the Republic of Salo on the shores of Lake Garda. This was simply a vassal of Germany. It seemed there was nothing that Mussolini would not do to impress Hitler, even to the extent of executing his own son-in-law and former Foreign Minister, Ciano. Later, when the war was almost over and he was escaping to Switzerland, the *Duce*, as he was still called, was captured by non-communist partisans who in turn handed him over to the communists who shot him.

The end of Fascism in Italy was soon accompanied by the end of the monarchy. Victor Emmanuel abdicated in favour of his son, Umberto, who was to be the last King of Italy, reigning only forty-six days. Twenty six million people voted in the referendum and by a majority of a little under two million a Republic was declared.

Italy after the war was in a catastrophic state. Of her railways 8000 km had been destroyed, together with a third of all bridges, 60 per cent of all goods wagons, 80 per cent of passenger coaches and 90 per cent of her mercantile fleet. In Florence, the Nazi commandant, Kesselring, had spared only the Ponte Vecchio. Ports had been destroyed, cities bombed to bits or bombarded from the sea. Since much of the north had been liberated by partisans, many of them communists, much of the administration was in communist hands. There was a great deal of summary justice dealt out before the new government could get Italy back onto a more normal course. A temporary agreement was reached with Tito's Yugoslavia whereby what is today's Friuli-Venezia-Giulia was partitioned between the two sides. Those in the eastern half still remember fifty years on, how hollow victory seemed at that time. They had suffered Germans, Austrians, Cossacks and Nazis only to find themselves under the communist Yugoslavs.

Out of all this chaos, physical, administrative and political, arrived Alcide de Gasperi, possibly the most able politician since Cavour and Giolitti. He had been a deputy for the Trentino at the Austrian Parliament in Vienna before the First World War. A Christian Democrat by inclination, he kept his head during Fascism and avoided certain *confino* by becoming a librarian in the Vatican. In the early post-war years he endeavoured to maintain an anti-Fascist alliance which involved governing with the socialists and even communists. However, in 1948 the Christian Democrats had their first overall victory and de Gasperi was Prime Minister until his death in 1953. It has been said that perhaps de Gasperi was to a degree responsible for the growth of corruption in political circles in Italy since he failed to notice its birth during his ministry. As has been said before corruption is part and parcel of Italian life and even the nicest and most honest Italians tend to think in a somewhat corrupt fashion when in trouble or when they want a university place for their child or a job for their brother or friend. Before one condemns this outright, one should remember that the old school tie, political affiliations and friendships can still be important factors in getting a good job in the Great Britain or United States of today, and seats on Government committees and quangos are still in the gift of ministers and politicians.

Until a few years ago, the Christian Democrats were Italy's most important political party and there are still parts of the country which remain staunchly loyal to their precepts. However, although perhaps the socialists were more involved in the corruption and sleaze allegations, the Christian Democrats were not spared and their portion of the vote has plummeted as severely as that of the socialists. Bettino

Craxi, a socialist and Italy's longest serving Prime Minister, now hiding in yet another country which has no extradition treaty with Italy, was judged, *in absentia*, to have been the most corrupt Prime Minister ever. Yet, Giulio Andreotti, who must have the world record for having been Prime Minister so often, may also have the dubious honour of being the only Prime Minister to be a paid-up member of the Mafia. He lost his parliamentary immunity and went on trial. It is believed he will die before the verdict is known.

The assassinations of several upright anti-Mafia judges and policemen in Sicily aroused the conscience of ordinary Italians. Little happened, for a time, until an investigating judge in Milan came across bribes being paid to people in the local administration. Untangling the sorry business led to further bribes being discovered, the involvement of politicians reaching so high as to include a Prime Minister; and so the campaign which came to be known as *mani pulite* or 'Clean Hands' came into being. Eventually, almost the whole of Italy was involved; even one of the judges, de Pietro, was accused, though promptly acquitted.

Long prison sentences and huge fines were imposed. A great number of people, including top industrialists, committed suicide rather than face trial. Internationally known designers such as Armani were accused of bribing the *Guardia di Finanza* (the Financial Police). He did not deny it, but said it was essential to pay them to keep in business. Given that Italy demands more than 120 separate taxes from its companies (as compared, for instance, with next-door-neighbour Austria's 24), one can understand Signor Armani's stance. It is also said that if Italians were to pay all the taxes imposed on them, they would need 150 per cent of what they earn.

The virtual demise of the socialists and Christian Democrats was good news for the old Communist Party now called the PDS or *Parti Democratico della Sinistra* and, to a certain extent, for the neo-fascists, whose ranks boast Alessandra Mussolini, the *Duce*'s granddaughter.

Lega Nord, led by Umberto Bossi, wants a new part of Italy called Padania to be separate from the rest of the peninsula. It would prevent the pouring of hard-earned northern money into the southern part of Italy which is still bitterly poor and would ban foreign immigrants from the old eastern bloc. Where the cheap labour would come from is anyone's guess. It is a party which panders to the electorate's basest instincts, gaining sympathy from those who have seen the centre of Turin become 'southern' and much of the workforce, building trade and above all the administration become Calabrese, Pugliese or Sicilian. No matter that the people who complain most did not want to do this sort of work themselves.

Lega Nord has its own paper *'La Padania'* where even the weather forecast ends at Perugia and Rome is firmly put among the rest of Europe's capitals. It is difficult to say whether or not Padania includes Tuscany, Umbria and the Marche. Almost certainly it does since Tuscany is a prosperous area and the two others are more or less on the same geographical, if not financial, level. One day these early news-sheets will probably be eagerly collected for their curiosity value.

For a short time Italy had a 'media' Prime Minister in the shape of Silvio Berlusconi who owned most of Italy's television stations. He used his television stations morning, noon and night to advertise his own political party, *Forza Italia*, and won. The Italians believed he had no axe to grind since he was rich already, owning things like the *Standa* chain, football clubs, TV stations, but in fact he wanted power and was prepared to pay heavily for it. It is against the law for a Minister or Prime Minister to have active business interests while in office. Silvio Berlusconi never once let the reins of his business leave his hands. Now, he too, is under investigation.

However, the most interesting aspect of Silvio Berlusconi's time as Prime Minister was that he needed the support of *Lega Nord*, which had approximately ten per cent of the vote, in order to remain in power. As a result *Lega Nord* had five of its members in the Italian Cabinet which is almost unbelievable when you consider their small numbers. All things considered, they are probably a party to watch in the future.

Today, as this is being written, the newest crisis is Albania which, deep down, the Italians regard almost as a colony. They like it less that so many Albanians should treat Italy as a second home. Signor Prodi, at one time considered an unlikely Prime Minister, is on the way to being a long serving one. Italian soldiers are acting as peacekeepers both in Bosnia and Albania and doing the job superlatively well. Naturally friendly people and great lovers of children they treat the locals as friends rather than as potential murderers. John Simpson, the BBC Foreign Affairs Editor believes the UN Secretary General regards them as the finest peacekeeping force ever and makes a mental note to book them for any future emergency. Considering their history this is quite a change. Whereas in the past they were not always brilliant soldiers, perhaps because they were forced to fight often against their will, they now have a role much more in keeping with their character – that of keeping the peace. Most Italians prefer it that way and probably so do most of the rest of Europe.

The economy, of course, is still in dire straits and likely to remain so for some time to come.

3
Leaving for Italy

It is quite amazing to discover how many people move from their own country to another without making the slightest preparation for what is bound to be a different way of life. They visit a country on holiday and decide, there and then, to buy a property or an apartment and set up house. If they have a grain of common sense they will at least make this move to a holiday home and if they are rather more careful they will rent a place on long lease for holiday living only, before deciding 'this is it'. Some do not speak a word of the language of their chosen country whilst others manage by regressing to their infancy in grammar, vocabulary and subject matter. This state of affairs can, and often does, obtain for many years.

Italian, except for the verbs, is not a difficult language and it is considerably richer than most foreigners think. There are several tenses which do not exist in English or French and slotting yourself into the state of mind in which you would need or want to use such tenses is one of the more trying aspects of learning the language. On an everyday basis you can make yourself understood quite easily but virtually any educated Italian speaks his language rather better than his British counterpart speaks English, and few short cuts are taken. Though there is a rich vein of slang in Italian, it doesn't mean the subjunctive tenses are optional. They are there to be used and used they are.

So, if you are serious about living in Italy on either a temporary or permanent basis, start learning Italian either by evening class lessons, by Linguaphone or similar methods or by private lessons. It will serve you well once you arrive because not all civil servants speak English and certainly your neighbours will not. It will also help you make friends which, as you will have left many of your own behind, would be a good thing.

If you leave learning the language until you reach Italy, you will still need lessons of some sort or the other and you should allow at

24

least a year before you will have any real fluency. English is one of the easier languages from which to learn Italian; I learnt from French, the grammar of which is totally unlike Italian, and spent, much against my will, five lessons learning about the continuous present which is something I was brought up with in English. I also had the further disadvantage of speaking relatively good Spanish and went through a dreadful period where I spoke neither Spanish nor Italian. Even after more than twelve years of speaking Italian I still tend to pronounce new words with a Spanish stress rather than an Italian one.

It is most important to consult the right people before leaving the UK. It is essential that the advice you get, from your lawyer and/or accountant, is not only up to date but given by someone who has a good knowledge of the laws of both countries. There are in the UK lawyers and accountants who have this knowledge, and if your own advisers do not, they should be encouraged to seek it from such sources as Italian banks in London, the Law Society and the Institute of Chartered Accountants all of whom will suggest suitable people. It is very dangerous to get separate advice in each country from people who have no knowledge of the other country's laws. On no account should you believe that, being members of the European Union, Italy and the UK are likely to have much the same laws. It simply isn't so.

For instance, ostensibly there is no longer any exchange control between EU member states, but Italy still has a form of exchange control by limiting the amount you can send at any one time without permission and by questioning you when you want to send money to the USA, Switzerland or any obvious tax haven. They cannot forbid your sending money abroad but they can make it a long process and such transfers are best made directly from the UK to their ultimate destination. Incidentally, there are no longer non-resident accounts for people from EU member nations.

Even if you intend leaving the UK for good, you may not wish to take all your assets or, if you do, to take them to Italy. Indeed, you would be mad if you did. Highly skilled professional advice is needed about this, particularly from a tax point of view. It is an absolute rule that you must never accept advice from kind friends who have organized their lives in a way which they say is ideal (for them). No two people have the same lifestyles or the same problems and you cannot apply their solutions to your needs. It is true that there is a sort of flexibility of thought in both legal and financial matters which is far more akin to British thinking than is, say, the very formalist approach in France, but there is a hidden danger in all this. In Italy, this flexibility can often stem from a desire to avoid complications or even to seem to be of help, and such an approach to dealings with the Revenue in the UK is pretty useless. Worse than this laxity is real laziness which I have recently come across. I had a VAT problem which I wanted solved once and for all since I import a great deal of plants from the UK and, worse, from the Channel Islands, which are not part of the EU. The VAT official had next to him a truly vast tome which obviously held the answer, but he was not going to open it. An Italian civil servant, he actually told me to forget about this particular knotty VAT situation and to 'lose' any profit and VAT in my accounts. He even said my accountant could help, a remark which did not please when I repeated it to the gentleman concerned! In the end I decided to import only from EU countries. Never, ever, become trapped into any form of tax evasion or dishonesty. On purely practical grounds you will never be fluent enough to wriggle out of the problem; more importantly why be dishonest in your new country when you would never seriously consider being so at home?

One of the most important things to get clear in your mind is your future tax position in the UK and whether, although you may spend very little time in the UK, you may still be liable for UK tax. The problems here vary from the most simple (leaving the UK for good with all your assets) to the most complex (thinking you are non-resident in the UK for tax purposes when the Revenue thinks otherwise). This is something you must discuss with your accountant in order to take advantage of arrangements which are available to you. Remember, for example, that people who are non-resident in the UK for tax purposes are treated differently so far as Capital Gains Tax is concerned and it can be to your advantage to use these allowances. Also it pays to investigate with your accountant the desirability of becoming non-resident before selling certain UK assets.

Domicile is another minefield. In English law, the word does not have the same meaning as 'residence'; but the Italian *domicilio* or even *dimora* should be translated as 'residence' rather than 'domicile' unless it is part of the phrase *elezione di domicilio speciale*, when, coupled with the context, it can take on a legal meaning. The odds are that you were born with, and still have today, an English or Scottish domicile and it requires a deliberate intention on your part to shed that domicile so that Italy henceforth becomes the place in which you intend to live for the rest of your life. The point is most important because Inheritance Tax in the UK is based on domicile and if the Revenue can prove that you have retained your original domicile, however long you may have lived in Italy, your family may find itself faced with Inheritance Tax payable on assets which you have carefully kept out of the country. Advice on this matter comes from your solicitor with whom you should also discuss, in the light of the guidelines at the beginning of this chapter and in Chapter 7, the question of Wills.

Equally if you do want to leave assets out of Italy, do not leave them in a country where, for want of advice, you may pay unnecessary tax. This is the province of the accountant who will be familiar with the various double tax conventions which are designed basically to ensure you do not pay tax twice on the same income in more than one country. Always remember that the Channel Islands and the Isle of Man are considered tax havens by many countries.

A thought should be given to bank accounts and currency. In very general terms, if you become resident in Italy you may maintain foreign bank accounts, and it is usually wise to keep your British account open but not over-filled on current account. Taxes deducted by UK banks from interest on deposit accounts do not apply if the holder of the account is non-resident for tax purposes in the UK.

Transfers of cash to and from Italy can take far longer than you might think normal. If you want to buy things in the UK no one will thank you for paying with an Italian cheque since it will take an age to clear. Similarly, you will find it an expensive operation to pay UK cheques into your Italian bank account. Organize yourself with Eurocheques and a Eurocheque card and use this method of payment in Italy whenever it seems convenient. All Italian shops, except very small ones, take Eurocheque. You can also use these cheques for cashing sterling into lire; today, you can cash up to 300,000 lire on any one cheque and you are allowed two cheques a day. If you are desperate for cash, and have it in the bank in the UK and know that your bank will not mind, you can cash several cheques in one day in various local banks. Italians, particularly builders and car dealers will take Eurocheques in large amounts. These will be outside the normal Eurocheque system and you should warn your bank of what you have done.

Certain items such as English books are extremely expensive in Italy since they are no longer cheap at home and paper is heavy. They are much more easily bought in the UK and will eventually arrive by post at a fraction of the Italian cost, even including postage and packing.

· It is wise to retain your British credit cards and use them in Italy, though there is no reason why you should not also have an Italian card as well. It is also a good idea to pay a minimum per month to these cards by standing order, thus obviating any non-payment due to vagaries of the post between the UK and Italy. The standing order can be topped up with a cheque when your account is received. I have worked out over the last five years that, for some unknown reason, one credit card account in seven appears to go astray in the post; if you have a large number of cards, this can be irritating on a large scale.

As to the currency in which you will keep your assets in the future, do not rush into lire, or into any other currency for that matter. No one can tell what the foreign exchange markets will do from one day to the next. Suffice it to say that the lire has not done well since the last edition of this book and advice should be sought just before you leave. On the whole, the UK has kept its island tradition of thinking only in sterling but this is changing.

There is no need to make special arrangements prior to leaving the UK, such as obtaining an entry visa. You simply arrive and whether you are permitted to stay (as you undoubtedly will be) depends on following the requirements set out in Chapter 7. Citizens of the various EU states have an absolute right to live and work in member states. Those taking up employment in Italy will be in a slightly different situation and their employers will help them with the various formalities. You have the right, after three months in Italy, to have an Italian Identity Card, which will mention your nationality. You should carry this with you at all times. In any event it is smaller and easier to carry than a passport. There is no obligation, even for the Italians, to have an ID card and Italy is not a police state, but you are expected to be able to identify yourself when asked to do so. The ID card will not be valid out of Italy so there will be times when you will have to carry your passport.

Importing your personal and household effects is now simplicity itself. You should use a British furniture removal firm since: (a) there are many more of them (the British move fifteen times more often than the Italians) (b) there are specialist firms for moving antiques (c) the insurance cover is better and any claims are paid within six or seven weeks, and (d) they are much cheaper. I had to pay more to move, within the same *comune*, half the furniture I arrived with from London; and in that short time there was severe damage to three items for which the expensive insurance policy did not pay. The Italians tend to stay put; if they do move, they go abroad for a long time and tend not to take their furniture with them. Perhaps this is due to bitter experience at home. Of course, there are good firms in the large cities such as Rome and Milan, but on average British firms tend to be better value. Whether you are importing goods for your permanent or holiday home makes no difference – you are at liberty to bring in what you like so long as it is for your own use. If the items are new it is as well to have at hand the various bills showing you have paid VAT at the time of purchase.

If you have a TV set you should declare it on arrival by going to the post office to pay the annual fee. You may well be stopped at the frontier and asked by the *Dogana* (Customs) to pay the yearly fee there and then. This is quite normal and you will get a proper receipt and later a *libretto* for the future. However, you cannot count on things being this way and if you are not accompanying the set it is unlikely you or your transporter will be asked. Do not try to get away without payment – the fines are as swingeing as in the UK. TV sets are on the same system as the UK but most you buy in Italy will take French TV as well. Satellite TV is common throughout Italy but if you want Sky you will need an English address and an English bank account for direct debit payments. It is impossible to telephone Sky about anything from Italy as they deliberately use a Freefone number. Therefore, if anything goes wrong with your card you will have to get a relation or friend to help you out. It is also quite expensive on top of a TV licence.

Radio, on the other hand, is free except for the price of the set, which should be chosen for its ability to receive short-wave transmissions. Since January 1990, Italian stations have been relaying BBC Overseas Service programmes on FM, so reception is perfect. Details can be obtained from the BBC – see Appendix F.

There is no quarantine for animals in Italy and you can bring your pet in at any time, provided it is accompanied by an International Certificate of Anti-Rabies together with a Certification of Freedom from Infection issued by your British vet. Ideally this should be countersigned by the Animal Health Division of MAAF, Export Division (at Hook Rise, Tolworth, Surbiton, Surrey). The Italian authorities are themselves unlikely to enforce these requirements: I have now imported two dogs into Italy without anyone even noticing the animals let alone asking me for any documentation. You will not, however, be able to leave England without the necessary certificates, which cost over £100. Your pet will, perforce, become a permanent exile from the UK until the racket of quarantine has been abolished. With modern micro-chipping and blood tests it should be necessary only to identify the actual animal on arrival; reducing the quarantine period to a mere month serves no purpose except to keep the kennel owners happy.

Anti-rabies inoculations must be given annually on the *exact day*, plus the various other jabs a dog or cat needs. There are one or two nasty diseases in Italy which at the moment have not come to the UK, but vaccines can be given for all but one. If you live between

200 and 800 metres above sea level, there is a possibility that your dog will contract leichmaniosis, which is transmitted by a mosquito sufficiently small to pass through a standard mosquito net. There is no cure and it is a terrible disease to watch in action. Cats are unaffected, but humans can catch it in the form of dum-dum fever, which, though curable, can leave a person seriously debilitated for some time. In the north and centre of Italy, you should, from the 1st May until the 1st November, give your dog a minute nightly spray on the back of its neck of DefendDog, which is available in most parts of Italy, as well as in France and the UK. In the south of Italy and the islands, you should apply this spray every night of the year. The bottle-spray releases too much at a time for such frequent use, but if the liquid is decanted into a fine scent-spray, one bottle of DefendDog, used solely for this purpose on one dog, should last for one whole year. Having received this nightly treatment, in conjunction with a monthly application of Frontline, my present dog is eight years old and perfectly fit, while 90 per cent of the village dogs are affected with leichmaniosis in one stage or another. With pedigree dogs the disease is somehow worse: I lost a cocker spaniel to leichmaniosis which gave her leukaemia, kidney and liver failure at the same time as a friend lost a magnificent Irish setter to kidney problems followed by paralysis. Take no chances; if you disapprove of small nightly doses, then don't have a dog.

Strictly speaking dogs are supposed to be muzzled in built-up areas but this is honoured more in the breach than in the observance. However, you cannot get your dog on public transport without a muzzle. This can be very difficult with certain breeds which simply cannot accommodate a muzzle such as Tibetan Spaniels or, even worse, Pekinese.

For many years there was an annual dog tax which probably became too expensive to collect. Then you had to declare your dog to the local *comune* and a dog tag was issued. The latest is that you declare one or more dogs, but no cats, when you fill up the form for refuse removal.

Strictly speaking, your dog should be tattooed with a number which is registered at the local provincial capital, but working dogs (i.e those living in the country) are excepted. Naturally, virtually every dog in the country is a working dog in the eyes of the locals. You should, in any event, always put a tag on your dog which gives *your* name, town or village and your telephone number; if you travel, mention that this information applies to Italy. If you lose your dog there is at least a chance you will get it back and it won't end up in the dog pound, slated for death. Do not put the dog's name on the tag because dogs are frequently stolen in Italy for a variety of reasons, the nastiest of which is for vivisection. The criminals who take dogs for this purpose will collect any sort of dog from mongrel to champion just to get 10,000 lire each for them. Be very cautious about allowing your dog loose in the forest or even more than a couple of hundred metres away from you. During the hunting season, which seems incredibly long in Italy, there is a good chance of your cat or dog being shot; I have even had reports of pets being deliberately killed by poisoning or traps.

I have been taken to task for not mentioning horses and have to admit that I was unaware that some people bring their horses here, particularly in the Rome area. Keeping a horse in Italy is expensive, far more expensive than in the UK, and straw, when obtainable, is a great luxury – shredded newspaper is far more common.

For a country famous for its leather, saddles and tack in general are not only expensive but rather poor quality when compared with British or French equivalents. Vets are expensive, but so they are in the UK. Many do not do equine work and it's best to make enquiries before bringing out a horse. Italian horses are rather like Italians, beautiful, well bred, intelligent, expensive but unpredictable.

Foreigners living in the Italian countryside complain about their Italian neighbours' lack of consideration. There is no law of privacy in Italy and hunters can come over your land, but not your garden, in search of their prey. Your neighbour can spread the most ghastly smelling manure on his land without so much as a by your leave. In my experience, neighbours are likely to help themselves to any tools left outside so lock everything away with a good padlock or even an alarm. One friend of mine found that her neighbours had been using her pool when she was away. On her return, they kindly told her that it needed to be re-treated 'urgently'. An automatic gate, alarm and even real or fake video cameras are good investments if you live in such an area. There are large parts of Italy where this sort of thing never occurs, but where there is a tourist industry be on your guard.

Finally, British newspapers are available in all large towns though they are rather expensive. (It should be remembered that it is the newspaper which sets the overseas price and not the Italians.) Often you do not get the magazines which go with the papers. The Telegraph group produce not only a *Daily Telegraph* and a *Sunday Telegraph* but a *Weekly Telegraph* which is a digest of all seven of the week's papers and represents the best value for money. Watch the dates very carefully since retailers leave them on the racks for weeks at a time.

4

Where to Live

As a reader pointed out to me, not everyone has the choice of where to live when they emigrate, but may have to go where they are sent either by the government or by their employer. Although this is very true, happily it can be said that most people do have a choice and usually the main constraint in Italy is the cost of property, which is absolutely astronomical in town but much less if you are able to live in the country.

That said, it should also be remembered that it is now considerably easier to find rented accommodation all over Italy, and at reasonable prices, particularly if you are prepared to invest some money in re-decoration, with the exception of real tourist areas such as Rome, Florence and Venice. Rome is the biggest problem of all because taking up the rural possibility means a long journey for commuters who work in the city, without the possibility of using a car since it is so difficult to park. Venice is much easier since the moment you get on to what the Venetians call *terraferma*, or the mainland, the availability increases, the prices decrease and the commuting is rather less difficult. Few foreigners have the joy (or otherwise) of working in Florence, where living around ten or fifteen miles outside the city is a pleasant possibility.

It is unlikely you will be able to take advantage of what is known as *equo canone* or 'controlled rent' property, and indeed, you may well find landlords who are not prepared to let to those who are bona fide residents in Italy. This is because as a resident you get a certain amount of automatic protection. As a non-resident you don't and the landlord has much more liberty to charge what he likes and not undertake repairs, etc.

For the newcomer it is perhaps useful to know where most of the English speaking foreigners live, be they British, Irish, American, Dutch or Scandinavian. In a word – Tuscany. Most foreigners in fact have chosen Tuscany and thereafter, in order of popularity, comes Latina (the region around Rome), Liguria, Umbria, Lombardy,

Campania and Sicily. To a lesser extent they are also in Piedmont, the Veneto, Emilia-Romagna, on the Adriatic coast near Ancona and, in a very small way, in Sardinia.

Difficulty in communications makes the southern regions of Abruzzo, Molise, Calabria, Basilicata and Apulia considerably less popular with the foreigner. Although these regions have been opened up to the public at large by the *Autostrade del Sole* (which is free in the south), the death-dealing summer heat and problematical water supply are not very welcoming factors for those from more northerly climes. Furthermore, society in this part of Italy is very closed and non-locals, including other Italians, cannot enter it. The standard of living and of eating is lower in the south than in the north. Life is lived on the streets and in the local bars and cafés if you are a man and, almost exclusively in the house, usually in the kitchen, if you are a woman. As with all generalizations there are many exceptions.

Although scenically very beautiful, the northern mountain regions of Val d'Aosta, Trentino-Alto Adige and Friuli-Venezia-Giulia tend not to attract foreigners except on a holiday basis and then mostly for winter sports, although spending summers in these regions can be a wonderfully worthwhile experience. All these areas produce excellent wine, among Italy's finest, and each is known as a hunter's paradise.

The other problem is that Italy is not what it seems on the map – it is really quite small when you consider that under a quarter of its land is agricultural and that it is more or less situated in the same place, the rather boring Po Plain going from Ivrea just north of Turin due east to just south of Venice on the Adriatic. There is another small plain down the west coast of Italy starting at the Maremma and finishing just north of Rome. South of Rome, there is one other agricultural plain made out of former malarial Pontine marshes drained on the orders of Mussolini.

Many of the vineyards are at altitude, particularly in the north, because vines will grow there where cereals will not. Something like 40 per cent of the country is at an altitude of more than 700 metres. These are hard geographical facts obtainable from any encyclopaedia on Italy and responsible for the history of agriculture in the country and for the state it is in today. There is a marked lack of water, and only in the heel of Italy has any effort been made to irrigate what was the arid plain of the Tavoliere and add citrus farming to the already indigenous olives and grapes. But it is all on such a small scale.

To help with choosing a place to live, the average temperatures and rainfall in ten large Italian cities are given below. From this it will be seen that Bologna has a slightly higher rainfall than Palermo which has more than double that of Eastern Sicily. As in Venice, it rains every month of the year in Bologna. Venice can be wonderfully sunny but most of the year it is grey and damp and, like Turin, rather a melancholy place. As the Italians say, you need large personal resources to be happy in Turin or Venice on a long-term basis. Strangely, Milan which, with its mountainous, continental climate, is often colder, wetter or hotter than the other big cities, also has its own, in many ways greater attractions. In the summer, the Lakes are visited not only by the Milanese but by most of Lombardy; this same area around Como, Maggiore and Lugano can also be very melancholy from late autumn to mid-spring with almost constant fog and damp. The English in particular regard it as extremely romantic. From April to almost the end of September it is the most perfect place.

Rainfall is shown in centimetres, temperature in degrees Celsius.

	Spring		Summer		Autumn		Winter	
	Temp.	Rain	Temp.	Rain	Temp.	Rain.	Temp.	Rain
Bologna	12	63	24	41	15	111	4	104
Cagliari	15	40	27	nil	20	50	10	55
Florence	13	60	25	75	17	98	6	60
Genoa	14	82	25	35	18	135	8	110
Milan	12	82	25	47	14	75	1	60
Naples	15	55	25	14	18	102	9	85
Palermo	16	65	26	6	20	120	10	140
Rome	14	2	26	6	18	123	7	75
Turin	11	74	23	65	12	60	0	10
Venice	13	77	26	37	15	68	4	60

Surprisingly, l'Aquila in the Abruzzo is the coldest city in the whole country; even the Government recognizes this by reducing their income tax. This also applies to other *comuni* which are above a certain altitude, usually 500 metres. Rome has a more or less equable climate but in its immediate surroundings things are not so pleasant and winters are rather cool and very, very damp. In the north during winter, it is always either snowing or raining.

The next thing to consider is price. In principle, the town is more expensive than the country and the north more expensive than the south. Parts of central Italy, including Tuscany and Rome, can be very dear indeed. Resorts also appear somewhat expensive when you consider they cost the same or more as Milan or Rome but offer so much less to the would-be resident.

Below is a table showing the price (in lire) per square metre of apartments in eleven of Italy's largest cities. The figures in the first column concern new apartments or those which have been completely and professionally renovated, not necessarily right in the city centre, but in a good, sought after district. The second column concerns old (and unrenovated) apartments, often in the historic centre of the city in question. Very often, in large and industrial cities, the historic centre has been taken over by immigrants from the south. This is because, many years ago when the first influx occurred, the historic centres were cheaper. Gradually, in many large and not so large towns, there is a moving back into well-renovated apartments in the historic centres and the ex-southerners are moving into newly built modern blocks on the outskirts of town.

There can be some wonderful bargains here if you are prepared to renovate them yourself. Italian builders are usually excellent at this sort of work and many seem to have a real feel for dealing with buildings which are four and even five hundred years old. There is no way prices can be given for individual houses but if you are prepared to build from scratch or renovate then there are bargains to be had.

	New/Renovated	Old and Unrenovated
Bologna	2,600,000–3,500,000	1,000,000–2,400,000
Florence	3,100,000–4,200,000	prices not available
Genoa	2,900,000–4,000,000	650,000–1,000,000
Milan	4,000,000–6,000,000+	800,000–1,750,000
Palermo	2,000,000–3,125,000	650,000–1,250,000
Perugia	1,450,000–1,850,000	950,000–1,600,000
Rome	4,400,000–6,250,000	2,300,000–4,150,000
Trieste	1,750,000–2,750,000	800,000–1,000,000
Turin	2,275,000–4,000,000	740,000–1,225,000
Udine	2,000,000–2,750,000	750,00–950,000
Venice	2,350,000–3,000,000	not applicable
(mainland only)		

Of course, by no means everyone wants to live in a city. For those who want to ensure that they will have beautiful scenery, good services, good restaurants and excellent communications, there are plenty of suitable resorts on the many lakes, in the mountains and by the sea. None is cheap, but around Como and Maggiore many of the old villas are being restored as four to six apartments with one or two bedrooms for much the same price as a faceless, ordinary apartment in a modern block in a less beautiful setting. However, a word of warning. It has not been unknown for people living all year round in one of these villas (or modern blocks for that matter) to find that they are the people running the place while all the other owners are living the rest of the year in Milan, Turin or Parma. The burden of these blocks is meant to be shared by all the owners, not just those left behind. Establish first that there are at least two or three other families who live all year round in your block or converted villa. One English woman found herself meeting aircraft at Venice Airport to take other owners' tenants back to the villa which she owned in common with two other families. Another passionate gardener found she was doing all the outside cleaning up, planting, buying the insecticides, mowing the lawn and paying for the help she needed for a two hectare garden. You must start such arrangements as you mean them to continue.

Perhaps because flats and houses in resorts are usually purchased as second homes, prices have not risen quite so much as in the cities. The following table gives some idea of the range of prices (in lire) of houses in a dozen different resorts. The first price can be regarded as the lowest and the second as the *average* maximum but in fact the sky's the limit in many of the resorts.

Bormio	2,800,000–4,000,000
Cortina d'Ampezzo	4,250,000–5,750,000
Courmayeur	3,500,000–5,000,000
Gardone Riviera	2,000,000–3,000,000
Porto Cervo	2,925,000–4,225,000
Porto Santo Stefano	2,250,000–3,750,000
Portofino	3,200,000–5,500,000
Rimini	2,250,000–3,250,000
Sanremo/Ospedaletti/Bordighera	2,600,000–4,500,000
Sestriere	3,000,000–4,000,000
Stresa	2,000,000–3,000,000
Taormina	2,400,000–2,900,000

Parts of Tuscany are almost entirely peopled with British and they have given the area the sobriquet 'Chiantishire'. The main attractions are large houses with enviable amounts of land all at a most reasonable price. However, there can, in the summer, be severe problems with the most basic requirement of all, water. Of course, it is possible to store thousands of gallons of water for the summer to come, but the initial outlay can be phenomenal. Usually if the place has been a farm (but not a vineyard only), there will be access to water. Often in Tuscany and other regions, you will have to generate your own electricity. Modern Japanese generators will produce AC current and are soundproofed. The only problem is remembering always to have a stock of diesel fuel. Petrol is far too expensive and too dangerous to have anywhere near the house. In towns and villages there are no or few problems with water and none with electricity.

Houses in Florence or Siena are as expensive as you might expect and are difficult to find. There is also the question of whether you will enjoy living in a town which is a tourist centre for six to nine months a year. This also goes for the smaller Tuscan towns such as Arezzo, San Gimignano, Prato, Lucca, even Grossetto.

The Tuscan coast is not really to be recommended, inundated as it is in high summer with tourists from all over the world. You can never park your car, get to market or find a table in your regular restaurant. In winter it is chilly, windswept. The sandy beaches become a series of moonscape dunes and the general atmosphere, as described by an Italian friend, is as though the place has suffered a nuclear attack. Some of the coastal resorts shut up shop completely in winter thus adding to the eerie atmosphere. Livorno (Leghorn) was bombed to bits in the war and now has little to recommend it except a few good restaurants. The general recommendation is to try for a property with water or water-storage facilities twenty or twenty-five kilometres from a largish town. Happily, there are still some left and at reasonable prices compared with their counterparts in the UK.

Perhaps by virtue of its proximity and its similarity to Tuscany, Umbria, with its centre at Perugia, has become the 'in' place in recent years. Even more favourably the prices in Umbria are half those of Tuscany and there is masses of property available. Water is not always such a problem as in Tuscany but nevertheless enquiries should be made and not just from the owner, his agent and local people who will all lie if they think a positive answer will please you more than a negative one. Communications are not wonderful although there is a *Superstrada* to Perugia and Assisi. This last town should be avoided for the most part – it is tourist-ridden virtually all year round, but is nonetheless worth visiting once or twice. Not without reason this area is known as the *Terra dei Santi*: there are those who say you need the patience of a saint to live there, though its name probably has more to do with the former poverty of the area. Now, with the influx of tourists, this has changed. Lake Trasimeno is one of the more popular places, but full-time residents (as opposed to summer visitors) should bear in mind it is foggy in winter.

The region of Latium tends to have its foreign population centred around Rome. Properties in the immediate vicinity of Rome itself are the second most expensive in Italy. The further from Rome the less expensive; Viterbo and its vicinity, all slightly north of

Rome, are not to be sniffed at. Do not be put off by some of the horrible modern suburbs but go for one of the three famous Lakes, Bracciano, Vico or Capraola, which also has the unmissable Villa Farnese. Estruscan remains abound so if you were to buy property you would always have something to show your visitors. Prices are fairly reasonable and properties are available, along with many workmen in this area who are good and serious people. Away from civilization or from the various lakes, water can be a problem so always make enquiries.

Further south is Campania, with Naples as its capital. No sane person would want to live in Naples which is too dangerous, dirty, noisy and hot to be a permanent dwelling place, but it is well worth several visits. Ischia, Capri, Sorrento, Positano and Amalfi are all expensive resorts with property prices to match. Little more is being built and there is a shortage of accommodation. Although there can be water problems in high summer, the climate is excellent all year round.

Liguria is the third most expensive area of Italy in which to purchase property. Its main problem is that the sea-level coastal strip is only ten or less kilometres deep before the terrain quickly rises to 500 or 600 metres, where one immediately loses the benefit of the best climate in northern Italy, particularly in winter. The coastal towns are universally expensive with an average minimum of 3,500,000 lire per square metre for a flat without a seaview. Fifteen or twenty kilometres from the sea the prices are a little lower and there are *rustici* for conversion. These are always on a small scale, often less than 50 square metres of living space and little chance of increasing it. Many foreigners dislike the Ligurian style though not the wedding cake colours of their houses. These are often tall, narrow buildings with angled flat roofs and the modern blocks of flats are not pretty. However, for the richer buyer there are many conversions of turn-of-the-century and earlier villas into most attractive apartments in some of the better-known resorts such as Bordighera and Sanremo. The gardens are well established with plenty of shade trees and sub-tropical plants and climbers. There are very few problems with water in the resorts; sometimes, in deep country, it has been known for water to get rationed in high summer, but this is almost a thing of the past. All water is metered now in Liguria.

Lombardy, with its capital Milan, is the most expensive area in which to buy. The flat in the city and a house on one of the Lakes are very expensive items indeed, mainly because the foreigner is competing with the Milanese who know their way around. There are bargains to be had if you are prepared to live in an old walk-up flat or to go outside Milan and away from the Lakes. Certain areas on the lakeside have a mild micro-climate and are much sought after. However, one can say without fear of contradiction that the climate of Lombardy is far from brilliant – in summer it is much too hot, yet Milan is colder than Copenhagen in winter. With all the modern *autostrade* into Milan, charming places such as the countryside round Piacenza, Pavia or Cremona are all within commuting distance of the big city. It pays to investigate.

Eastern Sicily has long been popular with the British, though inland the heat can be difficult to bear. The resorts which cater for the non-natives are probably a better bet in this case and the coast from Messina to Syracuse has much to offer the foreigners. Many of Sicily's resorts have become concrete jungles and, unless you actually like living in high rise blocks of flats (which the Italians do not know how to build anyway), you will have to choose very carefully. Non-Italians often ask if it is safe to live in Sicily or Southern Italy given that it is the home of the Mafia. Most people wouldn't know a Mafioso if they saw one and the presence or not of the Mafia in Sicily is not likely to concern the average foreign tourist or resident. However, there are those who counsel people living in *western* Sicily not to try to run a vineyard, an orange grove or a farm without first making their peace with the local Mafia. If this is the case then the answer is to buy your property elsewhere. Always remember that property may be cheaper on the island but the cost of living is considerably higher.

Much the same goes for Sardinia, though the people are considerably more closed and less gregarious than the Sicilians. Costa Smeralda is a development which, as a holiday resort, attracts a certain sort of person who wants to be quite sure of meeting the same type. It has little to do with the real Sardinia which as any local will tell you is a hard place to live, particularly if you till the land or farm in any sort of way, as do most of the natives. There is a famous Englishwoman who has made it her task to teach the Sards about composting their garden and farm rubbish instead of burning it, thus preventing fires. After fifteen years she has at last convinced a few of them that it is also cheaper. There is what the Italians call 'a terrible beauty' about Sardinia, where nature is at her wildest and most breath-taking. That said, I cannot imagine living all year round on the island.

One of the most neglected regions of Italy – neglected that is, by foreigners – is the *Marche* or Marches on the Adriatic. Before the unification of Italy in the last century, the Marchigiani were the tax gatherers for the Papal States and, judging by their rich and beautiful architecture, appear to have been pretty good at it. By tradition,

they were hated by the rest of Italy although it is only the old Papal
States which keep this up. They seem a perfectly normal, kind sort
of Italian. Ascoli Piceno is a small picturesque town said to have the
most beautiful women in all Italy. There are many other similar
towns and plenty of property available at reasonable prices. Urbino,
which is one of the few towns to look attractive in pouring rain, is
probably the only relatively expensive place in this region. Property
is very sought after here. Ancona is the big town and interesting to
see if not to live in. The countryside is green and lush most of the
year round and has the attractive backdrop of the Apennines. The
downside to this part of Italy is the weather. Due to its geographical location, sandwiched between the sea and the mountains, the
area can be subjected to terrible, violent storms.

Piedmont (*Piemonte*) has a similar countryside, much better
wine, wonderful autumns, pretty rotten winters, late springs, very
hot summers and no water shortages to talk of. The architecture is
of three types, beautiful, ugly, and faceless modern or Fascist. The
last will be recognized by anyone who has lived in Italy for three
months and Piedmont appears to be full of it in the towns.

Turin, like any big city in northern Italy, has lost a lot of its native
character due to the influx of immigrants from the south.
Nevertheless, there remains something solid and reassuring about
most of the Piedmontese towns. The countryside, particularly around
Asti and Alba, is incredibly beautiful. Alas, a great number of Torinese
have already got there and so prices for property are high.

Emilia-Romagna has Bologna as its capital, a city which is worth
investigating. It is extremely rich, very honest since it is run by the
Communist Party, and hardly affected by all the recent upheavals.
The architecture isn't at all grandiose, though it is pleasant to be
able to shop under arcades when it is raining, which is depressingly
frequent in Bologna. Many of the streets are named after
Communist icons such as Gramsci as well as Stalinist idols. And yet
it is a rich city where eating out tends to be expensive and property
keeps its value. There is very little available in the historic centre
since this has been virtually taken over by the municipality for
offices and public use as well as for making flats. The old facades
remain the same, but the insides are stripped out and rebuilt. All
this has been done to a very high standard. The suburbs are pleasant but unexceptional and generally property is quite expensive.
The quality of workmanship can be excellent and the restoration of
a house or an old flat is definitely a good idea, always supposing
you can find the right property to begin with.

To the west is Emilia with Parma, Modena and Piacenza and to the
east is the former Papal State of Romagna with Ferrara, Ravenna and

Rimini. Emilia, with Bologna, is the culinary capital of Italy and is famous for its trenchermen. Romagna, on the other hand, eats rather poorly in comparison. The locals say it is due to their clerical past. However, Ferrara has a long culinary tradition going back to their ruling family, the Este, who were so grand and so rich they were one of the twelve families allowed to marry with the Hapsburgs. Ferrara was also famous for its Jews and Jewish cuisine. Alas, most of the Jews have now gone, having either been assimilated into Italian society or having perished in the concentration camps. Anyone wanting to dive into Italian literature should read everything the Ferrarese Giorgio Bassani has written. It will be very rewarding.

The wine, notwithstanding Lambrusco's fame as the only red, fizzy wine which is drinkable, is frankly poor, particularly compared with the quality of the cuisine. However, there are plenty of good wines from elsewhere in Italy and the Emiliani are happy to import them.

This is a region where the towns are rather more interesting than the countryside, which can be flat and boring. Modena probably has the most perfect example of Romanesque architecture in its Cathedral of San Geminiano which was started at the end of the eleventh century and completed in the fourteenth. It has recently been cleaned back to a pale cream stone which enhances its beauty even more. The city is backed by the beginning of the Apennine mountains, a pleasant change after the flatness of the Po Plain.

The Veneto, the region which is Venice's hinterland and which bears endless reminders of the Serenissima's ownership long ago, is much loved by northern Europeans, including me. If ever I made my fortune I would buy a house in this area. Although the summers are hot, the area remains green and the wine is a great compensation for the bitterness of the winter which nearly always brings deep snow. However, the spring is beautiful (if a little late) and the wonderful autumn seems to last for ever. The people are among the most honest in Italy. Probably it is the winter which puts off so many would-be residents. Venice itself is an impossible place to live. There are far too many tourists virtually all the year round, it is very expensive and the weather is not always what it should be. The winter is cold, wet and foggy, romantic to some, but ghastly to others. The architecture is, of course, the overwhelming redeeming feature. This is an area which has several British enclaves around Asolo and Conegliano where the views of green, rolling hills and vineyards are much admired by foreigners. In spring, these same hills are covered with millions of wild bulbs.

When considering where to live in Italy, you should, if you haven't already fallen in love with somewhere, visit your chosen place in its worst season, that is to say winter in north and central Italy, and summer in the south. It could be a revelation.

Agrigento	AG
Alessandr.	AL
Ancona	AN
Aosta	AO
Arezzo	AR
Ascoli P.	AP
Asti	AT
Avellino	AV
Bari	BA
Belluno	BL
Benevento	BN
Bergamo	BG
Biella	BI
Bologna	BO
Bolzano	BZ
Brescia	BS
Brindisi	BR
Cagliari	CA
Caltanis.	CL
Campob.	CB
Caserta	CE
Catania	CT
Catanzaro	CZ
Chieti	CH
Como	CO
Cosenza	CS
Cremona	CR
Crotone	KR
Cuneo	CN
Enna	EN
Ferrara	FE

Regions and provinces of Italy

Firenze	FI	Mantova	MN	Pisa	PI	Taranto	TA
Foggia	FG	Massa C.	MS	Pistoia	PT	Teramo	TE
Forlì	FO	Matera	MT	Porden.	PN	Terni	TR
Frosinone	FR	Messina	ME	Potenza	PZ	Torino	TO
Genova	GE	Milano	MI	Prato	PR	Trapani	TP
Gorizia	GO	Modena	MO	Ragusa	RG	Trento	TN
Grosseto	GR	Napoli	NA	Ravenna	RA	Treviso	TV
Imperia	IM	Novara	NO	Reggio C.	RC	Trieste	TS
Isernia	IS	Nuoro	NU	Reggio E.	RE	Udine	UD
L'Aquila	AQ	Oristano	OR	Rieti	RI	Varese	VA
La Spezia	SP	Padova	PD	Roma	ROMA	Venezia	VE
Latina	LT	Palermo	PA	Rovigo	RO	Verbano	VB
Lecce	LE	Parma	PR	Salerno	SA	Vercelli	VC
Lecco	LC	Pavia	PV	Sassari	SS	Verona	VR
Livorno	LI	Perugia	PG	Savona	SV	Vibo-Valentia	VV
Lodi	LO	Pesaro	PS	Siena	SI	Vicenza	VI
Lucca	LU	Pescara	PE	Siracusa	SR	Viterbo	VT
Macerata	MC	Piacenza	PC	Sondrio	SO		

5

Communications

Air

Italy is in the heart of Europe from a communications viewpoint. Milan has two of the busiest international airports in Europe. Rome, on the other hand, together with Athens, is an important staging post on the way to the Middle and Far East.

Italy has international airports at Rome, Milan, Bologna, Turin, Genoa, Pisa, Venice, Palermo, Catania and Olbia in Sardinia. The domestic network is run by a subsidiary of Alitalia called ATI (Aero Trasporti Italiani) and this line, in addition to the international airports serves the following towns: Bergamo, Verona, Florence, Trieste, Rimini, Ancona, Pescara, Bari, Brindisi, Lamezia Terme, Reggio Calabria, Trapani, Pantelleria and Lampedusa. Sassari and Cagliari in Sardinia are served by Alisarda. There are also three other airlines: Transavia, Algiulia, and Aermediterranea, which cover destinations elsewhere in Italy not always served by Alitalia and ATI.

There are direct flights from Heathrow by both Alitalia and British Airways to Bologna, Genoa, Milan, Naples, Pisa (for Florence and Siena), Rome, Turin and Venice. In the holiday seasons there are extra scheduled and chartered flights out of Gatwick to destinations all over Italy. Both Air UK (Tel: 0345 666 777) and Meridiana (0171 839 22 22) do cheaper flights at certain times of the year. Another possibility much used by Italians and foreigners alike is to use the large international airlines on the first lap of their intercontinental flights. Instead of the full scheduled air fare to Rome or Milan of around £250, companies such as Air India, Jordanian Airlines, Air Kenya or even Quantas can offer fares as little as £100. It depends entirely on the time of year and the availability of seats; at Christmas, Easter and in the summer holidays do not expect too much. There is also a company Italy Sky Shuttle who do chartered flights (0171 748 1333) and can get cheap last minute seats with other carriers. From the United States there are two useful companies for cheap travel to Italy and Europe in general. They are Now Voyager and Airhitch who appear in most local Yellow Pages. Watch the newspapers in any event because lots of last-minute flights become available and are ideal for those not constrained by fixed dates.

Alitalia is a good airline. The pilots are excellent, the crews are polite and helpful (a bonus nowadays) and, incredibly, their time-keeping is on a par with other good airlines.

Air travel within Italy is not cheap; indeed there are absolutely *no* bargains. However, faced with the idea of driving or taking the train to Naples, Brindisi or Sicily from Genoa or Milan it has the merit of great convenience. Remember, from the north to the south of the country is often over 1,000 kilometres by land.

Sea

Apart from Sicily and Sardinia, Italy has many islands which are all served by some sort of ferry service from hydrofoils to putt-putt motorboats. The main ferries are run by six organizations: FS (Italian State Railways), the Tirrenia Company, the Trans-Tirreno Express, I Grandi Traghetti, Nav.Ar.Mar., Alimar-SVAV.

State Railways: Their ferries go from Civitavecchia (near Rome) to Golfo Aranci in Sardinia. It is a nine-hour crossing and there are several crossings a day on which cars can be taken.

The Tirrenia Company: This ferry goes from Civitavecchia to both Olbia and Cagliari in Sardinia. Passengers and cars; day and night. There are also crossings from Naples to Cagliari, Genoa to Cagliari, Genoa to Porto Torres, Livorno (Leghorn) to Porto Torres. Crossing times range from twelve to fifteen hours.

They also run a ferry from Naples to Palermo in Sicily which takes cars.

Trans-Tirreno Express: There is an all-year-round ferry service between Livorno and Olbia in Sardinia. Cars may be taken.

Grandi Traghetti: This ferry service runs out of Genoa and takes both passengers and cars. There is a service from Genoa to Porto Torres which takes eleven hours. Another service is to Palermo which takes twenty-two hours and another from Livorno to Palermo which takes eighteen hours. Unaccompanied cars may be taken but they must be personally delivered and met at the destination.

Nav.Av.Mar: This company offers a drive-on/drive-off service from both Piobino (near Grossetto) and Livorno to Elba and Corsica.

Alimar SVAV: Operates huge hydrofoils which go between Naples and Palermo in a mere five hours instead of twelve, so is obviously more expensive. It is also cleaner.

The Adriatic coast is served mainly by the Adriatic Company which is a large international line but also provides services between various Adriatic ports such as Venice, Trieste, Ancona, Bari and Brindisi. Takes passengers and cars. Also has services to foreign destinations such as Greece, former Yugoslavia etc.

Rail

Unless you are able to get the most enormous discount, going to Italy from the UK by train is an expensive, grubby and gastronomically miserable experience, the Channel Tunnel notwithstanding. If possible, route yourself through Switzerland rather than France because they often provide the restaurant car the French and Italians now shun. The only good reason for going to Italy by rail is that you can take a great deal of luggage. However, it is not difficult to get a private firm to bring your bags out separately on a part-load basis which, combined with an air fare, can still work out cheaper and certainly far more pleasant since your heavy luggage is delivered to your door.

To go to Rome costs around £200 return plus a sleeper or couchette and takes almost a whole day. You can get to Milan quicker, though hardly cheaper, by taking Eurostar to Paris and then the TGV to Lyon and onward to Milan. In all, about twelve hours.

Really the only way to go by train is on the Orient Express, the luxury of which is not all that expensive when compared with the £500 or so two people will pay to get to Venice and back from London without sleepers and without meals. It costs just under £900 for a double sleeper cabin *one way for two* including *all* meals. This once-in-a-lifetime splurge can be effectively combined with a return by air.

Italy has a vast network of railways, much of which is part of the European international system. The FS as it is known (*Ferrovie dello Stato*) was the first railway to be nationalized in Europe, in 1908, and has the dubious advantage of having had to start from scratch after the Second World War in which it lost almost 80 per cent of its rail and rolling stock due to either Allied bombing or retreating Germans.

It is often said that under Mussolini Italian trains always ran on time (they did under Giolitti at the turn of the century but that was conveniently forgotten by the Fascists) and that what is currently lacking is his guiding hand. Now that there are ostensibly no immigration or customs controls between Italy and France or Italy and Austria, many of the international trains run on time, but between Italy and Slovenia and Italy and Switzerland there can be hold-ups; the first as a result of attempts to bring in drugs via former Yugoslavia and the latter because of Italians taking cash out to put into Swiss bank accounts. On most occasions these trains are late. The Swiss have built these hiccups into their timetable and so, once in Switzerland, you arrive at the scheduled time.

Apart from an all too frequent lack of cleanliness on Italian trains, the greatest failing is the lack of restaurant or buffet cars. There are frequent trolleys which offer expensive sandwiches and warm fizzy drinks, but it is, nevertheless, possible to go from Tarvisio on the Austrian border to Taranto in the deep south, i.e. the length of Italy, without being able to avail oneself of any of these services.

A few trains leaving from Milan, Rome, even Bologna, and similar cities and serving Naples, Bari, Genoa, Trieste and Reggio Calabria have restaurant cars. Of these, two of them, namely Milan-Rome and Trieste-Rome have a service known as *tipo extra* – the prices are extra as well. They are indicated in the timetable by a letter E. Therefore, when in Rome do as the Romans do and take packed food and drinks on a long journey. Lines from Rome to Bologna, Genoa, Milan, Naples, Ventimiglia, Venice, Turin and vice versa sometimes, but by no means always, have self-service mini-bars for snacks and drinks. Passengers should check beforehand.

Apart from the international TEE trains there are four main internal TEE type trains. The Colosseum and the Ambrosiano travel between Milan and Rome; the Vesuvio goes between Milan and Naples; and the Adriatico between Milan and Bari. As elsewhere in Europe, the price of a ticket is at the first-class rate and a special supplement includes the cost of a seat since there is no standing allowed on a TEE.

Italy now has in service new high-speed trains capable of up to 250km per hour. They are designed by Pinin Farina and their livery is dark green and white with a small amount of red, presumably to recall the Italian flag. They are probably the most beautiful trains in the world – to look at, that is. Alas, the service is not always so beautiful but it is certainly better than most.

There are dozens of international night trains with sleeper and couchette accommodation (TEN). Almost always the sleeping arrangements must be booked through an agency rather than at the FS station. FS are not strong on logic either. Usually, if this service is offered at the station it is at a special counter marked *Prenotazione e Carrozze* or *Vetture Letti*. The price of sleeping cars has to be seen to be believed, particularly if you go first class in non-shared accommodation. Between Ventimiglia and Rome this costs over 250,000 lire which is more than a first-class hotel with bath and breakfast, neither of which is offered on the train. Hence the remark about the Orient Express being relatively cheap. Sharing accommodation immediately brings down the class to second and the price to 90,000 lire for the sleeper. Tickets for the distance are extra. Couchettes are still relatively cheap in Italy and, kilometre by kilometre, Italian railways are among the cheapest in Europe.

Be very careful of supplements and always pay them in advance otherwise you pay them on the train *plus* a fine. Pay all the supplements required and do not trust agencies to book your tickets – some are very careless, as I know to my cost. If necessary get FS to check your ticket before you take your journey.

Hardly anyone living in Italy pays the normal full ticket-price. Below is a list of reductions and cards available to the travelling public depending on age, residence, marital status, motherhood and much else. What is not available to the public are the free tickets available to many Government Ministers and their families (greatly extended of course) some of whom get these perks for the rest of their lives. I once travelled with a young girl whose great uncle had once been Minister of Transport and hence her first-class ticket was free. Italian Railways are run at a loss.

Ordinary Season Ticket: A season ticket or *tessera d'abbonamento* represents a substantial saving on the normal fare and there are also special workers' season tickets for even further savings. This latter requires a certificate from the employer as proof of entitlement.

Ordinary Return Fare (Biglietto di andare e ritorno): This represents a 15% reduction over a maximum distance of 250km in all.

Kilometric ticket (Biglietto chilometrico): A 15% reduction is offered up to a maximum of 3,000 kilometres in Italy for as many as twenty trips. Good for two months and can have as many as five names on it. Of more interest to tourists than to those living in Italy.

Group Ticket (Biglietto di Gruppo di [number of persons]):   There must be at least ten people travelling on the same train at the same time together. There is then a 20% reduction. Another group ticket for 20 persons gives a reduction of 30% under the same conditions. If you have the misfortune to be travelling in a group of more than 400 persons then there is a well-deserved reduction of 40%.

Family Card (Carta per Famiglia):   Costs 5,000 lire and lasts three years. The family must consist of at least three people and must travel together. Allows a 30% discount on all travel.

Silver Card (Carta d'argento):   Half price for those of retirement age on most trains and at most times. A Residence Certificate is required. Outside Italy this card doesn't give such a good discount.

Eurail Card (Carta Rail Europ):   Available for travelling out of Italy only, first and second class.

Tessera d'Autorizzazione: Pass authorizing rail travel at 40% discount.

Unlimited Circulation Ticket: Available only *outside* Italy, these tickets can be purchased for periods of eight, fifteen, twenty-one or thirty days in first or second class and there are no surcharges for TEE reservations or supplements. Sleeping accommodation is extra.

Children up to the age of four go free in Italian trains but should not occupy a seat – though they always do; from four to twelve they go at half price. Thereafter, when travelling, either on their own or with parents they can obtain one or other sort of discount including Interail and Trans-Alpino (BIGE).
    If you want to take your car with you on holiday or business but do not want to drive it to your destination, FS will transport it for you while you travel in the passenger part of the train. One paying person must accompany the car and in the case of leaving or arriving at Bari, Bolzano, Brindisi, Milan Porta Garibaldi and Rome Tiburtina that person must be the driver and able to drive the car on and off. Other stations with this service are Turin, Genoa, Verona, Calalzo, Bologna, Naples and Villa San Giovanni (near Reggio Calabria).
    Internationally, such trains can be taken from Venice to Vienna,

Verona to Hanover, Milan to Paris, Boulogne and Amiens (book well in advance), Milan to Dusseldorf and Cologne, Bolzano to Dusseldorf, Rimini to Paris and Rimini to Munich.

Only properly registered cars will be accepted and for international journeys which cross non-EU frontiers a Green Card is required. Check with your insurance company that you are covered for damage or loss of your car when travelling this way – it could be that you are not. The same applies when you are crossing the English Channel. The Channel Tunnel apparently counts as a road.

Trailers (but not caravans) can be taken at extra cost; in any event the total height must not exceed 1.57 metres. Places for cars and bookings for sleepers can be made up to two months in advance and as little as three hours before departure if there are places free. Caravans are seldom taken by rail but it pays to enquire.

Bus

For some years Italian bus companies tried to force the public to purchase their bus tickets in advance either at the bus company offices or at tobacconists, etc. The public and tourist outcry was loud and long since the system did not allow for last-minute change of plan due to weather or unforeseen circumstances. Anyway, tourists didn't understand the system. On Sundays it was impossible to buy a bus ticket anywhere except from a fellow passenger if there was one, if he had a spare ticket and if the would-be passenger had the exact change. The bus companies started losing money and finally relaxed and allowed people to buy tickets on board. Anyone using the local transport system a lot should purchase blocks of tickets at a discount. All tickets must be validated by the machine on entering the bus and inspections are frequent. Failure to have a valid ticket can lead to a fine of up to twenty times the fare.

A very few cities and towns allow discounts to the elderly and bona fide residents of up to 50 per cent off the normal fare. In all cases a Residence Certificate is required. The normally expensive ACTV in Venice gives a 50 per cent discount to bona fide residents and a further discount to OAPs who can produce a Residence Certificate and proof of their age. This discount applies to residents of all six *sestieri* as well as residents of the towns on the lagoon islands, Marghera and Mestre, where the bulk of the population lives. Other towns are not so generous and few private bus companies give discounts to the elderly, probably because there are too many of them.

Finally, the disabled get a raw deal in Italy. Only airlines and trains have anything organized for them. Always give advance warning of your appearance in a wheelchair. For such a caring, compassionate lot the Italians seem to have a blank spot for the disabled whom they heartlessly leave to shift for themselves. However, things are improving and more and more hotels and restaurants have suitable entrances and toilet facilities for the disabled. As always in Italy this sudden concern is carried to ridiculous extremes. All new shops, garden centres, restaurants etc. must, by law, provide facilities for the disabled which only results in people not opening new shops and restaurants since putting in such facilities *everywhere* is expensive and not necessarily needed and sometimes physically impossible. Few national museums, however, have any facilities for the disabled thus denying them an important pleasure.

Road

Italy has an enviable amount of motorways (*autostrade*), thirty-one in all, covering more than 6,000 kilometres of which more than 1,000 kilometres are toll-free. There are also *superstrade* which are often of motorway standard but are all toll-free. They appear mostly in tourist areas such as the northern lakes but there is no logic as to their positioning – places which cry out for them have none.

As well as certain free parts of motorway in the Mezzogiorno (i.e. Salerno to Reggio Calabria, Palermo to Catania and Palermo to Mazaro) there are toll-free areas near large cities such as Turin, Milan, Rome, Bologna and Parma. Most large cities have a ring-road known as the *Tangenziale* – often abbreviated to T.zle or Tanz.le on the road signs. These are always free, always crowded, even in the middle of the night, and are often, but not always, the easiest way to get onto the motorway.

There are nineteen companies operating Italy's motorways and the tolls vary enormously from as little as 79 lire per kilometre between Naples and Rome and also between Venice and Trieste to almost 150 lire per km. between Savona and Ventimiglia at the French border.

The following are sample tolls as at the 1st April 1998. These are for ordinary standard saloon and estate cars. A mini bus with more than eight seats or a camper would cost more.

| A1 | Milan to Bologna | 202 km | 17,000 lire |
| A1 | Milan to Florence | 287 km | 25,000 |

A1	Milan to Rome	556 km	47,000
A2	Rome to Naples	209 km	16,500
A4	Turin to Milan	127 km	10,500
A4	Venice to Trieste	126 km	10,000
A4	Venice to Milan	264 km	22,000
A5	Turin to Aosta	119 km	13,500
A6	Turin to Savona	144 km	13,500
A7/26/10	Milan to Ventimiglia	283 km	38,000
A9	Milan to Chiasso		
	(Como Grandate)	33 km	4,200
A18	Messina to Palermo	109 km	10,000
A20	Messina to Catania	78 km	5,000

The Riviera motorways, the Italian A10 and the French A8 which join at Ventimiglia are among the most expensive in Europe.

A safe and easy average is to allow 150 lire per kilometre and you will usually have a little change. It is also useful to know that the toll can be paid in certain currencies other than lire, especially near Italy's borders. Thus the Austrian schilling, the Swiss franc, the French franc are all accepted plus, of course, Deutschemarks and US dollars. The rates, except at frontier towns, are not always that attractive but the service can be very convenient on a bank holiday or a Sunday.

Although credit cards are not usually accepted for payment of tolls there are two other methods to be considered. One is only open to those who have a current account in one of the larger Italian banks. It is called *Telepass* and involves your putting a magnetized badge on your windscreen which allows you to whizz through a special lane without stopping. Your bank account is then debited each month with the amount of tolls you have incurred for that period. The other method, open to all, is to purchase a magne- tized card for either 50,000 or 100,000 lire which you insert in a machine to pay the toll demanded on the ticket. There are special lanes provided and both these methods help speed the journey, particularly in the rush hours or at holiday periods.

Although many petrol stations on the motorways take cards, not all do and you should have cash in reserve in case you cannot use your cards. Few, if any petrol stations off the motorway take credit cards. Indeed, compared with the rest of Western Europe, few Italian shops of any kind take cards.

Ordinary roads are divided into, *Superstrade, Strade Statale, Strade Provinciale*, and *Strade Comunali*, names which signify that they are kept up by the State, the Province or the local *comune*, respectively.

There are SOS boxes every two kilometres on motorways but do not be tempted to cross the motorway to get to a nearer one on the other side: the obvious danger aside, all boxes are linked to the police and indicate where you and your car are; the last thing you want is help on the other side of the motorway. After calling for help you should stay in your car, having put up the obligatory warning triangle as Italian law requires. On ordinary roads you dial 116 and explain your difficulties. If you are involved in an accident where anyone is physically injured the *carabinieri* should be called on 112. If this is beyond your linguistic capabilities, there are some officials who speak the major European languages though it could take some time to find them.

For residents and non-residents alike it pays to belong to an assistance organization operating a 'get you home' scheme. ACI (*Automobile Club d'Italia*) costs approximately 60,000 lire a year, but this expense is amortized by one tow off the motorway which is even more expensive on a Sunday. Most insurance companies operate national and international schemes and many of them use ACI's services in Italy. Possibly you get more for your money this way than with ACI direct, and as yet, ACI, unlike the AA or RAC, does not have reciprocal arrangements out of Italy. Europassistance is offered by many insurance companies as well as banks and for those who travel abroad a good deal it is well worth the premium.

6
Law and Order

Italy has special problems in maintaining law and order within her territory. Not only is the average Italian not naturally a law-abiding type, but there is also the age old curse of organized crime in the form of the Mafia, who have now branched out into the illegal drug trade. The only good thing to report since the last edition of this book is that the fear of urban terrorism has diminished to such an extent one is hardly aware of its existence.

It would be totally wrong to suppose, as a result of the above statements, that Italy is in any way a lawless country. It is, however, a country where either petty infractions are simply overlooked (particularly if the general consensus of opinion is that Rome has produced yet another law which everyone considers rather useless or irksome) or where the public is jumped on ferociously in order to avoid total anarchy – a state for which much of Italy has a secret longing.

Unless the fines were so enormous, no Italian would think of informing the authorities that he has now moved to a new house and is waiting to be taxed on his property ownership, his income and so on. Since he uses his car every day and the fines for not paying a road-fund licence or driving an uninsured car are incredibly high, to say nothing of the possibility of temporarily or permanently losing the use of the vehicle, he does make sure his car and its papers are *a posto*. Alas, the tax authorities are considerably more dilatory and require would-be tax-payers to register themselves. An incredible number do not and there is a Statute of Limitations so that anyone caught is only liable for the past five or six years' back-tax, plus a fine.

Then there are scandals on which the Italian reading public feast daily. Some are so stupid it defies belief. Much work is still black in Italy with no VAT payable and, more importantly, no income tax on the undeclared profit which is made. The most recent scandal in my own area concerns a builder and a marble supplier who endeavoured to perform an entire contract for a local port authority black, including not paying properly declared salaries to their workers, no National Insurance and of course no VAT on a contract worth approximately thirty million pounds. A fine of over eight million pounds was imposed on one of the perpetrators, which he was able to pay the next day. The other man has gone to jail unable to pay a rather less swingeing fine.

Given the prevailing climate in Italy, it is scarcely surprising that there are police everywhere looking for contraband drugs. Italy has become a European centre for drug trafficking particularly in the north-west where there is a long border with France. Much of the stuff comes in from former Yugoslavia and Albania. With all the problems in Albania there have been more than 16,000 Albanian refugees legally allowed to remain in Italy. Of these some 13,000 appear to have disappeared totally and are believed to be involved in drug dealing.

Do not be concerned that virtually all police are armed and that some tend to brandish machine guns. A simple roadside check is likely to involve a number of police of one sort or another, possibly with a *carabiniere* 100 metres further down the road with gun at the ready to catch those who failed to respond to the signal to stop. There seems to be a pat answer from all policemen in Italy to foreigners: 'We Italians are not law-abiding like you British and we must be prepared for every eventuality', including, it would seem, the possibility of encountering a murderer or cocaine dealer, both of which happened only a few weeks prior to typing this.

However you enter Italy, you may well see the frontier police, even though Italy has now ratified the Schengen Agreement on open frontiers. These frontier police are divided into: *Polstrada* (road), *Polfer* (railway police), *Polarea* (airport) and the *Guardia di Finanza* who are immediately recognizable by the brilliant yellow flashes on their uniforms, for which they have the somewhat pejorative name of '*becchi gialli*'. These last are the Customs and Excise, Fraud Squad, Tax Police and partial coastguard all rolled into one. At most of the big ports such as Genoa, Naples and Taranto you will see their sleek, very fast power-boats which they use to chase smugglers of everything from tobacco and jewels to gold and cocaine.

Every town of any size has its own municipal police called either *Polizia Municipale* or *Vigili Urbani*. In towns they control the traffic and work almost entirely in their headquarters where they take in the fines for road traffic and parking offences. They are not greatly loved by anyone, except perhaps their wives. In villages, where there is usually only one of them, they do similar work including collecting fines for infringements of the building code such as putting up walls without prior permission. All these police are under the Ministry-of-the-Interior umbrella.

Quite different and considerably more efficient are the *carabinieri* who come under the Ministry of Defence. Their nearest equivalents are in countries which maintain a gendarmerie, but there the similarity ends. The *carabinieri* have a somewhat romantic view of themselves, seeking and finding criminals, restoring order after an earthquake or an explosion, restoring stolen art to Italian galleries and so on. There is more than a little truth in all this. Geographically, Italy seems to be prone to natural disasters such as earthquakes, appalling floods and terrible summer fires and the *carabinieri* always appear to be on the spot in no time at all. They have fast cars, speedboats and helicopters to aid them in their work and there seems to be no sign of penny-pinching as there is with the other branches of the police. There is a large readership for the many books on the exploits of the *carabinieri* from the memoirs of a *mariesciallo* (a sergeant in a small town) to their role in history as an institution. It is strangely true that when there is anything rather nasty to be done, like arresting Mussolini or telling the King he has to leave Italy at once, it is always the *carabinieri* who do the dirty work. Certainly, they represent the greatest enemy of organized crime in Italy.

Apart from the occasional murder or *crime passionel*, and many burglaries (now almost as common as elsewhere in Europe), most crime in Italy is in the hands of the Mafia. This is an organization which Mussolini managed to break – the only really good thing he ever did. When the Americans and their allies liberated Italy they sent over, as interpreters and negotiators, Italian Americans, many of whom had Mafia connections. By no means all were involved but the seed was once again sown and the Mafia was re-born after the war, stronger than ever.

Today the Mafia has tentacles stretching from Colombia to Russia, the USA to Holland, and everyday their network grows. In Italy they are feared but also, in a strange way actually admired for their sense of honour and vow of silence or *omertà* as it is known. The idea is that a member of the Sicilian Mafia is trusted to keep his word. This went out of fashion somewhere around 1900, but old ideas die hard. Frankly, the only thing worth considering is that a member of the Mafia never forgives a slight; the *vendetta* and/or the Calabrese *faida* is alive and well.

On a lighter note this *omertà* or vow of silence is shown in all its glory in the following story. Someone has been shot in the market square of a small Calabrese town. The *carabinieri* rush in and question the onlookers who all say the same thing. 'I saw nothing, I heard nothing', or 'I was asleep and heard nothing and if I saw something it was in a dream'. After half an hour of this type of answer the *carabinieri* realized it was pointless questioning anyone in this town where the entire population was blind and dumb, but not stupid.

Sub-divisions of the Mafia are the Camorra in Naples and Campania, the 'Ndrangheta in Calabria and the Sacra Corona Unità in Apulia which used to be a rather honest part of the south only a few years ago. Cosa Nostra is an American name for the Mafia and essentially a name used in New York and Chicago. It is horribly near to sounding like Casa Nostra which is a wonderful organization bent on saving Italy's architectural heritage.

The biggest wine scandal ever known in Italy was said to be as a result of a Mafia settling of accounts. Be that as it may, the *carabinieri* have a very large department dealing with health and food and drink adulteration, and factory inspection units. Vineyards, farms and bottling plants are subject to spot checks as well. Out of a total of almost 25,000 visits over 4,000 firms were found guilty of some infringement or other but (excluding the wine and spirit trade) very few cases involved the closure of a factory or plant.

The most law-abiding regions in Italy are the Val d'Aosta, Friuli-Venezia-Giulia, Trentino-Alto-Adige, the Marche, Molise and Basilicata. Most burglaries take place in Milan and other Lombardy towns, as well as in Naples and Campania. On average, about a third of the burglars are brought to book, which is marginally better than the UK. One reads of antique shops where the entire stock turns out to have been stolen and there is quite a lot of stolen international fine art on sale in Italy. Whole houses, some of which have appeared in *Architectural Digest* or *House and Garden*, are pillaged to provide good antique furniture for collectors who have no idea of the provenance of their latest acquisition.

Urban terrorism appears to be a thing of the past – at least one hopes it is and the police are now less worried about people registering when on holiday. The local town hall prefers you to register your guests, if only for tax reasons. Be very circumspect about letting your house or apartment. You may let one year and declare the income only to find you will be asked questions in the following years even when you have not let the place.

On a very minor scale it is important to remember that, as in the UK you cannot just go and fish anywhere and you need a local licence to fish in all but special trout pounds. The local municipal offices will put you on the right track. In most places in Italy, you cannot collect mushrooms without a permit from the local authority and in many places you must be a resident. This is because the mushroom crop is diminishing yearly. In no circumstances, on pain of a fine, can you use a plastic bag of any sort for your mushroom collection. This is because dropped plastic bags tend to remain and prevent re-growth of mushrooms, and anyway look awful in a forest. For similar reasons you cannot pick wild flowers – particularly on mountains – and you cannot dig up bulbs or seedlings. Apparently the Dutch manage to take back to Holland all sorts of wild bulbs which appear in their catalogues two or three years later. Many of the species they advertise are endemic to one or two specific places in Italy and so could not have come from anywhere else. I have heard this same tale in Austria, Hungary and the Czech Republic, so it seems to be a general problem.

Lotteries are strictly controlled and pay out slowly, nothing like the National Lottery or the French Loterie Nationale. In one town recently, a man began legal proceedings against the authorities who failed to pay him on the grounds that too many (over fifty) people had already won. It won't come to court and he will be paid, but they will have had time to recover from the shock of having to pay out to so many winners.

There are four casinos in Italy at Campione d'Italia on Lake Lugano, Venice, San Remo (IM) and St Vincent (AO). They are all very closely controlled, but this still doesn't stop occasional scandals and closures.

7
Family Law

There can be no better place than under the heading Family Law to make a plea to the foreigner emigrating to Italy. The Italian system of law has little, if anything, to do with Anglo-Saxon tradition and it is quite pointless to rail against the vast amounts of paper and form-filling required or the time it takes to get a semblance of justice. As has been said before, a country gets the police it deserves and the same goes for the system of law. The Italians themselves are not particularly happy with their legal system and even though you may not have voluntarily chosen to live in Italy you are in no position to improve it. If you have fallen in love with Italy and decided to stay then you must accept the country on a warts-and-all basis.

The Italian national cannot do much without a certificate of some sort or another and a whole sheaf of these has to be presented even to get a fishing licence. Non-Italians, incidentally, are not allowed to vote in Italy except at municipal elections, however long they may have been resident in the country. Nonetheless, as an exercise in bureaucracy it is quite interesting to go through the process of getting on to the electoral roll.

In May 1997 a new law was passed, number 125/97, the idea of which was to lessen the burden of supplying endless new certificates for this and that purpose. From that date, certificates which have fixed dates and refer to fixed acts, such as birth, death, marriage, adoption or a university degree or diploma can be of any date and no person or department can demand a more up-to-date copy. Similarly, in the majority of cases it is no longer necessary to have your signature authenticated by the local *municipio* and you can make a declaration as to the veracity of any statement you can give. This new legislation can save a great deal of what the Americans call hassle and is to be gratefully received by Italian and foreign resident alike. Certificates of residence, *Stato di Famiglia* and similar certificates which can change according to circumstances will still have to be less than three or six months old.

Stato civile or civil status is part and parcel of life in Italy as in many other, particularly Latin, countries where the legal systems owe something to the Napoleonic Code.

On marriage, both husband and wife start a new family unit and all things affecting that family unit are inscribed in the family book known as a *Libretto di Famiglia* as well as in the anagraphic register (Register of Births, Deaths and Marriages) which is held at the local *municipio*. Thus the marriage, the names of the two parties, the type of marriage contract, the names of their children if they have any, their possible subsequent divorce and finally their deaths are all entered in this book and register. Strictly speaking, this *libretto* should be kept by the husband or wife at home but it is frequently left at the *municipio* for safe keeping and for them to fill in the various events as they occur.

It should be remembered that there is no reason why the Italian bureaucracy should demand less of the foreigner than it does of the native born. Certificates of civil status are often required for job application as are certificates which show your present *Stato di Famiglia*. They can show you as single, married, legally separated, divorced, widowed and so on.

The most difficult certificate is the penal certificate showing you have or have not been to prison since this does not exist in the UK and occasionally it is beyond the comprehension of an Italian that it is not obtainable. (In the old days before a united Europe, the other certificate which was extremely difficult to produce was one from the Mayor of your British municipality saying you owed nothing by way of taxes.) If the Italians insist on a Penal Certificate then you will have to contact the Embassy in Rome or your nearest British Consulate for them to send the standard letter of explanation. After some years in Italy you will find that your local *comune* will, in certain circumstances, issue you with a Penal Certificate stating you have never been imprisoned in Italy, providing this is the case. However, they are not required by law to do so for a foreigner.

There are also certificates to prove you are still alive (usually for pension purposes), of good conduct, of citizenship (*Certificato di Cittadinanza*) which for foreigners is provided by his or her passport. In fact, your passport is extremely useful in cases of civil status and many notaries will accept it in lieu of a number of certificates which are often demanded. Translations are not usually required but it is kind to produce one.

Italian law requires that you inform the authorities of your change of address, of marriage, of divorce etc. which have occurred out of Italy since at home these facts would automatically be registered in the local records. Italians in any event are rather dilatory about this and, except in the case of death, the fines are fairly minimal for not doing so and indeed, are often not even imposed.

Foreign children at Italian schools and universities when asked to provide a *Certificato di Stato Civile* or *Stato di Famiglia* should provide a birth certificate and its translation, done either by a translator attached to the local court or *Tribunale* or by a Notary Public and certified by the Italian Consulate in the country of its issue. This last is the slowest way of going about things since no Consulate appears to have any sense of urgency or service to the public even when it is paid for. As with penal certificates some Italian town halls will provide civil status certificates where others will say, categorically, that Italian law prevents them from doing so.

A Residence Certificate or *Certificato di Residenza* is the most frequently asked for document since it controls the price you pay both for telephone and electricity. Sometimes it carries a fiscal stamp of 20,000 lire and sometimes it does not: if it is being used for USL or Department of Health matters or for other Government requirements it does not; but if it is for ENEL, Telecom Italia or the purchase of a car it does. In most cases it should not be older than six months, in others less than three months old and in rare cases less than a month old.

Foreigners wishing to take up residence in Italy must have filled in, usually at the *municipio* of their local *comune*, an application for a *Soggiorno* (*Dichiarazione di soggiorno per stranieri*) which requires a stay of three months as a tourist in the first place. Thereafter, when finally issued by the State Police or *Polizia Statale*, it will last for five years if you are a member of the European Community and one year if you come from elsewhere. Renewals are done in the same office at the end of the stated period and failure to renew can lead to a whopping fine. You will need three photographs at the beginning and at the renewal and the demand, as it is called, requires *carta bollata* at 20,000 lire. Do not rely on offices, town halls etc. since they never have any fiscal stamps; these are ostensibly obtainable from all tobacconists but sometimes you have to go to several shops before finding one with the requisite stamps or paper.

Once you become a permanent resident your local *comune* will, at your request, issue you with an Italian identity card or *Carta d'Identita* which is considerably easier to carry around than a passport and less disastrous if you lose it through theft or carelessness. It will give all the necessary details of your civil status including your marital status and your nationality. It is not valid, however, out of Italy. This should not matter since you will have arrived with a passport from your own country. It is the piece of identification Italians prefer so for that reason alone is a worthwhile acquisition. The cost is nominal though constantly changing which is why it is not given here.

Births

It is obligatory to register any birth in Italy within ten days of the event, *irrespective of the nationality of the parents*. As in most civilized countries the majority of births take place in hospitals and two or three times a week a person from the *Stato Civile* department of the local *comune* comes round and issues birth certificates very much as in British and American hospitals. However, do not be surprised if this service is not provided since it is *your* obligation, not that of the hospital or local *comune* to register the birth. Anyone, including husband, grandparent, brother, sister etc. can register the birth as long as he or she can provide the necessary *Certificato di Ostetrico* or *di Levatrice*; this certificate is still needed even when the birth takes place without an obstetrician or midwife being present. Any doctor, midwife or hospital can arrange the necessary examination prior to issuing the certificate. There is a thriving trade in illegal adoptions, particularly in the south and this is why a physical examination of the putative mother is vital. *There is no fee for registering a birth in Italy* so do not let anyone charge you for this service. The birth does not have to be registered in the *comune* where it took place if that is different from that of one or both of the parents. To give an example; it is perfectly legal for the child, born in Viterbo to be registered in the *comune* of the father which could be Pescara or of the mother which could be Verona. However, do remember that wherever the birth is registered the *Certificato di Ostretico* or *di Levatrice* will be needed.

Birth in Italy to non-Italian parents does *not* confer Italian nationality on the child. This is only acquired after ten years of residence in Italy, not necessarily but preferably continuous. Thus a child who is born in Italy, whose parents continue to reside in the country for a further ten years and who then become Italian nationals, will automatically become Italian (and, if a boy, will at eighteen be liable for military service). Copies of birth certificates can be obtained either at the *comune* or at the regional registry of births. From time to time there are murmurs about making registration a national thing, as has been done with motor cars, but the sheer size of the undertaking is very daunting and such a change seems unlikely for some time to come. At this date it is still essential to know the *comune* in which the birth took place and also, though not essential, the date of birth.

Children born in Italy of non-Italian parents should always have their birth registered at the nearest Consulate of their parents' home country. Failure to do this can result in either loss of nationality or a great deal of paper work and inconvenience for all concerned. British nationals should consult Appendix B of this book which sets out British nationality rules. Also it can be very irritating to have a single birth certificate from a country of which he or she is not a citizen. Far better that a child should have the nationality of at least one of its parents.

Marriages

As in many countries the world over, the number of people marrying is going down rapidly and the number of illegitimate births is climbing steadily. The Italian State is not particularly kind or generous to single-parent families and it is generally up to the individual's family and relations to provide what the State manifestly will not.

There are both civil and religious marriages in Italy. Since Italy is predominantly a Roman Catholic country with a special concordat with the Vatican, *all* Roman Catholic priests are licensed to conduct marriages in church. Thus, provided one is Roman Catholic, there is no necessity to have both a civil and a religious ceremony. Otherwise, it depends entirely on the individual performing the marriage ceremony and on whether he is licensed to do so or not.

Irrespective of religion, or lack of one, the following documents are needed: a birth certificate and, if it is a foreign one, its translation by a court translator (*Perito del Tribunale*) or by the person's Consulate; a certificate of freedom (*Certificato di Stato Libero*), which can be difficult for the British to acquire, though in the case of Roman Catholics it is accepted in the form of a clean baptismal certificate; and if this does show a marriage, it should show either the date of death in conjunction with a copy of the death certificate, or a Vatican annulment; finally, a fiscal stamp at 20,000 lire (1998) is also required.

Although widows can re-marry immediately after their husbands' death, divorced women cannot and are obliged to wait nine months or obtain a special dispensation from the local court, known as a *Dispensa Speciale*. This is said to be because they could be pregnant by the former husband at the date of the divorce.

Apart from the fiscal stamp there is nothing to pay for a civil ceremony of marriage, though there are no limits on the cost of a church wedding. It depends entirely on how modest or grand it is. In Italy you can get married at any time of the day, any day of the week, including Sunday, but it has to be said that the local mayor is usually not best pleased to perform the ceremony out of normal working hours. There is a constantly growing number of civil marriages in Italy, entirely due to divorce being legal since 1970.

The romantically inclined are not allowed to marry at the British Embassy or the British Consulates in Italy. British Consuls are only empowered to conduct marriages where there are no other suitable facilities and Italy is considered highly suitable by the British Government.

There are special licences to marry urgently in Italy but they are only available in very limited circumstances and few apply to British or American nationals. They cover situations such as imminent death of one of the parties or his or her immediate imprisonment. No one appears to have heard of any British national availing himself of such a licence.

Irrespective of the type of wedding ceremony the banns or *Pubblicazioni Matrimoniali*, are, in the case of a Roman Catholic wedding, read out on two successive Sundays at the parish church of both the bride and the groom, no matter where they are. In the case of a civil wedding, the banns will be put up on the local notice board for a period of two successive Sundays plus four days. If one, or both, of the parties is from abroad then the banns are published in their own area be it Naples, Concord, Massachusetts or Alice Springs, Australia. Effectively, there is an eighteen day wait before you can get married in Italy and this is reduced only in the most dire circumstances, none of which is pleasurable.

You must be at least 16 years old in Italy and until you are 18 you will need the permission of both parents. In the case of no mother or father then the permission of the eldest near relative either in the direct line or laterally must be sought. If this is withheld then waiting is the only answer. There is no recourse to the *Tribunale* against this family decision.

Two witnesses are required at any marriage ceremony in Italy and for some inexplicable reason four witnesses are required at prison marriages.

A civil marriage is normally celebrated in the local *municipio* of either the bride or groom. The mayor (*sindaco*) who performs the ceremony is obliged to wear his mayoral sash (the green, white and red *tricolore*) and the room must be open to the public at large. The mayor reads out the various articles concerning civil status and marriage from the Italian Civil Code and asks the groom and the bride if he and she freely consent to the marriage. On receiving their assent he asks them to exchange rings (virtually all Italian husbands wear wedding rings) and then he gives a short speech on marriage directing the couple to help each other in time of need. This is said to mean that a modern Italian wife should go out to work when the husband is unemployed (which was previously unthinkable). He then asks the witnesses if they have heard and understood the ceremony. Once they say yes he turns to the couple and says '*Siete marito e moglie*' – 'You are husband and wife'.

There is no requirement in Italy for a wife to take her husband's name and, indeed, legally it is never hers and she retains her maiden name until death. However, most women are known by the husband's surname. In all documents she is bound to use her maiden name, followed by 'wife of so and so'. The most common way is for a woman to tack her husband's name onto her own, viz. Paola Rieti Dalmasso, Paola Rieti wife of Signor Dalmasso. However, just to muddle things some women put their husband's name first, e.g. Paola Dalmasso Rieti, but this is unusual. When this form is used it is often for professional reasons as with doctors or university professors.

In the recent past a foreign woman marrying an Italian was bound to take his nationality, but this is no longer a requirement. She can acquire Italian nationality as a right simply by being the wife of an Italian national and considerably more simply than the Italian wife of a British national can acquire British nationality. She is entitled to have dual nationality, i.e. not lose her nationality of birth, but cannot expect the help of the British Government against the Italian authorities in Italy. This seems perfectly normal and reasonable but such are the unreasonable expectations of certain British nationals that they take exception to this proviso.

A British (or American for that matter) woman whose passport is in her married name should either ask the passport issuing authorities to show her maiden name or she should show her birth certificate (for her maiden name) and her marriage certificate (to show how it was changed) to the various Italian authorities. Otherwise, it can still be difficult, for instance, to change from a British driving licence in your married name to an Italian one in your maiden name.

However, things are becoming considerably more relaxed in Italy and only recently I was able to hire a car in my married name, show an Italian driving licence in my maiden name and pay by credit card in a company name. Perhaps this was partly due to their not being able to get their money any other way but the whole transaction would have been unthinkable ten years ago.

Marriage in Italy, irrespective of nationality, is subject to one of two matrimonial regimes: community of property (*comunità dei beni*) or separation of property (*separazione dei beni*). Which regime is chosen depends on the persons and families involved but it can make a great deal of difference later on, particularly at the death of one of the parties if he or she is governed by Italian law. (See under Wills later in this chapter.) It is essential that this is discussed with a lawyer and perhaps also a notary. It is totally irrelevant that the parties might be marrying without a bean to their name. The situation is bound to change and then it may be too late.

Foreigners who come from countries without matrimonial regimes are usually shown as having married without regime or under the equivalent of *separazione dei beni* and any notary worth his salt will discuss this matter with husband and wife before drawing the document.

A wife's earnings in Italy are her own. She can have her own credit cards and credit arrangements without her husband's permission. She is not required to put her earnings in to the family kitty though she most frequently does. The days of grooming a girl to be wife and mother and nothing else are over. More and more women are going out to work to earn for themselves and are tasting both the delights and bitterness of being independent. Only in the deep south do the old mores obtain. There, women are still under the thumb of their menfolk and though many of them work they do so black and the money is sometimes even paid direct to their husbands. '*Un altra coltura*' they say. Indeed it is.

Divorce

Even though it may mean having to achieve a year's residence in the UK, British subjects should try to avoid getting divorced in Italy unless it is by mutual consent. In this case, it is virtually free, easy and proceedings can be started almost immediately after the marriage, should that be necessary.

Although Italy has had divorce for over twenty-five years the figures are still surprisingly low when compared with the rest of Europe. Except for divorce by consent it is a complicated process and perhaps many would-be divorcers give up halfway through.

The Italian courts have jurisdiction in the matter of divorce (a) if the marriage took place in Italy (b) if one or both of the parties is

Italian, and (c) if one or both of the parties has a permanent residence in Italy.

There are no restrictions as to marriage after divorce though a woman must wait nine months unless she gets a *dispensa speciale* from the court. If during the waiting period she becomes pregnant by her future husband, or indeed if she is already pregnant by him and gives birth before they can marry, he can formally recognize the child and it will become legitimate upon their marriage.

The waiting times for divorce have changed and now couples divorcing by consent need wait only three years in all to be divorced. Couples divorcing not by consent of one of the parties must wait five years in all once the fault has been proved.

Once a couple decides to divorce, they go before the judge who offers them one of two things. Either to try for a reconciliation for a year, or a formal separation (*separazione formale*) for a year. If there are any financial matters to be dealt with this is the moment a decision will be made. Where there are children, custody is usually given to the mother, though not always, and usually the father has access at weekends or on his day off. Incidentally, once the child is ten he or she can, to a certain extent, decide with which parent he or she wishes to live. By sixteen he can equally decide whether he wishes to live with either of his parents or none in which case the court will hand over his care to the social services. Usually it is the father who is entirely responsible for the maintenance of his children unless the wife is earning a fortune. So far as maintenance for a wife is concerned if the husband is suing her for divorce on the grounds of her proven adultery, the court will decide whether she is due money or not.

At the end of this year of reconciliation through which all couples must go, the next stage is either the said reconciliation or divorce on the grounds given below. This is *divorzio legale* and there is a further waiting period of either two years in the case of couples consenting to divorce or four years in the case of couples not consenting. There is little a woman, or a man for that matter, can do against a spouse determined to divorce and the only inhibiting fact is the cost. A divorce by consent costs virtually nothing whereas the other sort begins at around five million lire.

The grounds for divorce in Italy are: adultery by one of the parties, cruelty either mental or physical or both, desertion known as *abbandono di tetto coniugale* (which can, in certain circumstances be a criminal offence) and unsoundness of mind, but this last has to be legal insanity and not merely the opinion of the other spouse and his or her relations. It is far better and cheaper when divorcing, even in the case of adultery or cruelty, to agree to a divorce and a reasonable financial settlement than to wait two more years to get the same thing or less. Strictly speaking, there is no such claim as irretrievable breakdown of marriage but a good lawyer will organize things for you if this is what both parties believe has happened. Desertion usually requires a five-year wait (it used to be seven) before the final divorce is declared. Even if a deserting husband or wife writes from the other end of Italy or from abroad that he or she is never coming back, it doesn't seem to count so far as lessening the waiting period. However, even that may change in the future.

Maintenance, particularly to ex-wives is a knotty problem. As in any country, no husband likes to pay money to an ex-wife when he has a new wife to support. In any event he will be forced to pay maintenance for his children and there is a system of attachment of earnings in Italy to make sure he does. However, since most of Italy is self-employed (it has the highest rate of self-employed in the European Union) it becomes very difficult to enforce a system geared to salaried persons. Non-payment of child maintenance can lead to a term of imprisonment which most ex-wives wish to avoid since it doesn't feed the children and gives the father a criminal record. Things like this are put into the *comune* records – instead of a clear Penal Certificate he will forever have *un Certificato Penale Macchiato*. Likewise, foreign maintenance orders can be enforced in Italy and vice versa but it is uphill work.

Two final but important points. An Italian national obtaining a divorce out of Italy which ends a marriage celebrated in Italy must obtain in addition to his foreign decree an Italian one based on that foreign decree. It is usually a rubber stamp situation for which a lawyer does little but gets well over two million lire – and a lawyer *must* be employed. The same goes for a non-Italian in the same circumstances if he or she wishes to re-marry in Italy. Most divorces are recognized in Italy except those from places specializing in 'quickie divorces'.

Those fortunate beings who need and obtain a Vatican annulment of their marriage can marry again and in church since the first marriage has effectively never taken place. Italy, Ireland and Spain recognize Vatican annulments and count it as a civil divorce which is *not* the position in many, many other countries including the UK. Because of this, it is impossible to get a civil divorce in Italy after a Vatican annulment and you cannot obtain the necessary divorce decree document enabling you to marry anywhere other than Italy, Ireland and Spain. One way round this is to get a divorce elsewhere before or after a Vatican annulment or get married in one of the three countries who recognize the Vatican document.

For Catholics who do not wish to divorce but equally no longer wish to be married there exists a formal judicial separation in Italy. Your parish priest will put you in touch with a suitable lawyer.

Deaths

Deaths must be registered within twenty-four hours at the offices of the *comune* in which they took place. However, five hours should elapse before registration in any event. In the case of violent or suspected violent death the time limit is forty-eight hours. These time limits were worked out many years ago when there was little or no refrigeration in Italy and nowadays it is quite possible to obtain longer delays than before especially if the next of kin has to come from abroad. I know of people in Livorno who were able to keep a member of their family from burial for more than a week whilst awaiting the arrival of his son from the United States. However, in general these time limits are normally adhered to. Do remember though, that a special request must be made for such an extension and on no account must time be allowed simply to slip by until it is convenient to conduct the funeral since you will find yourself breaking the law and having to pay a large fine.

A death certificate is not issued unless two doctors, the treating practitioner, if there is one, or another general practitioner and the Local Health Authority Doctor confirm the death. Often a general practitioner fulfils both functions in which case only one signature is needed. Thereafter, unless there is to be a post-mortem, the coffin is closed within twenty-four hours and buried or cremated.

Italian death certificates show the cause of death and an international death certificate can be issued if the body is to be transported abroad for burial. Do remember that the transporting of a body over frontiers can be complicated, though less complicated than it was in the past; most countries, and certainly Italy, demand that it is embalmed, which is an additional cost to consider. International death certificates are also available for legal and insurance purposes out of Italy.

Cremation is becoming more and more common in Italy, particularly in the north. Though there was a time when it was actually more expensive, cremation nowadays is usually considerably cheaper. South of Rome, cremation is far less common; burial in the family vault is usually the order of the day. Anyone wishing to be cremated *must* leave written confirmation of his or her wishes otherwise the sorrowing relatives can find it hard to carry them out.

In any part of Italy where cremation is not very common it is as well to lodge this document with the notary having executed it before him. Alternatively your will can be an ideal place to make your wishes known. However, make sure that the family have access to your will before you are summarily buried because no one had read your instructions.

Some years ago, an Italian national married an Indian girl and changed his religion to Hindu which requires cremation at death. The widow had great difficulty, at his death, in avoiding summary burial in the local Roman Catholic cemetery since it was known he was Italian and had been Roman Catholic at one time. Only high-level diplomacy prevented this.

Anglicans or Nonconformists should contact either the nearest British Consulate or the nearest English Church who will put them on the right road. Muslims will already be in touch with their own community and Jews should contact the nearest synagogue in their area. One of the main problems for both Christian Protestants and Jews in Italy is that there are large swathes of Italy where none of one's own kind exists and help has to be called from afar.

Virtually every city and *comune* in Italy has its own cemetery or cemeteries. Only very rarely indeed can burial take place outside of a cemetery in Italy so try not to entertain any idea of being buried down by the stream in your garden and planting a cherry tree on top of the grave. Almost certainly you will not be allowed to have your wish. Most of the major religions have their own cemeteries scattered around Italy and it pays to make enquiries before you actually need the service. Almost all have a *camera mortuaria* where the body can be kept if the family do not wish to keep it at home. To a certain extent the local authorities try to keep the cost of funerals down but prices, as in all other countries, are rising and today a funeral will not cost short of a million lire and can be as much as ten, depending on what sort of monument you wish.

Northern Italians tend to have rather less elaborate funerals than southerners who all belong to burial societies and are great amateurs of the purple and orange funeral wreath. Never is a country so divided as Italy on the subject of death and funerals.

Finally, to scotch the commonly held belief that the Roman Catholic Church will not allow normal burial for suicides, it should be pointed out that Italy, in common with most other civilized countries and, moreover, the Church itself now recognizes that most, if not all, people who commit suicide are mentally ill, if only at the moment of their fatal decision, and it is very rare for a religious funeral not to be allowed.

Adoption

Adoption in Italy, particularly by foreigners, is a subject fraught with complications. It is a subject which brings out the worst on both sides and all the lingering reservations Italians have about foreigners and foreigners in their turn have about Italians are brought to the fore most unpleasantly. It is easier in the north in some ways, but not so much easier.

Should you see a darling little dark-eyed street urchin in Naples whom you long to take home with you, be warned that not only will it be expensive but also virtually impossible. *Never, never try to adopt privately. It is illegal in Italy, as it is in all countries in Europe. The penalty is always a very large fine and frequently a long prison sentence. Also the Foreign Office will not allow such a child to have its parents' British nationality.*

Many, though by no means all, of the orphanages are run by the Catholic Church and seem to have a vested interest in keeping their homes going for other reasons than mere charity. I wish I could explain the logic of this but I would not want to denigrate the few very excellent institutions who do superb work. There are many others who are far less worthy. Also many orphanages demand that future parents are not only practising Catholics but verging on saintly. Often the local parish priest and occasionally even the Bishop are involved. Underlying all this fuss there seems to be a general unwillingness to part with any child if it can be avoided. Adopting a child from the Third World is usually easier and cheaper, even taking the fares into account, but do make sure before coming to Italy that all the child's papers are in order.

Never undertake adoption without the support of an Italian lawyer who specializes in Adoption Law. Four to five years is usually the minimum waiting period.

Domicile

It is important to know where you are domiciled. You may think you are domiciled in Italy because you own a house there and pay Italian income tax. The British Revenue may view the matter differently and your family may be in for a very unpleasant surprise after your death when all your assets, worldwide, become subject to UK inheritance tax.

Most British citizens will be born with a domicile or origin be it England, Wales, Northern Ireland or Scotland and if you no longer wish to keep this domicile you must make it clear, in writing, to your solicitor, accountant and family, over and over again. Remember, it is not easy to argue about domicile once the person in question is dead.

Although under English law a husband and wife can opt for separate domiciles this is not something commonly understood by Italians and certainly not by the Italian Revenue. Also Italians use the word *domicilio* to mean dwelling house or where you live. If you own a house in Italy, Italian inheritance tax will become due on your death according to your relationship to the beneficiary. Ditto for other property held as well as Italian securities. There is a double-tax convention between the UK and Italy so tax will not be paid twice but will be paid at the higher rate, which is usually the Italian. There is no exemption between husband and wife.

Wills

There are two aspects to the making of every Will: its contents, and the formalities which must be complied with to make it a valid document. The reason why domicile does not have the importance in Italy that it does in many other countries is partly due to the fact that under Italian law, the contents of a Will made by a foreigner are governed by the law of his nationality at the date of his death.

On the other hand, the formalities needed to make the Will valid may be those recognized either by Italian law or by the law of the nationality of the testator at the time he makes the Will. Since the criterion is British nationality and people living in any one of the four countries which make up the United Kingdom all have the same nationality, advice may well be needed about this in your 'home' country. Some care is needed where a person domiciled in Scotland makes a Will of only English, Welsh and Italian property or where a person domiciled in England or Wales has property only in Scotland and Italy. Highly skilled advice is called for.

Hence, a British subject living in Italy may safely make a Will in English/Welsh or Scottish form and execute it in accordance with English/Welsh or Scottish requirements and it will, in every respect, be a valid Will in Italy. Indeed, this is almost certainly the most practical thing to do.

Lawyers love home-made Wills since they end up making a fortune out of them. Needless to say, unless you are particularly anxious to involve your loved ones in legal tangles after your death, you will consult a lawyer when you wish to make a Will and preferably a lawyer who has a knowledge of both the Italian and your own legal system.

Of course, you can make an Italian Will in any one of the three forms allowed under Italian law but do remember that in any event your property will pass in accordance with *your* nationality. In the case of English/Welsh law this may well be no different from what you say in your Will, but other nationalities such as French, German, Belgian or even Scottish can cause quite a difference. Therefore, on the whole, no matter how good your Italian, it is probably best not to use Italian as the language of your Will since it may give headaches when translated into English.

However, if you absolutely insist on making an Italian Will the three methods available are:

1. *Testamento Olografo*: A Holograph Will, the only requirement of which is that it is must be entirely in your own handwriting and signed and dated by you. It requires no witnesses and indeed should not have any. This is a very popular type of Will in Italy because of its apparent simplicity, wherein lies its main disadvantage: it is equally simple for it to disappear at the appropriate time, which is a fairly frequent occurrence, or to be forged or changed, which is less so. There is little sanctity about a Will in Italy.

2. *Testamento Pubblico*: A Public Will, so called because it is held by the notary before whom you make it in his 'public' records. This involves certain formalities as to the witnessing of the document. Of all Italian Wills this is the best type to opt for but you should inform your nearest and dearest of what you have done and where the actual Will is held, although you may well keep a copy for your own records.

3. *Testamento Segreto*: A Secret Will, a hybrid of the two former types of Will with the disadvantage that it, too, can be 'mislaid', sometimes forever. You prepare the Will and then hand it to the *notaio* in a sealed envelope accompanied by certain formalities. However, too often the Will contained in the envelope is of the home made variety and therefore, this third type is best avoided.

Since in Italy all foreigners' Wills are dealt with according to their nationality, the foreign testator avoids the problem of Italian succession rules and *legittime*. This is a rule of law found in quite a few western European countries, including Scotland, which gives certain relatives of the deceased an absolute right to a share in his estate even when he has expressed his wishes in his Will to the contrary. It is possible to disinherit children and close family members in Italy but not at all easy and usually costs far more than the small amount to which these people are entitled.

Therefore, unless a UK citizen becomes an Italian national, he will not be involved in this scheme of things which is so deeply foreign to him. He can happily disinherit his wife and children (unless he is Scottish with a Scottish domicile where *legitim* and *terce* play a part) and leave everything to the cats' home, though in this case there will be a larger than usual amount of Italian inheritance tax to pay since it will not be one of the three main charities which the Italian Revenue smile upon and allow gifts to go tax free. That said, his disinherited wife and/or children can go to court to apply to be 'cut-in'. This freedom to leave an estate where one wishes fills the Italian testator (sometimes) with amazement and his family (always) with horror.

Those living in the Alto-Adige region (Sud-Tirol), specifically in the province of Bolzano, or Bosen in German, are subject to a system totally different from the rest of Italy. Due to the province having been part of the Austro-Hungarian Empire until the end of the First World War, the law of primo-geniture can obtain. A foreigner living in the Alto-Adige has the extra option of making his Will according to the law of that region and a local lawyer or *notaio* will advise on this. However, should he die intestate, his property will devolve according to the law of his nationality and no other.

It is strange that no other part of northern Italy such as Trentino, Venice, Trieste, Friuli-Venezia-Giulia which were under the Austro-Hungarian Empire have this difference in law. Perhaps it is true, as many Italians say, that the Tyrol area of Austria and the Sud-Tirol or Alto-Adige in Italy one day intend to become an independent nation and want to hold on to their age old legal system with that in mind.

Legittime can be of great importance, and irritation to the foreigner. In the past, spurred on first by the Church then by Mussolini, Italian families used to be large, which explains why small fields in the country and tiny houses in towns can be split up between numerous owners. It can be more than merely tedious trying to buy a right of way which others in the meantime may have acquired by right of prescription. Most foreigners buying a country property have had the hassle of negotiating with anything up to ten or fifteen people. I know of one case where a prospective purchaser was asked to pay the inheritance tax due from the vendors to the Italian government plus the INVIM due on the profit made on the sale. All the Italians, including the estate agent and the notary, were surprised when she wouldn't pay pointing out that not only did the payment of INVIM indicate a profit but there was also several millions extra on which no taxes of any sort were going to be paid.

Although executors of a Will in Italy are totally different from those in the UK, Italian law accepts the powers and duties of

English/Scottish Executors and there are no problems on this score.

No one should fail to make a Will, but even if you do not make one, provided you are a British national, English/Welsh or Scottish rules will apply to the intestacy.

Do not worry about how the Italian system will cope with a foreign Will. Once a Will has been proven in the UK, an Italian Consul will certify the effect of the probate and send the Will to the notary of your choice who will take care of all the formalities.

Unfortunately, but perhaps not surprisingly, these comparatively simple rules about Wills for foreigners in Italy do not bring relief from Italian inheritance tax. As in so many other western European countries, the rates of duty depend on the relationship of the testator to the beneficiary rather than, as in the UK, the net worth of the estate in question. Also there is not, as in the UK, total exemption in Italy for the surviving spouse, though for them as for children and parents the rates are not particularly high.

Currently no duty is payable on estates below 30,000,000 lire and the highest rate of 31 per cent is reached on an estate in excess of 1,000 million lire. This latter sum is quite easy to reach, the price of real estate being what it is; estate planning with the help of a *notaio* and an insurance set-up would be a clever move to save inheritance tax. At the other end of the scale, where a beneficiary is totally unrelated to the testator everything above one million lire is dutiable starting at 3 per cent and rising to 60 per cent in respect of the slice in excess of 1,000 million lire. In between are brothers and sisters who pay more than children, parents and spouses, up to relations to the fourth degree who pay a little more.

Unlike the Anglo-Saxon system where the property of a person who dies belongs first to the executors who pay the death duties and then parcel out what is left, in Italy, each beneficiary inherits his share of the estate directly and is personally liable for the inheritance tax which he must pay *before* he can physically lay his hands on his share of the assets. This can sometimes cause problems but the payment of duty can be done by instalments or even be deferred, though incurring extra interest. Italian banks, as in the UK, will normally provide a bridging loan for this purpose. The *notaio* or a *commercialista* (accountant) can usually arrange this for you. Interest rates for this type of loan are currently higher than in the UK, and usually the minimum period for the loan is three months. If you need the money for less than two, it is cheaper to have an overdraft on your current account.

It seems that no country deals with probate as quickly as the UK or America. Certainly Italy is no exception to this rule and changing your *notaio* will not expedite matters. If things get really slow, employ an *avvocato* (lawyer) or specialist lawyer to intercede for you. Given the service he renders he will not be expensive. One of the best threats to be used if all else fails, is by writing by registered post, that you will hold the *notaio* personally responsible for any penalties you may have to fork out due to late payment of inheritance tax.

Finally, a little curiosity of Italian inheritance tax. Except for men and women in Holy Orders, the government, if you cannot produce evidence to the contrary, may want an extra five per cent over the declared value of an estate as non-declared jewellery. This is fine in the case of say a 100 or 200 million lire estate. But as said before, with property prices being what they are you can find an aged lady who wore only a good watch, a wedding and engagement ring and a pair of pearl earrings being worth 70 or 80 million lire in jewellery. Since manifestly this is not the case it is up to the beneficiaries of the estate to prove it. Many Italians, for good and sufficient reasons which are explained elsewhere, tend not to insure jewellery. In such circumstances as the old lady's it would pay handsomely to have all jewellery valued and insured at that value and then later included at that price in the inheritance tax accounts. When the estate is valued after death the valuation should agree, as to *content* not insurance values, with the last insurance cover. Even in Italy, valuations for probate purposes are always lower than insurance values. Of course, such things can be and frequently are negotiated both with the valuer and with the tax people, but it is better to know in advance what problems there can be.

Crime

Crime, as in many other countries, is on the increase in Italy, and in the cities much of it is drug related. The Italian police, in all its forms, has a difficult job keeping the peace let alone being tough on crime. No go areas in large cities are as common in Italy as in other countries. Never try to save money by parking your car in an unknown street in an unknown area if there is an alternative properly guarded car park.

Of course it is best not to get involved with the police anywhere and it is hardly edifying to see on World Cup television *carabinieri* charging innocent football fans merely because they had permission to do so.

Italy sometime ago went over to the English accusatorial system of criminal justice. The idea was to lessen the waiting time to come to court and empty the prisons. In the event the prisons are still as full as ever. It should be remembered that only the procedure and method of judgement have changed, not the Italian penal code. No British Consulate turns out fast for a possible drug charge and Italian prisons are places to be avoided especially if you don't speak the language. The new system notwithstanding, except on a murder charge, you can wait anything up to fifteen days before you even get a preliminary hearing. This is a facet of Italy you should never need to know about.

8

Property Transactions

This is the chapter for those who have accepted that real estate in Italy is extremely expensive though no more so than in parts of France, the UK, Austria etc. and have finally seen the house or apartment of their dreams. As in France, rural property is considerably cheaper than in cities, large towns and resorts which are the most expensive of all. Flats or even houses in the *centro storico* of small villages can be anything from a tremendous bargain to a very bad buy indeed. Of course the old north/south argument also obtains with property since one can purchase apartments complete with acceptable mod. cons for as little as fifteen or twenty million lire in Calabria.

Before you sign anything, get an architect or a really good *geometrà* to survey what you are buying. If it needs repairs, restoring, decorating etc., get him to give you an estimate of how much all this will cost including the administrative costs. It will be money well spent and will cost in the region of one to two million lire – rather less than a British surveyor would charge.

When buying or selling land, houses or apartments a *notaio* must be used. He is responsible to the Government for the correct and legal transfer of landed property, for collecting the taxes and stamp duties due. As has been said earlier, his first duty is to the Government and thereafter to you.

To the British who are still used to the inviolate rule of separate representation for both vendor and purchaser it may seem strange that usually in Italy only one *notaio* is used. He will prepare the documents and even give advice, but if you think it will be difficult for him to advise 'opposing' parties you, as purchaser, are quite free to use your own *notaio* or *avvocato*. Usually it is the latter or sometimes your own *commercialistà*, if you wish.

All three professions are surprisingly switched on from an international point of view and if you are going to live in Italy either permanently or for a long period you would be wise to have a *commercialistà* of your own since you will be paying taxes on your property and he can arrange their payment when you are not in residence. A word of warning though. Italy appears to be full of unqualified accountants and you should employ one only on recommendation from a good friend, your Italian bank or your UK accountant. Good accountants in Italy are not necessarily the larger firms, but the best usually have at least half a dozen young girls and boys doing dogsbody work in the office and learning the ropes before taking their exams. Usually a person working on their own doing everything is not an ideal set-up, if only because a qualified accountant can earn more advising than working a computer and filling in forms.

Perhaps this is a good place to point out that although there are professional bodies designed to protect the client it is very difficult to prove misconduct of a professional adviser to them or indeed to a court. Therefore, try to choose a *notaio*, accountant, lawyer and certainly doctor and dentist on personal recommendation. As an Italian lawyer once pointed out to me, '*Novanta per cento dei professionali non sono veramente professionali*', meaning that the professions do not behave in a very professional way. This can be seen right across the board. The Italians are great improvisors and whilst this can be very useful in some spheres, it is not something one seeks in a professional person.

Let us now take a sample case of a property purchase and follow it through to acquisition by a non-Italian. Italians are able to benefit from certain reductions in areas such as stamp duty and mortgage-rate interest where foreigners cannot.

Mr A. has seen a house he likes and decides to buy it. He signs nothing, not even the *compromesso* or *promesso di vendità* which the estate agent will undoubtedly push under his nose with the warning that there are other people interested in the property. This is probably untrue. As the purchaser, he is able to choose his own *notaio* or he can accept to use the seller's. He either gets the *notaio* or his *avvocato* to draw up a contract. In this document he agrees to buy the property subject, or not, to certain conditions.

This, as it is known, *compromesso* is the most important document for the purchaser since he can put in more or less any reasonable condition such as the obtaining of planning consent for repairs or restoration, the getting of a mortgage or bank loan for its purchase and so on. A good *notaio* or lawyer will usually cover every possibility under the sun, including many you had never thought of. Of course, the vendor has to agree to your conditions, particularly when some, such as planning permission, mean that he will not get his money very quickly; but even he will be aware that he will be required to wait with most would-be purchasers.

The normal deposit on signing the contract is 10 per cent and this should be paid direct to your *notaio*, *not* to the estate agent. If you do not complete the contract for any reason not mentioned in the contract, this is forfeit. The contract usually states the whole price you are going to pay which will not necessarily appear on the final transfer document. This is done also, to establish the amount of commission due to the estate agent; 3 per cent from each of you.

There has been a recent case where vendors claimed the 10 per cent deposit which they had already received for the purchase of an apartment in Rome. The purchaser died and therefore was unable to complete. He had, in fact, asked for a mortgage and the inability to obtain this due to death was held to be sufficient reason not to complete. It seems that had he not included the mortgage condition his estate would have lost the 10 per cent paid. In the UK it is extremely simple to get insurance cover for such a situation and for such a short time, particularly if you are going to take out mort-gage-protection insurance later.

Of course, a vendor may well not agree to the contract if the damages for his non-completion are too high. If a sum is not mentioned then Italian law provides for damages from the vendor for non-completion: double the deposit paid by the would-be purchaser. Thus gazumping is not common in Italy.

Planning permission takes about three months to get and purchasers should be wary of land sold without a passed project (*Progetto passato*) or a certificate of urbanization (*Certificato di Urbanizzazione*). Buying where there is also extant a passed project will lessen the waiting time to completion. By and large, agents will not accept land as building land without planning consent or a *prog-etto*. In any event, never take anyone's word but get the necessary certificate from the *comune* in which the property is. By the time you have found your ideal property you should be employing an architect or a *geometrà* to do this sort of thing for you and to protect you from the following racket.

It is a relatively common practice for smaller agents to quote building land at a third more than they are going to give the vendor. They tell the vendor that he will get 'x' net and no commission to pay. Thirty-three per cent commission is a great deal and some agents are not beyond charging you, the purchaser, the otherwise normal 3 per cent, which is usual as well. The agent pockets either 36 or 39 per cent instead of the rather more normal 6 per cent in all. Needless to say this 'windfall' is never declared to the Italian Revenue. This is a highly dishonest transaction all round and no purchaser (or vendor for that matter) should be party to it. Another thing less than honest agents often do is quote a price to the vendor of 'x' million on which 3 per cent commission is due from both parties plus 50 per cent on anything more he can get over and above the quoted price. Incredibly some people agree to this.

Assuming Mr A. has obtained planning permission, or does not need it as the house is already built, and that he has the sum required to complete the transaction, he can then arrange for the funds to be transferred either within Italy or from outside the country.

Although Italy no longer has any Exchange Control you should have some documentation as to where money for large purchases has come from. Therefore, do this particular transfer from your bank in the UK or wherever (preferably *not* Switzerland since the Italians smell a rat over Swiss accounts for anyone who is not a Swiss national) to your bank in Italy. Of course, if you are never going to become resident in Italy it doesn't matter in which country you have your money. If you haven't already got a bank in Italy you will certainly need one for the future payment of electricity, telephone and water bills. Banks are very expensive, not particularly efficient, bureaucratic but very polite. Once the money has been cleared and a certain number of days have elapsed to satisfy 'international anti-Mafia requirements' you ask the *notaio* for the final figure needed for purchase, stamp duty and his fees. Meanwhile, you also ask your Italian bank for a certificate stating that you have imported this sum into Italy. The *notaio* will also mention this in the *atto* provided you nudge him to do so. Do not be brushed off with the 'Italy has no Exchange Control nowadays' response – it is not really true since you cannot take out more than 20 million lire on any one day. This too, is said to be an anti-Mafia and anti money-laundering measure but it prevents any vast sums going out in one transaction. When you want to export large sums from Italy you must ask for permission from the Banca d'Italia (on an indefinite strike as I write this) approximately three months before you need to carry out the transaction.

You can either give a personal cheque, though no vendor will be thrilled by this, or pay by bank draft. Normally, there is no charge for a bank draft in Italy which is known as an *assegno circolare* and should be made out to your *notaio*. It will also be a record of how many lire you received for your pounds, francs, dollars etc. The entering of Italy into the European single currency will change nothing except, perhaps, to increase the price of property very slightly.

It is common to find that your neighbours will tell you they have had a right of way over your land for this and that reason for the last twenty-five or thirty years or even since time immemorial. You can ask for confirmation from other people and the *comune* as to his right to pass over your land. Unless it appears in your vendor's *atto* it is not a right of way – unless, of course, you choose to grant one. Many so-called rights of way can be dismissed out of hand. There are others which cannot, such as a *servitù di necessità* which can occur when, for instance, the only access to your neighbour's land is over yours. You cannot refuse this and in any event it will appear in the document.

However, this does not necessarily mean he has a right of vehicular access over your land and you should check exactly the sort of access it is. If you discover your neighbours insist on using your land, picking your fruit and telling you they have the right because the previous owner gave it to them in perpetuity, shout back at them *all' italiana* or call the *carabinieri*, always providing you know you are right and they are wrong. Another answer, of course, is to enclose your land which can be rather expensive, and have a locked gate. Once done it is far more difficult to gain access.

Mortgages in Italy are provided by specialist credit institutions often via a bank. Your own Italian bank is bound to have one. However, do not jump at the first offer. Normally the period is ten years, occasionally it can be more. The interest rates, compared with the UK are not that high and, if it is your first house in Italy and it is new, you can sometimes get a further percentage knocked off the interest rate to encourage the building industry, ranging from as low as 8.5 per cent (you will be lucky if you get that) to around 13 per cent. The most common is just under 12 per cent. Not unreasonably they will require evidence of your ability to service this loan. You pay back both interest and capital and it is very important to say at the outset how you wish to repay – monthly, quarterly, half yearly or yearly. *Once these dates are in the mortgage deed it becomes very difficult and extremely expensive to alter them, involving as it does a completely new notarial document.*

To give an idea of the repayment of an ordinary bank or finance company mortgage of 100 million lire repayable over ten years: it will cost around 15 to 16 million a year at 11.4 per cent and only after the five-year mark will you see larger capital repayments. In all it will cost around 148 million and the early years will be the most expensive. As elsewhere it is you who has to supply all the bits of paper and documentation and you who pays for the survey of the building. Normally, you can get up to 50 per cent of the value of the house. Mortgages on property in course of construction are also common and the lender will make stage payments as and when needed. It is always better to go for the survey option otherwise

these institutions tend to lend a percentage based on the price of the
land register or *Rogito*.

The building is insured through the bank but you may well have
to have a separate policy of your own because the bank will insure
more or less only for the mortgage sum.

Few British institutions or banks will lend on property abroad
but the Abbey National, who are in Italy (in Milan) with a view to
lending to the Italians with less hassle than normal, also invite
British enquiries. When property is being purchased with a mortgage, it is usual to execute the mortgage at the bank or financial
institution; your own *notaio* has to come to the bank to do it and
charges you accordingly. Moreover, the bank, in addition to all
other charges on the mortgage, charge *you* for this execution.

If you are buying property in the country and your immediate
neighbours are what are known as *coltivatori diretti*, i.e. those who
earn more than 70 per cent of their income from the land, you and
the vendor must ensure that they have no prior claim on your land
and your house. They have the right of pre-emption on any adja-
cent land, even though it may have a house on it, at the price which
appears on the land register or *Rogito*. Therefore, it is unwise to
cheat in any way on the price in the purchase document and it is
equally unwise even to mention what you have paid for it.

None of this need arise if at the time of purchase, or preferably
before, a *casa rurale* is re-registered as a *casa urbana*. Certainly the
annual taxes will be slightly higher and the *rendità*, of which more
later, will be a little more, but it is a small price to pay for peace of
mind. Alternatively, before signing anything establish that the house
you are going to buy is a *casa urbana*.

The cost of converting from a *casa rurale* to a *casa urbana* is
around a million to two million lire including *geometrà*'s fees for
the obligatory interior plan. The cost varies from province to
province and there are still certain parts of Italy in deep country
where you are not allowed to convert from one to the other.

If you are in the unfortunate position of selling such a house
where you have put in a great deal of money for various works,
often without paying Italian VAT, then it is essential to get a clearance from your *coltivatori diretti* neighbours before even putting
the property on the market. Anyone selling to you in such circumstances should do the same thing. Alternatively, if all else fails then
a payment of between ten and fifteen million lire for the necessary
permission will clear things up. However, with some forethought
such a situation should never arise.

The next problem is at what price to buy and sell – officially that
is. There are still Italians who believe they can sell below the offi-

cially allowed price and any *notaio* who allows such a thing is equally stupid. It is common knowledge that absolutely no one declares the full price and some is always paid to the vendor black.

Basically the Italian Revenue will not investigate any property which is sold at the official rate which is, for 1998, 105 times the annual *rendità* as previously set by the *Catasto* or Land Registry when the property was registered.

Bearing in mind that it is for the owner to arrange for his property to be registered at the *Catasto* and that the local *comune* will not always ask for tax on non-registered property, it pays to have your property registered since the values remain the same for a long period and only the co-efficient changes. A *geometrà* will do this for you for a fee and it is something which is difficult, if not impossible, to do on your own. Naturally a property registered in 1985 is going to have a lower *rendità* value than one registered in 1996 and it is better to have the co-efficient applied to a property registered when it should have been than when penalties for non-payment of rates, interest and what the Italians charmingly call, *morosità* are applied, to say nothing of a higher value on which the *rendità* will be calculated.

When selling or purchasing apartments, the price you sell at, or pay, must be in line with other apartments in the same block, i.e. the official price plus what anyone else may be adding for the same apartment.

Do not think the Italian Revenue stupid. They are not.

For example the house Mr A. wishes to buy costs 500,000,000 lire on the estate agent's card. Its *rendità* value at the *Catasto* is 2,700,000 and multiplying that by 105 will give a figure of 283,000,000 lire and this is the *lowest* sum which can appear on the document. The average *notaio* would quite likely round this up to 300,000,000 lire at least. Always be guided by the *notaio* who knows the Italian Revenue people rather better than you do and anyway is accountable to them.

When all is arranged, Mr A. and the vendor will be convened to attend the *notaio*'s office. If one of the parties cannot be present he can appoint an attorney. Most Italian Consulates have printed forms ready for the appointment of attorneys. When signing a Power of Attorney before an Italian Consul the person appointing will need his birth certificate, his marriage certificate, his passport for proof of nationality and details of the property to be conveyed. Some proof of identity of the attorney should be produced together with his date of birth etc. His marital status is of no interest. Equally yours is. Your *notaio* can also prepare a Power of Attorney for signature before an Italian Consul or a Notary Public. In the latter case do not forget to remind him that it *must* have the Hague Convention Apostille or the notary's signature legalized by an Italian Consul or the Power will be absolutely useless in Italy. The preparation of such a document by an Italian Consul, *notaio* or Notary Public incurs a fee plus stamp duty.

For foreigners purchasing property in Italy it is not necessary to make a Will (though obviously far better to do so) since you may leave your property to whom you wish, as explained in the previous chapter. One of the easiest and cheapest ways of purchasing property is to buy in joint names and leave it to the children with a life interest to the spouse. The duty paid by the children is less and paid only once and the property cannot be sold without the consent of the life tenant. Life interest is *usofrutto* in Italian.

The most important thing to remember in Italy when purchasing property is that the advice of the *notaio* may well be excellent but you will need also advice of the tax side, particularly as to inheritance tax. At the moment, accident, life and certain endowment policies carry no inheritance tax and a policy can be written for the person who is going to inherit your property which will cover any future inheritance-tax liability. This can be combined with a mortgage protection policy and is not expensive, though probably cheaper out of Italy.

Although property can be purchased by a UK or an Italian registered company, this has absolutely no tax advantages in Italy and it is not to be advised. Trusts and trustees are not recognized in Italy in the same way as in the UK. (They do have a type of trust in Italy known as a *fondazione* but its aims are different from the average family trust.) You will find the trustees will be considered the beneficial owners – often to their, and your, disadvantage.

Selling property is rather less complicated than buying, but if only one party of a marriage is involved in a sale then he or she must prove he or she is entitled to the proceeds of sale. The *notaio* will need both a marriage certificate and a certificate from an Italian Consul in Great Britain stating that matrimonial regimes imposed by law do not exist in the UK. Those who have married under a matrimonial regime should provide the certificate together with a translation which should be done by a court interpreter (*Perito del Tribunale*).

The current stamp duty on land is around 17 per cent and 10 per cent on houses and apartments, and these are based on the sum shown in the *atto*. In Mr A's case this would be 300,000,000 lire, but there are certain reliefs allowed. *Notaio*'s fees vary – some are more expensive than others, so as said before, try to go to one on personal recommendation. In all cases of property purchase, it is the purchaser who is liable for these duties, for the *notaio*'s fees and the fees for preparing the mortgage, which are very expensive compared with the UK.

The vendor is very often subject to a form of Capital Gains Tax called INVIM which stands for *Imposto sul valore immobiliare*. However, any property built or purchased after December 1992 is subject not to this tax but to something very similar still based on the cost of the property, often with a form of indexation compared with the price you are selling at. In all cases, the tax usually turns out to be fairly minor and is not to be worried about. It should be remembered that both these taxes are personal taxes due from the vendor and there should be absolutely no question of a purchaser undertaking to pay them. In fact, with peasants in the country and *coltivatori diretti* you may well find yourself paying them because they otherwise refuse to sell. It is not to be encouraged. Before purchasing make quite sure, via the agent if possible, that you will not be paying the vendor's tax bills otherwise it can creep up on you unawares.

In principle you should be able to move into your new property the moment you have both signed the deed, unless there has been any other prior arrangement between you. One of these prior arrangements should be for ENEL or another supplier of electricity to read the meter on a given date, the purchaser having already told them the date of moving in. You will not be able to sign a contract before you move in – not until you have a certificate from the *notaio*, in fact. However, if you are already an ENEL (or similar) customer they will move a little more quickly for you. Exactly the same applies to the gas and water people. The quickest of all are Telecom Italia who can change telephones in less than half a day, but the charge can be up to a million lire depending on where you are and whether you are taking your old telephone number with you or are having a new one which has to be run in. ENEL charge around 750,000 lire for a change-over and often check the electrical installation. They can condemn installations out of hand if they consider them dangerous. The petroleum companies which supply propane or methane gas are also quick – they will come and read your *bombolone* (large holding-tank) and apportion the cost between the vendor and purchaser. Do not be surprised when your vendor insists he left more than the company tells you – this is standard practice.

Having bought your property you will be subject to several communal taxes such as collection of rubbish (*immondizia*), and main drainage for which you are charged until you can show, via a receipt for the septic tank or a declaration from a *geometrà*, that you are not on main drainage. It is quite monstrous that *comune* after *comune* engages in this fiddle when they know full well exactly where there is, and is not, main drainage in their town or village. If you are more than 400 metres from a municipal rubbish bin then you do not need to pay for this service. There are very few places which are caught out by this lack of rubbish bins though it must happen.

Then there is ICI which is a local communal tax *Imposta comunale immobiliare* which for the average house is between 500,000 and 750,000 lire per year. Some provinces also impose property taxes but these vary depending on which part of the country you are in. All in all, it is considerably cheaper than in the UK although you get little advance warning of the tax arriving and precious few days to pay it in. Most of these taxes are accompanied by a post office *bolletino* but if you prefer to pay by cheque you can do so but do take a photocopy of the *bolletino* they send you and send it back with your payment.

Fnally Mr A., or anyone else for that matter purchasing property in Italy, should realize that he cannot do anything to it (except internally) such as increase its size, change the building line, its windows, sometimes its shutters, put in a swimming pool, put up a garden shed, a greenhouse, garden walls, a pergola (if it's large) without prior permission from his local *comune* and possibly also the *provincia* and the *regione*. For instance, unlike in many other countries, swimming pools always require planning permission and the fine for even starting the excavation can be enormous. Permission is usually given where the size of the house is not involved. Having obtained it, the owner of the property or his official attorney must go in person and sign for it at the *comune* offices.

It is regrettable to have to report that the normally charming and kind-hearted Italians are also great snoopers on their neighbours and will denounce them to the authorities on the slightest whim. Therefore, be very circumspect about doing any building work without a licence.

By the same token if you find your neighbour is putting up a huge reinforced concrete wall (allowed absolutely nowhere in Italy) which cuts out your view or light then ask if he has permission to do so and check up to see whether his answer is true. Whether you denounce or not only you can decide. Personally, I find it an intrinsically unattractive system (it was codified under Mussolini) and it would annoy me that I would have to do it on *carta bollata* at 20,000 lire, and in perfect Italian. Living in deep country as I do I would be worried about my dogs, my house, my car and my garden being got at by my newly minted enemies. If you feel really strongly about some abuse of the building code the best way to denounce is to use an architect or *geometrà* and get him to do it for you. Similarly, it is wise to employ one of these people to get permission for property developments in the first place – quite painless, except financially, to the property owner.

Since so many Italians break the law regarding what is known as abusive construction, the government, every now and again, declares a building amnesty or *condono edilizio* where the transgressors pay a fine which amounts to approximately twice (occasionally three times) the amount of taxes they would have paid had they received permission. The advantage is that they get to keep an extension or an increase in the size of the house for which they would never have received permission in fifty years.

It is daunting, and almost part of everyday life to receive a demolition order for some work you have done in good faith. Unless it is built on *comune* property, or is dangerous or truly, unspeakably ugly, it is unlikely you will need to tear everything down. A good *geometrà* or architect will get you out of the jam and his reward will be a fine fat fee for making everything official. In the long run it is an economy to involve the architect or *geometrà* from the start. Nevertheless, some prefer to add on another room or bathroom for which they would never receive permission.

There is strikingly little fraud in property transactions if one excepts the non-declaration of the true price paid, and even that seems to have been more or less codified by the government. There are occasional scams where apartments are offered to the public 'on plan' and which exist only in the mind of the promoter. Timeshare as such does not exist in Italy though occasionally a UK company will own property in Italy and offer it on a timeshare basis. This is nearly always done with an English document since an Italian one cannot exist. You, therefore, have absolutely no protection for your investment in Italy. Properties in Italy under the Holiday Bond Scheme are completely different since you are purchasing weeks of holiday with a choice of properties virtually all over the world. The houses, villas and apartments remain the property of the Holiday Bond company and would-be bond owners are protected by British Government consumer legislation.

Nevertheless, in spite of the foregoing, *caveat emptor*.

9
The Condominium

When seeking a flat in Italy, it is important to keep several things in mind if you want it to be an investment rather than merely a place in the sun.

Most important of all – location, location, location, as the Americans say. Of course, you will pay more for an apartment in Portofino, Courmayeur, the fashionable districts of Milan or Rome, but there it will be a long-term investment and, at the worst, should certainly keep pace with inflation, which is an important consideration if you are using hard currency for the purchase. Location includes not only the situation but the actual setting of the apartment block, whether it has a view of the sea or the mountains, whether its street is tree lined, free of public transport, well lit, etc. A block of flats set in beautiful gardens, even though this increases the service-charge bill, is infinitely preferable to one with shops and dry cleaners underneath or non-professional offices in the block. Underground garages are desirable since vast areas of parked cars do not give an enchanting outlook.

The second important consideration is the age of the block and here there is a period to avoid. Flats became common in Italy rather earlier than in the UK and by 1860 were firmly established in the major cities as desirable (and undesirable) residences. Apartments built before the First World War will usually be extremely well built with thick walls and double-glazed windows, and will have a wealth of decorative fittings unobtainable nowadays; alas, these flats will also nearly always have communal hot water and central heating, and a rather antique lift-system. Few lifts are replaced until the insurance company absolutely refuses to cover them.

Apartments built between the wars until about 1935, when Italy went on a war footing and no longer imported building materials from abroad, are also well built but less interesting architecturally unless the Fascist period happens to interest you. They also have collective hot water and central heating.

Post-war blocks should be avoided since up to around 1960-65, when Italy's economic miracle took hold, the quality of the building materials was poor, the design was ugly, there were few blocks which were landscaped in any way and none, not even as late as 1965, was properly insulated.

Around 1980 Italy suddenly woke up to the fact that insulation was a good thing and that people, particularly the foreigners to whom they were now trying to sell apartment blocks in the better-known cities and resorts, absolutely hated collective hot water and central heating systems which forced them to pay an annual fee for something they didn't use for eight or nine months of the year at best. Sometimes, they were only in Italy in the summer months and then for less than six weeks and yet they received a huge service bill for hot water and heating. Enter the age of individual heating. This is often supplied by town gas which in many places today is methane or *il gas azzurro* or, less commonly, oil fired. The boilers usually have to be the same make for each apartment, but with different capacities according to the size of each apartment; they can be serviced annually at a specially low fee. This latter is now not a great deal lower than you would pay as an ordinary individual customer. It is ideal for the holiday apartment owner.

More and more apartment blocks are going over to individual heating, even in blocks over a hundred years old. There are very strict rules governing gas boilers in Italy and many will be found outside on balconies. If your block happens to go over to individual heating you will find it a long process because in most cases all the individual boilers have to be installed before they can be connected to the supply. There is little logic behind this, but it is as well to carry out this work in high summer since you can be without hot water for as much as six or eight weeks. Indeed, it should be done by the end of July – otherwise you hit August when all Italy and all Italian suppliers and plumbers' merchants go on holiday. Nevertheless, in the long run it is worth all the suffering. If you can arrange to be away when the changeover takes place so much the better.

Around the lakes north of Milan and on Lake Garda, as in some of the seaside resorts such as Sanremo, Bordighera and Taormina, quite a few of the big villas and hotels built around 1880-1890 are being converted into apartments with individual hot water and central-heating systems. Many are in landscaped, well-established gardens with beautiful old trees. Nearly all have a new swimming pool, which is often too small if all the apartment owners are in residence at once. With the nostalgia for past times and for a gentler pace of life these apartments are much sought after and very expensive. However, it is unlikely they will lose their value in the years to come.

The condominium (*il condominio*) is a method of apartment ownership by no means unique in Italy. It is a form of joint ownership applicable to virtually all blocks of apartments or any other building, part of which is owned by more than one person or entity. In fact it is almost impossible to buy an apartment in Italy which is not part of a condominium. This means that you will be the absolute owner of your apartment plus a certain proportion of the common parts of the building and also part of such vital things as drains, hot and cold water and central-heating pipes, electric wiring, entrance halls and corridors. Furthermore you will own other items such as your share of the land on which the building stands, together with all the amenities provided with the block such as swimming pools, tennis courts, solaria and gardens.

For better or worse the condominium has come to the UK though as yet it is not as common as the purchase of a flat on a long lease, under which a small ground-rent is paid to a landlord to whom the actual building belongs and an (all too often) high service-charge is also payable either to the landlord or to a company charged with the maintenance of the building and its amenities. The British flat owner usually has the landlord as his traditional enemy as well as the maintenance company. Every other flat owner in the block is certain to make common cause with his neighbour against these two enemies by means of a tenants' association or similar arrangement.

With a condominium this is not the case: since each flat owner is part owner of the entire block, each is the potential enemy of all the others. Except in very small blocks of less than five apartments, it is obligatory to have a managing agent (*un'amministratore del condominio*, a newish profession in Italy) who manages the property on behalf of all the apartment owners, and who gets little thanks for his task beyond a fat fee and endless brickbats.

The proportion (*l'unità immobiliare*) of the common parts (*l'ente condominiale*) which each apartment owner acquires depends on calculations made at the time the block was built. These are usually expressed in 1/000ths up to so many parts of 999,000ths of a building (which would be very large). If a building is bigger than that it is usually sub-divided into smaller blocks or floor by floor, but this is unusual. This proportion reflects the size and position of the apartment and it also governs the service charge (*il conto consultivo*) for each apartment, but in very few blocks can you apply them in a straightforward way to maintenance or central heating. Garages, cellars, parking places which come with apartments each have their proportion. To give an example or two: no person on the ground floor pays towards the cost of the lift unless his garage is at least two floors below his apartment or unless there is a solarium or a swimming pool on the roof. Moreover, in the case of older apartments, i.e. pre-1960 where there is collective hot water and central heating, the proportion of service charge is bound to be different from that of a modern block where most of the central heating is paid by the owner on an individual basis.

At the time of purchase every new owner should receive what is virtually a bible to the block, in which is set out all the relevant information on service charges and the rules and regulations concerning the use of the flat and its surroundings. It should also contain the general rules and regulations about the management of the block: the appointment and removal of the *amministratore*, the meetings of the flat owners and a schedule of certain works which require the special authority of the owners either by a straight majority or by a unanimous decision, which is very rare indeed.

Each flat owner is entitled to vote according to his share of the *condominio* at any meeting of the flat owners. A flat owner may vote in person or by proxy, about which more below. The law requires that there is at least one annual general meeting, the quorum for which is fifty-one per cent. If one is not obtained then a future date and time is set, usually seven days later when those present will form the necessary quorum whatever their number. It says much for the native ingenuity of the Italians that it is not uncommon, if an *amministratore* thinks he will not get a quorum at the first attempt, that he calls his meeting for one minute to midnight on a given day so he can almost certainly adjourn it to a convenient time on the next day or, if he is particularly intent on getting a small attendance, to one minute to midnight on the following day.

It is much to be recommended that if you own a flat in Italy but are not always in residence you appoint a proxy to attend meetings for you and to vote on your behalf. It is not a good thing to be an absentee flat-owner; even if your votes by themselves achieve nothing they may be valuable together with other votes in obtaining what you and others want done. Standard questions such as the approval of accounts require a simple majority, but certain other matters require larger majorities as laid down by law. More importantly the person you appoint as proxy should be someone who can receive the annual service charge accounts, explain them to you and report to you what happened at each meeting. Obviously it is not ideal to have a friend in the block who speaks no Italian and will not be listened to because of his nationality. You will automatically get the minutes of the meeting, but unless your Italian is good they will not be very clear to you.

Unless you deal with the proxy problem by way of a formal power of attorney, you will find that you need to have a fresh proxy for each meeting, and often you will not have time to appoint someone and get the authorization back to Italy in time for the meeting. One solution is that, having found someone to represent you, be it a friend who is permanently resident in Italy or possibly your *commercialista* (see Chapter 13, Tax in Italy), you give him or her a series of undated proxies and arrange with the *amministratore* for notices of meetings and the minutes to go, in the first instance, to him rather than to you. These will certainly arrive long after the meeting has taken place if they go to any address out of Italy.

The *amministratore* of your block can be your proxy but this is not always an ideal choice and you may well find that he will always vote his way rather than yours. In some cases, it need not be a fellow owner in the block, though this is not always so and you should check with the *notaio* at the time of purchase.

There is a single form of proxy for such circumstances; it could for instance read in English as follows:

> I (name of owner) the undersigned, delegate (name of proxy always with his place and date of birth) to represent me at the Flat Owners' General Meeting which will take place on the (date) at (place of meeting – not necessarily in the block). I give and confirm this proxy for my delegate to use on my behalf as and when he considers opportune.
>
> (Your signature)

It should be written in Italian as follows:

> *Io, sottoscritto* (flatowner's name) *delego* (name of proxy with place and date of birth in Italian) *di rappresentarmi alla Assemblea del Condominio* (name of block) *che avra luogo il* (date in figures) *alle* (time in figures) *presso* (place of meeting). *Dando per rato quando la mia delega considera opportuno di decidere in mio nome.*
>
> (Your signature)

Insurance of the building is effected by the *amministratore* on behalf of the condominium and your share of the premium is based on your proportion of the common parts. Such insurance does not cover your flat or its contents, nor any public liability you may incur, nor, for example, damage caused to your allowing your bath to overflow into the apartment below. More and more condominiums are requiring flat owners to insure their flats particularly as to public liability. Incredibly there is no legal requirement, but you would be unwise not to take out at least a very basic insurance.

Service charges are asked for in various ways and no two blocks are the same. Half-yearly, quarterly, in advance or sometimes all in arrears. This last is not very common and never occurs when there is a concierge to pay. A concierge can put as much as 50 per cent onto your service charges simply due to the fact that he cannot be paid black, he must be given accommodation rent-free and *all* his social security INPS must be paid up to date. You are, therefore, along with other flat owners, paying all the charges relating to his flat, his light, hot water and heating whether collective or individual, his salary, his pension and social security payments.

When buying a flat in a newly constructed block, be very circumspect about the estate agent's estimate of service charges – they will be absurdly low and although you will probably not have repair bills for several years, you will have to iron out other problems. Adding at least 30 per cent to his estimate would be wise.

On a sale, service charges are apportioned, but the practical problems which greet both purchaser and vendor as to payments in advance and in arrears are the province of the *notaio*. On the other hand, Italian law requires that when an *amministratore* asks a flat owner for service charges he *must* supply the account on which the figures are based. This is one way to find out whether the apportionment figures were correct or not.

In some, rare cases, the condominium system applies to houses where they are on an estate which supplies a swimming pool, gardens, tennis courts and generally anything the house owners own in common. Again it is up to you whether you insure your house or not, but you would be wise to do so.

All communications to the *amministratore* (and indeed to any other official body addressees in Italy) should be by registered AR letter (*lettera raccomandata*). It is your only chance of knowing that your letter was received in a country where reactions to letters are not automatic. Indeed, the law very often requires letters to be sent in this way, much to the great pleasure of the Italian Post Office.

Finally if you are thinking of buying a flat, do remember that the Italians are not the quietest of people and you cannot rely on them to keep your hours. I still remember renting a holiday flat in Sanremo where my neighbour had piano lessons at 6.30 in the morning. The smarter your block (*signorile*) or (*di prestigio*) the less will be this type of inconvenience, but the word for privacy in Italian is *il privacy*, which seems to indicate in the nicest possible way that it is not endemic to the country.

10
Cars and Driving

Even though you may own property in Italy, provided you are *not* resident you may bring in your car from elsewhere as frequently as you like. The Italian police prefer you to have an International Driving Licence, probably because it has a photograph, but this is not absolutely essential if you are from an EU member country. The car must not only have insurance but also a Green Card and it is surprising the number of people who omit to get one before leaving their home country. The insurance cover given by your policy without the Green Card is of the most basic sort, and in certain circumstances you can end up paying huge bills normally picked up by your insurance company. This does not happen with the big companies such as the Swiss companies, the AA, RAC and all other well-known British companies, but it can happen with some of the cheaper concerns who give cut-price cover, second-to-none in the UK but rather poor abroad – so be on your guard. In certain circumstances, though it will take time, a charge can be put on your property in Italy to ensure you will foot the bill for an accident of which you were proved the cause. This is extremely rare and in any event, given the wait for court hearings, takes enough time for you and your lawyer to arrange matters.

The purchase of a second-hand car is not permitted to non-residents, which is probably just as well since it costs over a million lire to effect the transfer from one owner to another. It is said that there is in Tuscany and Umbria, a thriving market in second-hand British and foreign cars for holiday use, but it pays to be very cautious before parting with your money. Equally, if you are not resident, you are not allowed to purchase a new car with Italian plates. If you purchase a tax-free car you must, again in theory, export it within the week. It will have EE plates (standing for *Estero* or foreign) and according to the specific insurance rates it would seem, in practice, that you can run them in Italy for at least six months. The people who sell the car will know the latest requirements but it is best to know beforehand and to get the details in *writing*.

If and when you take up permanent residence in Italy, you should, strictly speaking, import your car (if you have one) officially, which will cost you around a million lire if it is not of EU manufacture. Alternatively, you can buy a car in Italy – even a second-hand one. Again, as an Italian resident you should not drive any car in Italy (except a hired one) that does not have Italian plates. This means that as an Italian resident you should not drive your British, French or German friends' or relations' cars. Foreigners who are non-resident in Italy should not borrow cars with Italian plates. However, of recent years these rules, though still in operation, have been relaxed somewhat; if you find it is impossible to avoid lending your car to a non-resident, then a simple signed declaration is all that is necessary. It should mention your name as owner of the car, your address, the name and address and driving licence number of the person to whom you are lending it. *However, if the person who is going to borrow the car is going to take the car abroad this declaration must be made before a notary or the insurance will be invalid. You must also inform your insurance company of this.* If, for instance, you are driving from Italy to England in your Italian-registered car, your friend, brother, mother (etc.) cannot drive that car abroad without your written permission sworn before a notary – even though you may be sitting next to him or her. What you do about lending your British registered car is entirely up to you; so it is not difficult to see why so many people endeavour to hang on to their British cars in Italy. All these rules do, apart from irritating people to the point of distraction, is allow you the privilege of paying tax and VAT on your car at Italian rates.

Should you, an Italian resident, find yourself driving a car which does not have Italian plates, the easiest way around this is to use your British driving licence when doing so. Certainly it is illegal, but unless you have done something very stupid or are drunk it is unlikely the police will question you – a foreign car most frequently goes with foreign plates and foreign driving licences. However, do not do this where you are well known to the local police and do not admit you are an Italian resident.

People who have become newly resident in Italy strictly speaking have only six months in which to exchange their British driving licence for an Italian one. The old one will be given back to you and you should hang on to it for future use. An Italian driving licence is a very important document and you should keep it in a safe place and keep a photocopy of it in your car with the car's log book or *libretto*. You may well be asked to present the real one at your local police station or to your local *carabinieri* barracks within three days. This in itself is an improvement since previously one had to carry both the original licence and log book.

You can import a new car into Italy but not necessarily tax free as in the past. If you have paid VAT, you will be allowed to change the plates to the Italian sort; if you have not, you will need to have had the car for six months prior to registering it in Italy and you will then pay VAT on a second-hand car of far lower value. If your car is not of EU manufacture it will need to pass a *collaudo* or registration examination. The car's agents in Italy can arrange this but all in all it will cost nigh on a million lire to make it an Italian car. If the car's agents will not do this you will have to go to a *Pratiche Auto* agent.

It will be seen from the foregoing that it is probably cheaper to buy all but the most expensive foreign car in Italy. At least the million lire goes to you rather than to the Government. Also, in certain circumstances the Government will actually pay you to change your car. If you can produce a wreck more than ten years old they will pay out a considerable sum to keep it off the road if you buy a new car. Any good car agent or *Pratiche Auto* agent will have details – the sum varies from time to time and in any event is subsidized by Brussels. It is better to buy a new car in Italy or trade your old car in and let the garage have the irritation of doing all the work.

However, if you either wish to hang on to your old car or are forced through other circumstances to keep it you should hand everything over to the *Pratiche Auto* agent. He will arrange for the car to have an Italian logbook and change your driving licence. Normally it is up to you to purchase the road-fund licence (*bollo*) and arrange insurance but an agent may well do it for you, for a further fee. Apropos of which it should be remembered that a *bollo* for a diesel vehicle will cost around half a million lire more than for a petrol driven one due to the *sopra-tassa*. This is required because diesel fuel is so much cheaper than standard or lead-free petrol and the Government want to get their tax from somewhere. If, however, you do more than 20-25,000 kilometres a year, a diesel engine becomes a cheaper option and the servicing, whilst not cheaper, is less frequent.

The car's logbook is known in Italian as a *libretto di circolazione* and should be carried at all times. When you are stopped you will be asked for *patente e libretto*. As well as losing your licence, in Italy you can also lose the car's logbook if you have committed some (serious) offence. Often, people forbidden to drive for drink-driving, have their car 'stopped' as well. Other reasons are when the car is not road worthy or has not passed its MOT, when it has undergone alterations which are not noted on the *libretto* (including change of colour), and most common of all is when it has changed owners and not been registered to the new person. You have just ten days in which to register the change of ownership and therefore, it is imperative you or your agent do this in person. A mere change of address can be done by registered post. The advantage of an agent is that he can issue temporary circulation documents. It should be noted that most Italian offices are open in the morning only and close at the curious hour of 1.20 pm.

Another, less common reason for suspension of the car's papers is carrying merchandise when the car is registered for private use. It is easy to get this changed and it does not affect your insurance unless you are carrying on a bona fide business in which case the car should be in the name of the company. This use is called *uso promiscuo* which always causes a titter among the British though its translation is 'dual-purpose' or 'mixed use'. (Other uses of this adjective are *matrimonio promiscuo* = mixed marriage, and *scuola promiscua* = a co-educational school, and *coltivazione promiscua* = mixed planting.) Large purchases should always be accompanied by a docket or a receipt from the shop (if the purchase was in Italy). If you are transporting goods for sale from one place to another you need either an accompanying docket, a bill or a very good explanation. This tends to concern only people doing business but it is worth mentioning. In a country where more than 50 per cent of the trade is done black it is against the law to transport goods without a docket which will give rise to an invoice or the invoice itself.

The Italian driving test is very thorough and somewhat on American lines. Luckily all EU citizens are entitled to a straight exchange of their licence after passing a simple medical. For some, like me, this is just as well since the Italian driving test includes both theoretical and practical examination of the car's inner workings and the ability to change a tyre and, in snowy regions, the putting on of snow chains. No one, even the most practised, relishes putting on snow chains. The exchange of your British licence for an Italian one is something which can be done personally and since there are agencies which charge almost a hundred pounds it is worth doing yourself, particularly as they require to look at you personally, if only for a moment or two. You report to your local provincial prefecture armed with a Residence Certificate from the *comune* in which you reside. They will arrange for a medical examination, on the spot if you are lucky, will take your British licence and give you a receipt for it so you can drive (but not hire a car, so choose your

dates carefully) for up to thirty days. Once you have passed your
medical which includes a sight test and questions about your health,
you pay a small fee to the local authority doctor and wait to receive
your new Italian licence (*patente di guida*) accompanied by your
British licence.

The licence is a small pink document with your photograph and
mentions if you drive with glasses or contact lenses. Incidentally,
you are obliged to mention the fact that you wear contact lenses or
have had a cataract operation. If there are mistakes on it, such as a
mis-spelling of your name, place or date of birth it should be altered
only by the issuing authority and not by you. I was born in a place
beginning with Great shortened to Gt, which always foxes the
Italians and they nearly always get it wrong. I once altered it myself
and the *carabiniere* was shocked to the core at meeting someone
who had had the temerity to touch 'an anagraphic document'. Now
I just leave such mistakes as they are.

Driving licences last ten years for those under fifty and for five
years for those over fifty. At the end of this ten or five year period
a medical examination must be taken (mostly eyesight) and sometimes with the elderly a medical certificate from their own doctor is
required. In any event, it is unlikely you will be allowed to drive
after the age of eighty, though there are cases where this has been
allowed.

Italian driving licences are made out in the maiden name of a
married woman. Therefore, before handing over your British
driving licence in your married name it could be a good idea to
write to Swansea and explain the circumstances. This saves problems at the Italian end. If you cannot do this, or forget to do so in
time, then your application and British driving licence should be
accompanied by your birth certificate (and some authorities
demand a marriage certificate) – all translated at great expense. So
it pays to use the kind ways and flexibility of the British Civil
Service if you can. There is a sort of logic in all this. In Italy a
woman only ever has one name – the one she was born with –
whereas in the UK after a few years and a few marriages all trace
can be lost of who a woman once was. As an Italian once pointed
out British insurance companies are fussier about birth certificates
than are the British authorities. He had left out credit rating agencies which apparently can plough through all sorts of marriages,
cohabitations and name changes.

It should be noted that if your British licence carries endorse-
ments these are not carried over onto the Italian version. However,
if the licence has been suspended you cannot get an Italian one.
Dangerous driving, or driving under the influence of alcohol will

come to light when the Italians check with Swansea – and check they do, if only to ensure that you have passed a test.

There have been cases where Italians have said they were British residents and therefore had British licences which they wished to change for Italian ones – something they are entitled to do if they have had a British licence for more than five years. It is an easy way to get a bona fide Italian licence without passing a test, particularly if the British licence is a phoney one, as these were. In Naples you can purchase Italian driving licences for around 750,000 to a million lire – apparently it is for people who can't read and therefore are incapable of doing the test.

Since the last edition there is now a form of provisional licence and learners are allowed to practise in the family car on all roads other than motorways accompanied by a driver with more than five year's experience. The car must carry a large letter P on the back. P stands for *prova* from the verb *provare* which can mean to try. There is no way to take a test in Italy without going to a recognized driving school. Most bookshops have an up-to-date copy of the Italian Highway Code and you need to know it off by heart before taking the test. To take the test you need to be a bona fide resident and have a good working knowledge of Italian, to say nothing of re-vamping all your ideas on logic.

To many Italians and foreigners living in Italy it is a great sadness that the Ministry of Transport has scrapped provincial number plates for the rather ordinary sort which have two letters then two or three numbers and again two letters. However, the good thing is that you do not have to change the number plates of your car if you change provinces; indeed, you can buy a car with Bari plates and run it in Bolzano without changing anything but the owner's name on the log book. At the new central registry every Italian motor vehicle is on computer and changing owners or addresses is now very much simpler. Naturally it is no cheaper. It is also simpler to chase offenders and non-payment of parking fines. People complain that you cannot tell where cars come from and to this end there are now several companies who will put your new modern numbering on a plate which shows both your region and your province. Apparently they are doing a roaring trade. There will be provincial number plates on the road, both of the old sort with red letters and the new with black on a white background, for many years to come.

Italians are good drivers and, although impatient, very courteous compared with their neighbours. There are no ridiculous rules such as giving priority to people coming in from the right and they do stop at intersections which is a nice change. They have a slightly strange way of turning right or left at intersections which can seem a bit odd to British drivers and it is as well to remember that accidents on mountain roads, even write offs, frequently result in payments of only 50 per cent of the cost of repairs less any franchise – so be warned. The only way you will get around that is to prove the other person had been drinking.

Anyone who has driven in Italy for a number of years will moan about the motorcyclists and the young on Vespas and their lookalikes. They weave in and out of the traffic, overtake on the wrong side and jump the lights – and if there is an accident, somehow, against all logic, it's always thought to be the car driver's fault. On mountain roads where they frequently roar around corners on the wrong side of the road car owners should drive very cautiously indeed.

You will find that in exchange for a full British A or AE licence you will get an Italian *Patente B*. This covers you more or less for everything you could drive at home, including towing a caravan. There are slightly different rules about towing caravans on a *Patente B*. Basically the overall laden weight of the caravan should not exceed the unladen weight of the towing vehicle by more than 70 kilos. Thus a Fiat Regata which weighs 890 kilos kerb weight can tow a caravan of 950 kilos. Anything bigger than that and you need a BE licence. It is said that you could be tested on your manoeuvring skills but this is rarely done when you apply for a *Patente BE*. If you are going to tow a large van, point this out at the time of changing your licence. Otherwise a *Patente B* will cover you for most farm machinery, etc. but not for steamdriven vehicles.

There are limits on the widths and lengths of trailers. With one axle it is 6 m long by 2.3 m wide by 3 m high. With two axles it is 7.5 m long by 2.5 m wide by 3 m high. The maximum speed for vehicles towing a caravan (but not for Dormobiles and similar) is 80 km/h.

Now that Sweden is in the European Union there are fewer problems about tow bars, though Japan occasionally causes some problems particularly with Nissan so always check your tow bar has been passed for Italy.

Insurance

Car insurance is dealt with in a later chapter. However, it is as well to point out that in Italy it is the car, and not the person, which is insured. The person, his age and his driving record influence the obligatory and the all-risks part of a separate policy. Also obligatory insurance – third party only – does not cover fire and theft. Seven years plus, free of accidents, entitles you to have one accident and retain your no-claims bonus. All Italian car insurance works on a bonus/malus system.

Therefore, in principle, *all* cars in Italy are insured and that should prove comforting since on that basis you cannot have an accident which involves an uninsured party.

Although insurance claim limits are going up each year they are still not up to those of many of the EU countries. As at today's date you still cannot purchase obligatory insurance out of Italy and they are in trouble with Brussels for this. You can cover separately for All Risks Comprehensive but foreign companies are not queuing up for this sort of risk!

Should you have an accident in which you are injured, or in which your car is a write off, or in which you are not at fault, you should do all or some of the following:

1. If you or the other party is injured call the *carabinieri*. They won't come out unless there are injuries.
2. Get a medical report from the hospital to which you were taken.
3. Make sure the other party is breathalyzed, particularly from midday to around 2.30 p.m. and in the evening. I failed to do this in the Friuli (a region known for drinking neat *grappa* at any time of the day) when a young man came straight out of the bar and drove into my parked car and wrote it off.
4. *Consult a lawyer as quickly as possible,* preferably near where you live and not where the accident took place. Many car insurance all-risks policies carry this cover and can supply their own lawyer. Be guided by them in these circumstances. They too want a good outcome.

If you are taken to hospital after an accident you are certain to be either breathalyzed or given a blood and/or urine test. If you are considered drunk – and there are still doubts about what constitutes drunkenness in Italy – your insurance cover will immediately be reduced to third party only and the damage to your car will not be covered *even if the fault of the other party.* If the report says you were not drunk, the insurance company will pay, but will do so slowly unless you have a lawyer to speed matters along.

If the doctor suspects you are an alcoholic he will send you for further tests and if there is positive proof that you are such your licence will be taken away for good. Needless to say, the Italians have many ways of getting around such regulations, and until the breathalyzer becomes as commonplace as in the UK there will always be some drunken driving. As a nation, the Italians are not heavy drinkers, sticking to wines and *amari*. The further south you

go the less they drink. In the Veneto where they do drink strong
spirits they usually tend to stay at home and do it. As well as losing
your licence virtually on the spot for drunken driving the current
fine for being in charge of a car under the influence of alcohol is
around 2,500,000 lire and/or prison.

In spite of what you see to the contrary *seat belts are obligatory
in Italy*.

It is not recommended that those lucky enough to have a driving
licence other than an Italian one get an International Driving Permit
in Italy. For those holding a British driving licence, it takes about
three minutes and costs under five pounds to get an international
one at the AA or the RAC, neither of whom demands that you be a
member. It can also be done by post, which takes a little longer as
your driving licence has to be checked with Swansea.

In Italy, to get the same result you have to:

1. Supply a sheet of *carta bollata* at 20,000 lire
2. Supply three photographs, one of which must be authenticated
   by your local *comune* (cost 1000 lire)
3. Pay Automobile Club d'Italia almost 50,000 lire
4. Wait three to four weeks for its issue.

The Italians have a genius for making the simple complicated
and costly. The cost alone should put off any non-Italian. Italians,
alas, have no alternative but to pay up and wait. The following are
among the most common offences which all carry fines.

If you call out the *carabinieri* unnecessarily after an accident, i.e.
when there are no injured involved, you may well find your car
being looked at closely for what they call 'anomalies' – just to teach
you a lesson. You would be surprised what a trained eye can find
wrong with a car which has just done a long journey – all legal and
above board, so be warned:

a) not having a red warning triangle
b) not having a first aid box
c) not stopping at a red light
d) not having indicators, stop lights, rear lights, brake lights in
   perfect order
e) not having extra lights in pairs
f) driving too fast in fog, rain or snow
g) not having mudguards when you have studded tyres, which are
   legal only between 15th December and 15th March except by
   special provincial prolongation (in the Dolomites for instance)

h) speeding, which can lead to an on the spot fine and immediate suspension of your licence (Italian or foreign) for up to three months and with no appeal to the court.

Speeds in Italy are governed by the capacity of the car. In a built-up area the maximum speed is 50km/h and there are a lot of radar traps. These are rarely used and some have rusted into disuse, but it is impossible to know where they are. In my own locality there is a spot in a built-up area where everyone, including me, does around 55 to 60km/h. About every eighteen months they check the speeds for one morning and evening and collect more than 10 million lire in fines at around 55,000 lire a time.

Elsewhere the speed limits are as follows:

Car Capacity	Autostrada	Out of Town Roads
599 cc	90 kmh	80 kmh
600 to 900 cc	110 kmh	90kmh
901 to 1,300 cc	130 kmh	100 kmh
over 1,300 cc	130 kmh	110 kmh

These speeds are reduced when using studded tyres, to 90km/h for vehicles up to 1,200 cc and to 110km/h for all others. During *all* school holidays the maximum speed allowed on both the roads and the *autostrade* is 110km/h. I fail to see the logic of this at a time when most of the children are *not* on the road going to and from school. Usually it is flashed up at the toll booths if not on the *autostrada* itself.

For those going to Switzerland it is as well to remember that in no circumstances are studded tyres allowed, so if you are a frequent visitor you must, as the Americans say, 'winterize' your car in accordance with Swiss requirements.

There is a legal obligation in Italy to give first aid in an accident and to call assistance. Italian insurance companies pay for internal damage to a car when transporting wounded people to hospital. The *carabinieri* will give the necessary certificate. The Italian driving test includes examination in basic first-aid and artificial respiration. Obviously, if there are already people assisting there is no need to interfere.

Lead-free petrol (*senza piombo*) is available all over Italy and more and more stations are supplying propane gas, though quite a few towns forbid the passage of cars using this fuel.

11
Banking

When you are next standing in a queue at the bank wondering whether you will be served before closing time, reflect on the fact that the Italians actually invented not only the cheque but also the forerunner of modern banking.

Since that time of the Great Fairs in the thirteenth and fourteenth centuries when the Genovese bankers issued what amounts to the modern bank draft, or *assegno circolare*, Italian banking sometimes seems stuck in a time warp. For instance you see either the most modern computers or manual typewriters, yet no equipment for the interim years before the computer became commonplace.

Banking and banking services have come a long way in the last ten years and, like the telephone and television industries, seem to have skipped many of the stages other European nations have used and, indeed, are still using. Another example is credit cards. Italians did not really like credit cards and hardly any service stations, motorway toll booths or smaller shops took them. For years the department store la Standa held out against them. When you did give a card in the more expensive dress-shops for instance, you had to wait for a telephone authorization. Now many, many more shops, restaurants and service stations on the motorways take cards. As in any modern country, they have a permanent connection to an authorization link and the credit card holder can now pay at the end of each billing period either the full sum or a percentage. Of course, being Italy, the interest rates are horrendous – often as much as 30 per cent.

Like so many European, as opposed to British, banks, the Italians love value dates. Value dates work like this: you pay in a cheque for a million lire; if you are a known customer, they will allow you to draw against this amount immediately but you will find on your account that in fact the money was not really in your account until four or five days later and that you may well have been technically

104

overdrawn during this waiting period. Unlike France, Italians do not give value dates for cash or bank drafts, or rather they give the day the money was paid in. However, worse is yet to come. If you draw a cheque on the 18th of the month for instance, and take cash on that day, you will find that the amount will have a value date of the 14th or 15th of the month at which time, although your account may well have been in the black this cheque, of a later date, may make you 'technically' overdrawn, especially if they are clearing a cheque you have paid in. Who said the Italians can make a simple transaction complicated?

There seems to be a difference of opinion as to resident and non-resident accounts. There are banks which run both and banks which insist that there is now no difference between one account and another except the currencies they are in. Being able to have other-currency accounts is a new possibility in Italy, but choose carefully as many people have been caught by the fall in the Deutschemark. You can pay as much as you like, in any currency, into any account you may have, but *all* accounts carry the restriction of not being able to draw more than the equivalent of 20,000,0000 lire on any one day. Again, permission can be obtained fairly easily to export larger sums; for instance, after the sale of an apartment or a boat. It is the person who is restricted; you cannot draw 20,000,000 lire from say, each of five accounts in any one day – although probably you could from several different banks. Also, *assegni circolari* can be made out for any sum to be *paid* into somebody else's bank account. So you are not as restricted as it might first appear.

There are several types of account at Italian banks, ranging from a current account, *conto corrente*, to savings accounts. Utility bills can be paid direct from your current or savings account by means of a *domicilazione* document, but you will need to furnish the various account or client numbers to the bank from the electricity, gas, water or telephone companies. For anyone not living all year round in Italy this is undoubtedly the best way to ensure nothing is cut off. Do remember, however, that both electricity and gas have a balancing-up account twice yearly (this is due to billing you only on an estimated consumption during the interim period – see Chapter 17, Utilities) and the amount can make a very large hole in your bank balance.

Most savings accounts are subject to a withholding tax of 30 per cent, although certain non-resident savings accounts are not. These latter accounts are not always open to residents. Frankly, there are far better things on offer in other countries, especially when you realize that interest on deposit accounts is credited on the sum you have lent for the past twelve months on the 31st December of each year. If you remove it on the 15th November, for instance, you can often receive absolutely nothing by way of interest. No lending overnight money, or money on seven days' deposit – Italian saving is still in the dark ages for the customer and only the bank profits on such accounts.

That said, Italian current accounts do pay interest at a rate of around 2 per cent. Every six months you get a balance sheet from the bank in which you will see a summary of all the times you were in credit and debit, how much these sums were and how many transactions you made at so much, a general sum each month for dealing and posting your closing balance, a six-monthly sum and so on and, finally, you will see that you owe them a certain amount of lire or, if you are lucky, thay they owe you.

Usually it is you who owe them. Only once in fifteen years have I ever received money from an Italian bank and then it was a mere 26,000 lire. Normally I pay around 500,000 lire every twelve months to a bank which, by Italian standards, gives a good, prompt and understanding service but by British standards is pretty ordinary. I am seldom overdrawn because I consider it costs far too much for the convenience but I am forced to pay private bank or Swiss bank prices for merely so-so service. In London I would probably pay nothing at all.

It is debatable whether it is a good idea to have Italian credit cards. Visa is the commonest in Italy with American Express next. Mastercard and Diners are less used and most other cards are usually not acceptable. CartaSi is the generic Italian Visa card and is issued by most banks. You sign a contract to pay the whole sum within ten days of the billing date – the date is shown on the invoice – or you can opt to pay each month a percentage of the sum owed. Certainly it is useful to have a Bancomat card to enable you to withdraw money from a machine. Unlike some UK machines, this sum is immediately debited to your credit-card account and often, even if you use an Italian Visa card, it is debited to your current account. This is because a credit card is intimately linked to your current (or other) account and you cannot have a bank's credit card, Visa or otherwise, unless you have an account with them. Incidentally, it is worth knowing that not all Italian Bancomat machines will accept foreign (British or American, French etc.) cards – sometimes they will just swallow them. You should get a list from your own bank of the Italian banks which accept other countries' cards. Failing that, there is very often an EC or Eurocheque sign on many of these money machines and these will accept foreign cards.

Eurocheques can be cashed at any bank showing the EC sign up to around 300,000 lire per cheque at a time, and usually two cheques are allowed. If you want more money than that you will have to go from bank to bank – though nothing is marked in your cheque book. The amount will always be paid in lire and there is usually a commission which starts at 5,000 lire per cheque. Hotels, certain shops and restaurants all take Eurocheques provided you have the Eurocheque card. Moreover, Italians are quite happy to take larger Eurocheques than the guaranteed amount. It should be remembered that these are then dealt with outside the Eurocheque regime and nothing is guaranteed. In fact, your own personal cheque would do just as well but somehow Italians prefer Eurocheques. No other country's banks will accept Eurocheques in more than the guaranteed amount, but certain Italian banks will and it is a quick and easy way to cover an Italian overdraft should you need to. Equally, your Italian bank will happily accept an ordinary cheque on your UK account. This flexibility and kindness is somewhat marred by the rotten value date they give you. You remain overdrawn for quite a long time in spite of the cheque you have given them.

Sending money to Italy is bad enough and the quickest way is by your bank using Swift, but sending money from Italy is quite dreadful. More and more countries, including the UK, are using a central foreign department of their bank to deal with foreign transfers. Your bank may be very quick and mindful of your needs, but by the time the instructions get to London the urgency is forgotten and ten days is not unknown for a transfer from London to Milan. Imagine a transfer from Little Boddington on the Sea to Millefiori al Mare which has gone via London and Milan and you will get some idea of the problem. Also, little effort is made by the copy typist (you probably thought such a person no longer existed) to copy your very foreign name at all accurately, and so the whole business either gets held up, misdirected or even lost.

Probably the quickest and easiest method is to use your own personal cheque drawn on your British bank account. It would be kind to warn your bank in the UK of what you are doing and also to allow at least a week or ten days for the cheque to be cleared and the sum credited to your Italian account. The main advantage of using this method is that the entire transaction becomes the responsibility of your Italian bank. You can also use a Eurocheque as explained above.

If you are someone who is a bit careless in running your financial life and who tends to have an overdraft more often than not, all Italian banks offer a cheap insurance to cover an overdraft in the event of your death. Usually, the policy also pays a lump sum if you die in an accident, more if you die in a road accident. These cost from between 5,000 and 9,000 per month and must represent some of the best value for money in Italy.

As said in an earlier chapter, you would be mad to bring all your assets to Italy, if only because the lire is not particularly strong as a world currency; although much improved, the political climate of Italy, to say nothing of the economic, is not the most enviable in Europe. Virtually every large purchase you make in Italy, as well as your payment of every utility bill, goes down on your *Codice Fiscale* account. If you are non-resident this is of no interest but if you are resident and paying tax it is. It is pathetic to try and convince the Italian Fisc, which is not stupid, that you have an income of say 15,000,000 lire when your *Codice Fiscale* bills alone show you have spent considerably more. Therefore, resident or non-resident, buy most things via your British credit cards which usually obviates the use of a *Codice Fiscale* number since foreigners and most non-residents don't have one. However, you cannot avoid being caught on purchasing a house, boat or motor car.

Italian banks have the same secrecy code as British and a court order is required to look at your bank account. Usually such a request would be made by the police or the Italian tax authorities, and by the time this sort of thing happens you are in deep trouble. It is unlikely anyone else will be allowed to look at it. Credit rating, except for credit cards, is still a fairly local affair.

One other service Italian banks offer is mortgages. Mortgage interest, especially for a first house, is not particularly high, but the actual cost of preparing and registering the mortgage is unbelievable. You have all the usual things, many of which building societies and banks have done away with in the UK, such as: a valuation and survey by the bank's surveyor; the cost of the notary who is obliged to put himself out and come to the bank rather than the reverse, all at an extra cost; an insurance policy via the bank on the house (but not its contents); and possibly an insurance policy on your life as well. The less expensive taxes due on the purchase of a first house are allowed only in certain circumstances, but nationality is not a bar. A notary will advise you. See Chapter 8, Property Transactions.

Most people find writing foreign cheques a trial; Appendix L shows how to write an Italian cheque. The place named is mentioned because it governs where any court action will be heard, so that although you may live in Turin when you make a cheque out in Milan you mark it Milan. However, when you send a cheque from Turin to Milan you mark it Turin. It is where you make out the cheque which is important. In any event, very often, invoices mention the Tribunale which will be involved in the case of any court action. Next comes a space more or less on the top line for the date which for simplicity's sake you should keep in numbers, though if you know Italian you can use words for the month. If using numbers it should be day/month/year order *not* the American way. Immediately next to that is the space for the figures. The next line requires the amount in words and here you must either have learnt the Italian or get a person in the bank to help. Then your signature. Italian cheques are open and on the back is the word *Girate*. This means it can be endorsed over to someone other than the payee you have mentioned on the front. If you want payee-only you write the words *'non trasferibile'*. A word of warning here. You cannot live in Italy three weeks without someone asking you to leave the payee section blank. This means he wants to pass it via someone else's account. The problem is that nine times out of ten you do not even know the name of this person. If you can, try to avoid this type of transaction since it will prove impossible to stop such a cheque.

Even if you make a cheque out to yourself, *mi-stesso/a*, you will be required to endorse it. Every bank is different about paying out money – some pay your cheque there and then whilst others give you a slip to go to the *cassa* – but most will fill out your paying-in slips. Indeed, nowadays, since everything is on computer they prefer to do so rather than to try and read everyone's handwriting. I am reliably informed that optical readers are not that common in Italy, but then their volume of cheques is about a tenth of Great Britain's.

Equally confusing are banking hours. They vary from bank to bank though the big banks such as Credito Italiano, Banca Commerciale, etc. keep the same hours in all their branches. They all tend to open at 8.30 in the morning and close at the magic official time of 1.20 p.m. (to coincide with government offices perhaps?). Do not rely on this because I have come across banks which close promptly at 1 p.m. and then open for an hour in the afternoon between 2 and 4 p.m. Should you find your favourite bank closed and you need money, you will often find some other bank's one hour in the afternoon is at a different time. I know that Ambrosiano-Veneto open half an hour earlier than Banca Commerciale, and that the latter is open half an hour later than the former so you can usually arrange something.

Normally banks are not open on Saturday, but in holiday resorts and large towns in the tourist season one or two banks open from around 10 to 12 on Saturday mornings. For a list of bank holidays, see Appendix N.

12
Insurance, Health and Pensions

There are four important things to remember about Italian insurance policies.

First many, many policies are for *ten* years and it is very difficult to get away from a particular company unless you die, sell your house or leave the country. Marriage is not a reason for automatic cancellation, though they may listen sympathetically. They will dog you for the premiums, even though you have insured with another company and legally they are entitled to their premium under the contract you signed – including all the premium increases.

Secondly, if you insure with a foreign company you will have to pay not only all the taxes due on an ordinary Italian company's policy (and there are many) but also a special tax currently making the total tax just under 20 per cent plus Italian VAT. In any event many Swiss, German and French companies are now active in Italy and this has jolted Italian insurers out of their former lethargy; these concerns are now Italian; however, much of the way they are run is dictated by their head office abroad.

Thirdly, you cannot, as yet, insure your Italian-registered car out of Italy. Certainly you can insure the all-risks part of the policy, but not many foreign companies are keen on giving only that sort of cover.

Fourthly and finally, you will find that very few companies indeed will give you all-risks insurance for your jewellery, furs and precious objects. You are insured only when they are at home with you and then you must have a properly approved wall or floor-safe to put them in. However, you are insured for cash kept in the safe and so, naturally, everyone has the maximum of cash in their safe when they are burgled. Do not cut corners on fitting a safe. It may well be that the company will take your word and not come and look at the safe, but should there be a break-in they will see it soon enough and will almost certainly consider it quite useless unless it is a top Italian name. You should insist on their coming and approving the safe at the outset. Usually, a certificate is issued by the company selling the safe and, again, you should ensure that this make and its fitting is approved by your insurance company.

You cannot insure jewellery, *objets d'art* and pictures of value unless they have been valued by an Italian fine-art dealer or jeweller. If your things have been valued by top dealers elsewhere in Europe they will put you in touch with the relevant people in Milan or Rome. You will find that Italian prices for jewellery are rather less than in the UK, though gold is always 18 carat and not 9 or 14. Generally speaking, Italians, jewellers and customers alike, do not use top quality stones; the look of the thing is more important, though the superb workmanship is far cheaper than most places in Europe for similar quality. Solid-silver dinner services cost considerably more in Italy than in the UK. However, unless you have a previous valuation from a British dealer, they cannot understand why a George II service should be worth at least three times as much as a Victorian service which is twice as heavy. Caddies and caddy spoons together with other specialist collectables should either have the bill from where they were purchased or valuations from really top London dealers. Good Sheffield Plate is well understood in Italy and most good dealers in the larger cities have books of British and international hallmarks. Those insuring with Lloyds or other foreign companies should ask where the company wants its valuations done, rather than spend a lot of money having them done in the wrong country.

Given this rather discouraging line-up, it is scarcely surprising that many people with furniture and objects they treasure prefer to insure with Lloyds, who also give you cover against earthquake – something which no Italian company (or foreign company in Italy) at present offers.

Ordinary household cover is not expensive in Italy though the premiums, as anywhere else, are calculated according to the risk. Therefore, the large cities are more expensive than the small towns: starting with Naples, Milan and Rome, so the premiums descend. There is also a general feeling among Italians that if you live in the country you do so because you cannot afford to live in a city, which they consider to be infinitely preferable. Even with a *casa padronale* it is felt you are silly to spend your money in such a way. Foreigners coming to Italy are beginning to make the Italians revise their ideas but it is only at the seaside and in mountain resorts that such new ideas apply. There is also a prevalent feeling that the more neighbours you have the more valuable your house – quite the opposite of what obtains in the UK – and a house entirely on its own on the outside of a village is less desirable than one surrounded by others. Certainly, neighbours lessen the risk of being burgled in Italy.

As said before, ordinary household cover in Italy is not expensive mostly because there are, particularly compared to their British counterparts, a great number of things on which the companies do not pay out. Taking what they do cover first: fire, theft, thunder and lightning, burst pipes (but not due to old age or freezing and usually the payment is made to the third party who suffered and not to you), objects falling from the sky (but not nuclear objects), explosion (or implosion for that matter, which can make just as much mess and cause just as much damage), glass breakage (but not due to supersonic bangs), damage to electrical installation, damage by road vehicles and, of course, public liability. Don't be surprised when you are asked for the number of the vehicle which crashed into your wall. Without it they are quite likely not to pay. They do not pay out on any sort of water damage (such as your washing machine going on and on and on with dire results, or your deep freeze being without current for more than 48 hours), or a tree in your garden falling on your roof, or a wall in your garden falling down. Indeed, it is better to reckon you are not insured for anything except the most basic and dire happenings and perhaps you will get a pleasant surprise. There is nearly always a excess of the first three to five hundred thousand lire to pay.

At the time of taking out the policy, you should produce bills and valuations. For instance, except in the largest cities, Italians do not understand why curtains should be lined and interlined and cost around 75,000 lire a width to make. They normally have embroidered linen panels at the windows though these can cost well over a hundred pounds each. Remember also, that a dinner service is not a dinner service but eighty-four pieces of china and unless you insure this correctly you may find you can only claim on a percentage basis. Ditto for silver cutlery.

You cannot insure for earthquake on an Italian policy. It is possible to find earthquake cover and given that Italy is one vast earthquake zone it is probably worth the extra premium. If there is an earthquake, the government takes over the responsibility but this is limited to the amount on which you pay your annual communal tax ICI. There are people sitting in houses worth almost a thousand million lire (*un milliardo di lire*) who would get only a fifth of that if they lost their houses in an earthquake.

The fine art of insurance companies not paying claims has surely reached its apotheosis in Italy. Two typical examples illustrate admirably the official Italian attitude to disaster. Mr A. went off to ski for a fortnight. His lavatory cistern washer had perished and allowed water to flow all over the apartment ruining the floors, carpets, the wall decoration and, worst of all, it seeped through the floor to ruin his neighbours' ceiling and decoration. In addition to having to repair his own apartment at his own expense, he also had to pay the excess of 750,000 lire when the company paid for his neighbours' damage. Italian insurance law requires that you turn off the water, including the lavatory cistern feed, if you are more than twenty-four hours away from your house or flat. The number of Italian home-owners who do that must be minuscule.

Mr B. lived in the country and had divided his property into two in such a way that he had a formal garden surrounding the house which he had fenced with iron railings. The rest of the property had no protection because he had no problems with his neighbours, and in any event nobody could get in since there was a locked gate and drive to the whole property. One night a troop of wild boar got in – this is common enough in the countryside in Italy, but Mr B. had been sufficiently fortunate over a period of fourteen or fifteen years that he had not even considered this problem. In their search for food they dug and dug and weakened the wide bases of several very well-built dry stone walls, to say nothing of destroying most of his fruit trees, red currants and ornamental shrubs. He conservatively assessed the damage at around nine or ten million lire. His neighbour had a similar claim. Neither was paid a lire on the grounds that all property should be properly fenced. This is not part of Italian law nor does it appear in any Italian policy, but it is certainly Italian insurance practice not to pay out on this sort of disaster. The Great Storm of 1987, had it happened in Italy, would not have made any difference unless a neighbour's tree happened to fall on your roof, or one of your trees damaged your neighbour's property. One would think that being struck by lightning is a disaster which can hardly be argued about, given that it is completely beyond the control of the policy holder. The usual result of being struck is that the whole electricity installation is damaged beyond repair and the house or apartment must be re-wired. Also, the television, refrigerator, and often though not always the washing machine and dishwasher are struck. Hi-fi equipment is sometimes damaged. Unless you have *specifically* insured these items you will receive a derisory sum. You will be asked when the house was last wired and if it was relatively recently, say within the previous five years you will be required to produce a receipted and 'vatted' invoice plus the *certificato di conformità*. Unless you are extraordinarily lucky you will find yourself paying out rather more than the excess on a new installation. Under no circumstances can you be seen to *profit* from such a disaster (as if such a thing were possible). Your hi-fi equipment was of rubbishy quality and your kitchen appliances were on their last legs according to the insurance company. Therefore, be very circumspect about what is covered and what is not and try to get it in writing from the insurance company just what their drill is for paying out as a result of a natural disaster, earthquake excepted. Alas, insurance assessors do not exist in Italy for domestic insurance matters, more's the pity.

Although there is, or should be, a general insurance policy for a condominium, this policy covers only the fabric of the common parts of the building and never any individual flat. This is why it is so cheap – it gives the very basic legal minimum. You will need a further private policy to cover your flat, third-party problems, etc. Most blocks of flats now demand to see your annual premium receipt. In any event, you will find it very difficult to claim personally for damage caused by a neighbour without your having an insurance policy too. Most insurance companies will not even entertain such claims and you are likely to find yourself at the lawyer's office. This is considerably more expensive than paying an annual premium, so do not economize.

Those taking out mortgages may well find the company requires at least an accident policy on the mortgagee's life, if not an endowment policy, and it will almost certainly have to be with an Italian company. Often they will insure the property themselves (though you will pay the premium) and this insurance usually covers only *their* loan, so do not regard it as adequate insurance – you will need to take out another policy. For cover against any form of death you can take out a policy for a period of ten years (usually the period of the loan); as an example, a premium of two million lire a year will give you cover of one hundred million, double that if you die in a road accident. At the end of the period you get your twenty million back plus another five and, so far as can be assessed, there seem to be no problems with this type of insurance. Of course if you have some serious disease you would be foolish to hide it since they are bound to investigate the matter at your death and not pay if anything was hidden from the company. Exactly the same would apply in the UK, so one cannot complain. Otherwise life insurance is best purchased out of Italy, either in the UK or the US, where investment is better understood. Whether things will improve once Italy joins the single currency remains to be seen but certainly it would seem that Italy will have to pay at least 2000 lire for every Euro and this does not augur well for your Italian life assurance policy.

Car Insurance

The most important thing to remember about car insurance in Italy is that so far as the obligatory third-party insurance is concerned it is the car, and *not* the driver which is insured. Certainly the driver's background affects the premium but that is as far as it goes. The idea is that there is no such thing as an uninsured car on Italian roads, and by and large this is the case. Of course, there are dishonest people who manufacture false insurance policies and receipts, just as they manufacture false tax discs, but these are very rare. This is why, when the *carabinieri* stop a vehicle, they solemnly take down all the numbers.

The next most important thing to remember is that Italian motor policies, and *only* motor policies, are now for a period of twelve months and can be cancelled by giving a minimum of two months' notice in writing by recorded delivery. Other policies to do with your motoring, such as family insurance, breakdown insurance, legal assistance etc., can all be for either twelve months or ten years – be very careful indeed.

The sale of a car does not necessarily cancel a policy since it is assumed that you will carry the policy over to the new vehicle. You yourself must cancel it and say you are selling your car. If at the time of this declaration you can also quite truthfully say you have not got another car and can confirm it in writing, again by recorded delivery, you may just be able to change companies. Many Italians buy their new cars just as their renewal comes up and have already given notice two months previously. It takes some arranging but is often worth it. Incidentally, most insurance companies will write your cancellation letter for you to sign so you have no need to worry about how to word such a letter in Italian.

Obligatory insurance costs are now calculated on a points system that is much fairer than the previous method, which merely took into account the province in which you live and your driving record. The new method takes into consideration the following: the province or city in which you live (and the points allotted are very revealing), your age, the horsepower of your car, the amount of cover you require for third-party insurance, your place and the car's place on the bonus/malus scale. There are 18 classes on the bonus/malus scale and a new car comes in at class 13, i.e. 100 per cent of the premium, which at the moment is worth 703 points. However, if you are at class 3, for instance, because of your record, you will pay only 56 per cent of that premium. On the other hand if you have the misfortune to be at class 15 because you have had an accident, you will find you will be paying at least a further 30 per cent on the basic premium for obligatory insurance. All-risks cover can vary from company to company and depends also on what car you drive as well as how much they offer. The greatest differentiator of premiums, both obligatory and all-risks, is your place on the bonus/malus table and the province in which you live. Italians seem to prefer this system; certainly it has pulled down accidents quite dramatically from nearly 300,000 in the seventies to almost half that figure in the nineties, which is quite remarkable given the doubling of road traffic.

Below are tables showing the points value of each province, followed by the points value given to the place you have on the bonus/malus scale and the horsepower of your car. Also, it should be remembered that, as in the UK, young people pay more than middle aged and the elderly.

Province	Points	Province	Points	Province	Points
AGRIGENTO	10	GENOVA	587	POTENZA	10
ALESSANDRIA	272	GORIZIA	429	PRATO	641
ANCONA	467	GROSSETO	429	RAGUSA	10
AOSTA	192	IMPERIA	346	RAVENNA	517
AREZZO	429	ISERNIA	10	REGGIO CALABRIA	375
ASCOLI PICENO	272	LA SPEZIA	703	REGGIO EMILIA	467
ASTI	272	L'AQUILA	192	RIETI	272
AVELLINO	10	LATINA	467	RIMINI	467
BARI	272	LECCE	192	ROMA	587
BELLUNO	272	LECCO	375	ROVIGO	192
BENEVENTO	105	LIVORNO	467	SALERNO	192
BERGAMO	467	LODI	375	SAN MARINO	375
BIELLA	346	LUCCA	703	SASSARI	517
BOLOGNA	641	MACERATA	429	SAVONA	517
BOLZANO	272	MANTOVA	272	SIENA	272
BRESCIA	402	MASSA-CARRARA	703	SIRACUSA	105
BRINDISI	375	MATERA	192	SONDRIO	402
CAGLIARI	517	MESSINA	192	TARANTO	467
CALTANISSETTA	105	MILANO	375	TERAMO	272
CAMPOBASSO	10	MODENA	467	TERNI	272
CASERTA	272	NAPOLI	467	TORINO	467
CATANIA	192	NOVARA	272	TRAPANI	105
CATANZARO	272	NUORO	346	TRENTO	272
CHIETI	192	ORISTANO	225	TREVISO	288
COMO	375	PADOVA	375	TRIESTE	587
COSENZA	105	PALERMO	192	UDINE	192
CREMONA	346	PARMA	375	VARESE	375
CROTONE	272	PAVIA	346	VENEZIA	388
CUNEO	272	PERUGIA	346	VERBANO	272
ENNA	10	PESARO	346	VERCELLI	346
FERRARA	346	PESCARA	402	VERONA	346
FIRENZE	641	PIACENZA	375	VIBO-VALENTIA	272
FOGGIA	272	PISA	587	VICENZA	272
FORLI	467	PISTOIA	641	VITERBO	192
FROSINONE	192	PORDENONE	192		

Fiscal Horsepower	Points
Up to 8	10
9–10	317
11–12	541
13–14	603
15–16	821
17–18	999
19–20	1157
More than 20	1396

Bonus/Malus Position	Points
1	10
2	68
3	123
4	175
5	225
6	288
7	346
8	402
9	455
10	505
11	575
12	641
13	703
14	843
15	965
16	1109
17	1263
18	1396

Another thing which can change your premium is how much you want for third-party cover. The minimum cover is for 1500 million lire and normally the maximum is around 15,000 million lire, though there are certain large companies who set no final limit. If you look at the table you will see that the cover is not that expensive; this is not the area to economize.

Maximum Cover	Points
1,500,000,000	10
2,000,000,000	49
3,000,000,000	68
4,000,000,000	78
5,000,000,000	96
7,000,000,000	123
10,000,000,000	141
15,000,000,000	201

As can be seen, fifteen milliards of cover only cost just over twice the premium demanded for five milliards of lire cover.

Below are three typical examples of obligatory insurance from the most expensive to the cheapest, passing through a very normal person, not living in a large city and not driving a powerful car but having had his car damaged in a parking lot by a hit and run driver.

A young man aged 22 with a 2 litre new BMW living in Tuscany in the Province of Lucca.

	Points
2 litre BMW	1157
Max. cover third party	
15,000,000,000 lire	201
Resident in Prov. Lucca	703
Age of owner – 22	59
Position Bonus/Malus 17	1396
TOTAL NUMBER POINTS	3516 or 4,903,000 lire premium
12 H.P. Fiat	541
Third Party cover up to	
7,000,000,000 lire	123
Resident in Udine Province	192
Age of Person – over 40	10
Position Bonus/Malus 4	175
TOTAL NUMBER POINTS	1041 or 413,000 lire premium
Fiat 600	10
Third Party minimum cover	10
Resident in Avellino Province	10
Age of Person – over 40	10
Position Bonus/Malus 2	68
TOTAL NUMBER POINTS	108 or 162,000 lire premium

It is rare to come across anyone with a bonus/malus position of 1 though it must exist somewhere. All insurance premiums carry various taxes including VAT at 20 per cent and of course, the moment you get all-risks cover, which is a separate policy, the prices increase enormously. Nevertheless, the above examples do show the wide variations in more or less the same type of insurance from one part of the country to the other.

Companies like Admiral and Guardian Direct simply do not exist in Italy and in practice the maximum no-claims bonus you can get here is a miserable 30 per cent. Forty years of blameless driving often only gives you 30 per cent. The premiums are universally high and the service is frankly poor in comparison with the UK,

Switzerland, Germany or the US. Once in the so-called 50 per cent no-claims bonus bracket you can earn the right not to lose a no-claims bonus even though you have had an accident – no matter whose fault it is but only certain companies offer this and only to those taking out all-risks cover.

Like so many things in Italy, the bonus/malus system does not tell the whole story. It should be remembered that except in the categories 1 and 3 where you can have an accident without losing your no-claims bonus, an accident means you move down one place when your next premium is due, even though you may change companies. You will receive each year a *Certificato di Sinistro* and this will show anything from none to, heaven forbid, half a dozen accidents. Remember too, that, if you are involved in an accident judged to be your fault and more than your own car is damaged, each car, including yours, counts as a separate accident for bonus/malus purposes. So most of the time at least two cars are involved bonus/malus wise.

I have been driving in Italy for over fifteen years and have a different car every two or three years, never more than 1600 cc. The car is insured all-risks, owner-only driving, and yet I still have around 30 per cent no-claims bonus, and of course the premiums have soared into the stratosphere. I pay 1,736,000 lire a year for something that would cost me less than £400 in central London. As pointed out previously, you cannot win with an insurance company and there is no insurance competition in Italy.

Unless you lose your licence, Italian insurance companies are obliged to give you third-party cover; they are not obliged to give you all-risks cover, and anyway at this level – No. 18 – the premium would be somewhere around 4,000,000 lire for a Renault Clio 1200 cc plus a hefty obligatory third-party insurance premium.

Many insurance companies try to sell the excess system where you pay the first 750,000 or 1,000,000 lire of any damage. Often, that means *any* damage to your or someone else's car. In the higher bonus categories it is definitely a false economy to pay this excess.

Comprehensive cover for your car does not necessarily cost the same throughout Italy and you should shop around. Also very few companies pay out on things, including radios and tape recorders, left in the car. Without this type of insurance, you are not covered if you skid into a ditch, get written off by an unknown lorry or have a tree fall on you.

Being drunk and involved in an accident will almost certainly entail the suspension, if not cancellation, of your driving licence wherever it is from. Therefore, always drive in Italy on an Italian licence and not on a British one. There is as yet no law on what constitutes drunkenness in Italy, though there is a great deal of solid practice which means if a doctor, as a result of a blood or urine test, or both, considers you drunk, you are. No arguments. There is no appeal and your comprehensive cover automatically becomes void. You do not get a return of premium. Your third-party cover (the car's) remains in force but of course is of little use to you personally.

As stated earlier you cannot insure an Italian car out of Italy. However, it is possible for you, whilst driving anywhere in Europe, to effect an accident insurance which will cover you and your family if involved in an accident. Europassistance is on offer throughout Europe via banks, travel agents and even insurance companies. Certainly their get-you-home plan is far better than ACI or many Italian organizations can offer. In any event they are excellent for that extra cover whilst on a driving holiday. Not everyone drives as carefully as you.

Should you have the misfortune to have an accident, you will, provided you are still *compos mentis*, be required to fill out a declaration. This is known in Italian as a *costatazione amichevole di incidente – denuncia di sinistro* and is a combination of declaration and claim form. Each party, A and B, fill out their respective forms making sure beforehand who is A and who is B, otherwise the form is useless. Great care is needed when you are in a highly agitated state, but filling out this form does not constitute an admission of fault so all is not lost. The form, though in different languages, is the same throughout the European Community. It requires the name and address of the parties, their insurance company and policy numbers, the number of vehicles involved, the type of driving licence held by the drivers concerned and their numbers together with the expiry dates. Italian law requires that even though you may not have this *costatazione* form you must give the information to the other people involved. In between the two parties' details are a series of circumstances which may or may not apply to your particular case. You mark the relevant boxes with an 'X' and thereafter you both sign and address a copy to your own insurance company.

If the damage is slight you will often find the other driver offering to pay the garage bill. Be very circumspect until you have found out the extent and cost of the damage. I was caught once when someone damaged my back bumper and gave me the equivalent of forty pounds for something which cost almost a hundred and thirty, and I had no idea where he had gone. You should have a sight of his car's papers, his driving licence and the insurance company and policy number on his windscreen. There is no law against arranging things between yourselves (unless someone has been hurt) but it needs more than a modicum of caution.

Health

It is not cheering to learn that one of the easiest degrees to get from an Italian university is a medical one. Admittedly it is very basic and in order to practise as a doctor you need considerably more than this first degree. However, that is why you get people like Mussolini's granddaughter, quite truthfully saying she is a doctor though she has never even entered a hospital or consulting rooms, except as a patient. It gives her a handle and the magic *Dottoressa*.

Italy in fact has a large body of excellent doctors and, as in most countries, recommendation is always the best way to find a good one. If you are in the Italian national health system it is quite complicated to change doctors and requires at least a couple of visits to your local Italian Social Security Office, known as *Unità Sanitaria Locale* (or USL for short), to do so. The system works rather similarly to the old NHS in the UK and, in principle, you should not pay for consultations unless you call the doctor to your house when it will cost from 50,000 to 100,000 lire a time. If you have broken a limb and cannot drive or walk then call the Guardia Medica and ask their advice on how to see your local doctor.

Nurses in Italy are changing radically. Firstly, in the north the Church no longer has the majority of hospitals so the nurses are not nuns. The general tendency is to have better-qualified people with considerably less vocation. In north and central Italy, this has led to better hospitals, better beds with linen supplied by the hospital and better food. It is less common in these parts to see patients' families supplying all the necessities as well as the luxuries of a hospital stay.

Ideally, you should arrange to have private insurance to cover hospital care and use the Italian national health system for everyday minor problems. For really serious operations away from Piedmont, Lombardy and the north-east of Italy, arrange to have them out of Italy. Apart from anything else they will be cheaper. To give an idea: a simple cataract operation in Italy can cost from 5,000,000 to an incredible 15,000,000 lire privately but exactly the same operation costs a mere 1,000,000 lire in France, complete with a night's stay.

The problem of Italian private medicine is that it is badly organized in most parts of the country and all its doctors, without exception, make an absolute fortune in the private sector. It is for this reason that private health insurance is so expensive in Italy. There is also a semi-private insurance which picks up the tab the social security sector refuses to pay – it is called a *mutuo* and the care it provides varies from being very good to very bad indeed. They are not for the foreigner unless he is employed in Italy.

Although expensive at first sight, the British offer some of the best value in private health insurance in the world and it is well worth shopping around for the best deal. Even if you have no private insurance and are very ill you can return to the UK for treatment. However, it must be remembered that the British government will not pay for your repatriation – you must get there at your own expense. Most of the big private health insurance schemes will repatriate their members but it is as well to read the policy carefully. Certainly PPP and BUPA have schemes for repatriation.

In the first instance you should arrive in Italy accompanied by a form E111, which entitles you to treatment in Italy on exactly the same basis as the Italians. This form can be renewed after three months but not, of course, if you become non-resident in the UK. However, as with Italians, you will undoubtedly be called upon to contribute something towards your doctors' bills and hospital treatment. Once you become employed or resident in Italy, you will be liable for tax and national insurance contributions known as INPS. On the other hand, if you do not spend the whole year in Italy there is little point in giving the Italian State almost 10 per cent of your gross income for what is, at best, a very doubtful, health service. Most people find a basic private health insurance the best bet.

The Automobile Association St. John Alert is an emergency service open 24 hours a day and they have lists of English-speaking doctors throughout Italy. If you are a member of the AA they will give you this information and if you enrol in their scheme they can also arrange for repatriation to the UK.

Pensions

If you are a pensioner who has retired to Italy, or intends to retire there, you and your spouse will be entitled to most of the benefits you would get in your home country, i.e. free medical treatment and free medicines etc. The DSS will send you the necessary forms which you then take to your nearest USL. If you become entitled to a state retirement pension in the UK before you leave for Italy, this can either be paid in Italy or in the UK as you wish. If you reach retirement age having already taken up residence in Italy, you simply need to tell the Overseas Branch of the DSS in Newcastle of your address and they will make the necessary arrangements for payment of your pension wherever you want, as well as free medical care. You will also be dealing with the Italian social security services, which will be an object lesson in how very helpful and efficient the British civil service can be.

If, after becoming entitled to a state retirement pension, you do any work for which you receive remuneration in Italy you can find yourself liable for payment of INPS. You need to earn at least 10,000,000 per annum and after 15 years you will be entitled to free health care (this time from the Italians) and an earnings-related pension (also Italian). However, you will find that occasionally the Italian authorities require you to swear that you have *no pension arising in Italy* which, until you become entitled to this famous Italian pension for which you have paid fifteen years' contributions, you can truthfully say you have not. It has always been a matter of wonder why they should ask this. Does it mean they would not pay an Italian state pension if you already had a British one? At a time when the Italian Government is increasing taxes and trying to reduce both present and future pensions, one cannot help but surmise that it will become 'illegal' to receive two European Community pensions – no matter if you have worked or paid for both. Therefore, it would seem fairly sensible to try to be paid elsewhere than Italy if possible. Of course, if you are an ordinarily employed person then you will have to pay into the state pension fund and hope for the best.

A final comment on Italian life in general. The Italians are second only to the French in waiting to retire, though unlike the French they usually continue to work in some way or other. Provided you do not set up a business or work too obviously, no one asks questions; certainly as an energetic 70-year-old you are unlikely to be questioned about your status of OAP as long as you keep a low profile. The Italians, or rather the Venetians, have a saying, '*La verità non a ogniuno*'. On the other hand, your conscience may require you to reveal all.

13
Tax in Italy

In the previous four editions of this book, it has been pointed out that nothing is more difficult to discuss than tax in Italy. Italians don't like paying taxes and probably end up paying considerably more of them than most people in the European Union. Tax is rarely discussed except for ways to avoid paying, and even then no one gives free advice or boasts of his or her successes in this field. Indeed, as a friend commented recently, 'Tax in Italy is like sex in Ireland – you simply never mention it.'

Nevertheless there are lots of taxes out there, most of which you cannot avoid paying:

There is IVA, which stands for *Imposta sul Valore Aggiunto* and is currently at 20 per cent on virtually every purchase you make as well as on utilities' bills. There is IRPEF, which stands for *Imposta sul Reddito delle Persone Fisiche* and is the Italian form of income tax. There is ICI which sands for *Imposta Comunale Immobiliare* and amounts to local rates.

There was INVIM, which has been phased out for houses built and completed after 1992. It was a form of capital gains tax on real property. You still pay tax on the profit you make on selling your house or apartment; as yet, there is no new name for it but that doesn't stop the imposition. Ordinary capital gains tax hardly exists in Italy and is only charged when a person, owning or purchasing more than two per cent of a quoted company's share capital, sells shares and makes a profit. If you restrict yourself to large companies when purchasing shares such as MonteDison, Shell, AGIP, Fiat or Generali you will be safe from this imposition. However, it does apply to all quoted companies, perhaps including your own in Italy; no matter how small it is, having more than two per cent of the shares incurs tax when selling at a profit. There is, as yet, no capital gains tax on selling antiques, paintings, silver, jewellery etc., but I am reliably assured this is in the pipeline so make merry whilst you can.

The old ILOR is to be replaced with a new tax called IREP

which, as its letters indicate, is a regional and provincial tax on real property. As with ILOR, it will be based on both the property you own and your income. In the absence of property ownership it will be based on income only and will be part and parcel of your annual tax declaration.

Then there are taxes on your gas and electricity, which add anything up to 20 per cent to the bill. As if this were not enough, you then pay IVA at 10 per cent on the whole of the bill including the provincial tax – i.e. taxes on taxes!

Television licences are a sort of tax at over 100,000 lire per annum. This is one of the few areas where the Italians do not cheat since the *carabinieri* have powerful detector vans and the fines are truly horrendous. There is a tax on petrol, apart from all others, which keeps Italian troops in Bosnia and probably there are many others no one, including me, knows anything about.

There remain oddities about the Italian tax system. You still have to declare yourself at the local finance offices once you have taken up permanent residence in Italy. Usually you get a year's grace but not if you are an employee whose employer will declare you at the end of the financial period and therefore, you must declare yourself and match your employer's figures. If you own a house and you do not make a tax return you will be charged a certain amount of IRPEF on the grounds that you need some income to keep up the fabric of the house or apartment.

Of course, if you are non-resident you do not need to make a tax return but you must prove you have no income arising in Italy. This is where a *commercialistà* comes in handy. He will organize the various returns which have to be made, warn you of the taxes which have to be paid and probably tell you that the easiest way to prove you are non-resident is by showing the Italian Revenue last year's British tax declaration.

There are masses of foreigners in Italy who, over the years, have managed to pay nothing by way of tax except when they purchased the land, house or apartment they now have. Even VAT or IVA is avoidable. There is an entire Italian army of plumbers, electricians, suppliers of wood for fuel, upholsterers, odd-job men, gardeners and the like waiting to work for you or sell to you free of IVA. Be very circumspect about whom you employ. Builders should be registered, as should plumbers, electricians and other craftsmen; if they are not and are working black you get absolutely no guarantee or come back. You get precious little when they are registered (short of going to court, which is something to be avoided in Italy) but at least you are not breaking the law. There are inspectors from the local Sanitary Unit or USL who, from time to time, target an area to find out where the black labourers are working and for whom. Be careful about employing the elderly or *pensionati*. Very often they can have an invalidity pension which means they *cannot work at all* hence the pension to replace the incomes they are incapable of earning. You may be totally innocent and unaware of your jobbing gardener's private finances but you will be fined if you are caught employing such a person. You will also be asked why you are not paying National Insurance or INPS (*Istituto Nazionale di Previdenza Sociale*) contributions.

There are lots of other taxes too, such as *carta bollata* at 20,000 lire each time you have to make some application to a government department or similar body. There are stamp duties to pay on all the various certificates from the local *comune*, taxes on hire purchase documents, service agreements, leases of property, purchases of property, boats, Italian passports, local taxes on gas, electricity and fuel bills, taxes on petrol (even unleaded) apart from IVA, a tax on gas oil and an extra tax for your car radio which is added to your annual car tax. There is practically a new tax of some sort each month, on employing people (in a country where unemployment is very high indeed), on prescriptions, on certain hospital beds, and luxury taxes on such things as fur coats, non-working shoes, (virtually all except heavy boots and wellingtons), quite a lot of fish and shellfish are classified as luxury and, of course, caviare and champagne (to look after the *spumante* and *Prosecco* industry it is said). One could go on for ever.

If you own property in Italy you will have been given a *Codice Fiscale* number on its purchase if you had not had one already. If you do not own property in Italy but rent or stay only from time to time you will be able to avoid this 'branding' by the Italian government by producing your passport and proving you don't live in Italy. Otherwise, all large purchases with a proper invoice, all electricity, gas and fuel bills as well as leases and certain other documents must carry this number. It is a brilliant idea which quite literally codifies the average Italian and watches how he spends his money. It hasn't happened yet but there could come a time when Mr X spends more than fifty or sixty million lire on goods and services when he is only declaring an income of twenty-five or thirty millions. The Italian Revenue can, not unreasonably, ask where the money has come from. Even buying BOTs which are a type of Italian Government bond requires your *Codice Fiscale*.

The *Codice Fiscale* can be obtained, indeed must be obtained, when purchasing property, from the local tax office (*Intendenza di Finanza* or *Uffici Distrettuali delle Imposte Dirette*. For individuals or *persone fisiche* as they are known in Italian, the code is made up of letters and figures whereas for companies it is made up of figures only. A person's code is made up by taking the first three consonants of the surname (or fewer if there are fewer consonants) and the first, third and fourth consonants of the given name. If that name has only three consonants then all three are given, if two then two and so on. The year of birth is shown normally, e.g. 57, but the months are shown from A onwards, F being June. The day of birth 1–31 is for males and 41–71 is for females. Every *comune* in Italy has a code which then appears but for foreigners the country of birth is put in full.

Thus a man, Francis Carter born on the 30th April, 1943 in Great Britain would have the following *Codice Fiscale*: CRT FRC 43D30 plus Gran Bretagna on the next line down instead of a number.

Husbands and wives have different *Codice Fiscale* numbers since the wife keeps everything in her maiden name in Italy. This must be used on all official correspondence and when making your declaration. However, the number is not in fact a personal tax number but is used principally for VAT and social security purposes. Nevertheless, in spite of these protestations to the contrary, it would be all too easy to make the connection and that day is probably not so far off.

There are certain people in Italy who need not make a declaration and they are the following:

Those who have no income and are dependent on someone else for their existence, i.e. a huband or wife, child or parent.

Those who have income exempt from tax such as a war pension, an invalidity pension, State pensions and old-age pensions. This does *not* include private pensions.

Those whose income is solely from source where tax is deducted before payment such as bank interest, BOTs, share dividends, mortgage interest etc.

Those who are employed on a salary basis where tax is deducted at source. Lots of Italians get away with simply declaring what they earn as a salaried person without declaring anything else and probably this causes the biggest hole in the tax system. Far too many Italians are self-employed without any form of registration or supervision.

If you are in one of these categories you need not make a declaration, at the moment. It seems this will change in the not too distant future and everyone over the age of 18 will have to make some form of return even if it is a nil return.

If you are not one of the above, and particularly if you have income arising in Italy or have moneys on which tax has not been paid anywhere, then you should make a declaration. Similarly, if you have regular sums remitted to you in Italy you should make a return. Most foreigners who make a return declare only part of their income and the rest somehow gets lost in order to pay foreign credit cards and similar items. This is a case for both your own conscience and the advice of your *commercialista*. One thing to be very careful about is letting property. For instance, in Tuscany, many British have discovered they can get vast sums for their property in high summer which happens to be a time they would prefer to be elsewhere. It is difficult to persuade the local *carabinieri* and *comune* that you have such a wide circle of friends to whom you lend your house and in any event summer tenants do not keep their mouths shut. Also, should you quarrel with your help or anyone local they will probably denounce you. Before embarking on letting, and later declaring or not declaring your income from such an enterprise, you should gauge the feelings of the local powers that be. I know of one person in Tuscany who now spends all summer there in order to be near her tenants and convince the xenophobic, left-wing *marisciallo* of the local *caribinieri* that they are her close friends – he in turn watches her like a hawk.

Declaration Forms 740 are available from the offices of the local *comune* and the completed form together with a cheque for the taxes can be handed to them or put in the post to the local tax offices. This is about the only time you don't have to stamp an envelope to a government department. One of the three copies is for the *comune*.

Husbands and wives can make separate declarations or they can make joint returns. This must be done between the 1st and 31st May of each year. It is constantly said that this will have to change to come into line with other EU countries but so far nothing has happened.

The final paragraph of the leaflet showing you how to make your declaration sets out the fines which can be imposed for making a wrongful declaration, deliberate or not. As some of these can reach over a million lire a time, it is frankly unwise to complete your own declaration unless you are a qualified *Italian* accountant.

Once in the tax system and having paid your first year's tax you will become automatically liable for a percentage of that the following November. If you have earned less you will definitely need to consult a professional. You must claim a rebate within eighteen months and repayment can take as long as two years, so it is best not to put yourself in the position of lending interest free to the Italian Government.

The most valuable piece of advice to a foreigner living in Italy is to consult a good commercialista.

In your nearest big town there is bound to be a *commercialistà* specializing in international work. Do not leave it until May to consult him since by January of the New Year you will know what your income was for the previous year. He will tell you what taxes you simply must pay, what you can set off against taxes (not something which happens when you make a declaration on your own), he will fill in and file your declaration for you and charge you, considering what he almost certainly saved you in tax, a derisory sum, particularly compared with British or American accountants.

Of course there are good and bad *commercialistàs* but no one stays with a bad one for long and a good *commercialistà*'s office should be a hive of industry. The days of negotiating your tax with the local *ispettore* are over, but a *commercialistà* is the next best thing. If there is a language problem then take along someone as an interpreter. For heaven's sake don't give up a good *commercialistà* due to a language problem.

The provisional rates of tax for the year 1999 are as follows:

Up to 15 million lire	19%
15,000,001 to 60,000,000	27%
60,000,001 to 120,000,000	34%
120,000,001 and above	45%

At first glance this would seem to be more a 'soak the poor' rather than 'soak the rich' tax schedule. However, although the tax threshold is lower and the taxes for the higher earners are greater than in most of the EU, the majority of Italian incomes are between 15 and 120 million lire a year and here the tax compares very favourably with the rest of Europe, including Great Britain. Quite a pleasant surprise in fact, and one which is supposed to encourage the Italians to be honest about paying their income tax.

14
Gardening in Italy

Like so many other things in Italy, gardening has all the delights and all the drawbacks of gardening in the UK, only more so. 'Sunny' Italy offers such a variety of climates and soil that newcomers should be on their guard and look very carefully at what grows both wild and in nearby gardens before planting any well-loved favourites.

I remember giving three or four camellias to a friend who lives on Lake Maggiore (I own a nursery so it's not all that generous) and arriving at her house to find forty-feet-high hedges of a dozen varieties of camellia. At least I had the comfort of knowing they would do well but it certainly wasn't the luxurious present I had intended.

Italians are brilliant horticulturalists – witness the flower industry in Liguria, Tuscany around Pistoia, Lombardy and Piedmont – but they are not particularly talented gardeners, at least in the eyes of northern Europeans who lament the lack of colour in their garden design. The Italian garden has evolved over the centuries as a place of shade and protection from the elements rather than as a place of botanical interest. Moreover, the Italian character is one that prefers the security of the tried and true to the possibility of attempting something new and failing. Architecture is an important factor in Italian garden design, and rightly so, but not to the extent that statues take the place of living trees, flowers and shrubs.

Statues are very expensive, even their faked copies in cement or imitation marble, and more and more Italians are having to think in terms of trees, shrubs, climbers and trellises, and of course the ever-lasting *pelargoniums* or *gerani* as they call them. Two staples of Italian gardens I should like to see banned are all forms of *Cupressocyparis leylandii* and magenta geraniums.

Although Italy now produces many of her own trees, shrubs and plants, and indeed has a thriving export trade, it also imports a vast quantity, mostly from Holland. Now, anyone can import plants from any other part of the European Union, but it is always chancey and should be confined to items you really cannot find in Italy. The post is not always reliable and, failing being able to bring the items over yourself or having a friend do so for you, then overnight courier is a good, if expensive idea. Certainly in Italy it works out cheaper in the end. One or two companies or organizations in England send out small seedlings by post. The choice is limited but they are well packed and it is a good method of getting *osteospermums* and other perennials by airmail. Cannington College, in Bridgwater, Somerset is one place which offers this service.

One of the main problems is that Italians are often careless about naming their plants and only recently I was told (and this is professional to professional) that Lespedeza is the same as Desmodium, that the Camellia Janet Waterhouse is the same as Mrs E.G. Waterhouse because her name was Janet (one is pink and one is white) that there is only one sort of Clivia (ditto Amaryllis), and that *Chamaecyparis lawsoniana* is the same as *Cupressocyparis leylandii* – forget about the many forms of these two species. Even olive trees have to be bought from a true specialist or you can be fobbed off with what they have but under the name you have requested. It is almost impossible to tell one olive tree from another until you see the fruit and therefore you must be very careful that you are dealing with a reliable nurseryman.

Dotted around Italy there are many excellent nurserymen and garden centres usually called a *vivaio* or 'Garden Centre' in English to lend it authority. It is true that many cater to the taste of the general public, which is not very sophisticated. I myself have found that Italians do not understand clematis, except the larger flowered sort which do badly in most parts of Italy; they have never heard of *ceanothus*, though mine are much admired; and they like hybrid tea roses, because they bloom all summer, and ignore the fact that modern shrub roses and the Charles Austin English roses do the same. I have actually had someone tell me, standing next to a *ceanothus* in full bloom, that 'that sort of plant would never grow here,' which is really not believing your eyes. Roses do well in Italy and more and more specialist nurseries are appearing. However, because they believe they cater for a rather exclusive band, i.e. the connoisseur, the prices are steep, anything from 14,000–25,000 lire a plant. The names of suppliers are given at the end of this chapter. I myself provide around 250 varieties of old-fashioned and modern shrub roses all at 12,000 lire each, inclusive of VAT, so they need not be expensive.

Bulbs are not much used in Italy, except for the odd tulip or daffodil in winter, and this is a pity because many, many parts of the country are suited to bulb culture. Perhaps one should include corms as well: such as cyclamens and also many varieties of iris.

There was a time when practically every Tuscan olive grove or even vineyard was underplanted with *iris germanica 'florentina'* (or *iris pallida*) to give orris root, which is mostly known through orris-root biscuits but which today is used in violet perfume. Many of the summer-flowering bulbs, often from South Africa, do well: *acidanthera, brodiaea, brunsvigia, chionodoxa* of which the *sardensis* variety is a superb native, *colchicum, crocosmia, cyclamen* spp., *eremurus, eucomis*, virtually all the *fritillarias, galtonia, gynandriris* – another Italian native, *gladiolus, hedychium, hippeastrum,* many *iris* spp., *moraea*, many forms of *lilium* (though extra care may be needed), *oxalis* in a wild garden only, *pancratium, puschkinia* in winter, bulbous *pelargonium, ranunculus, romulea, schizostylis, sternbergia, tigridia pavonia, triteleia, tritonia*, bulbous *tropaeolum*, tulips in winter, *watsonia, zantedeschia* to name but a few. These are quite apart from the run-of-the-mill bulbs one can buy for spring flowering.

Probably the most important problem which besets gardening in Italy is water. The situation is partly bureaucratic and partly natural. As the natural side gets more and more difficult so the bureaucratic side for some reason becomes easier.

Water has been largely privatized in Italy and, as elsewhere, the price of this essential commodity has shot up. In most of Italy water is metered which at least has stopped people stealing it, more or less. The north of Italy tends to have far fewer problems than the centre and south of the country. Anyone with a swimming pool knows how essential it is to fill the pool the moment the danger of frost has disappeared – before the possible imposition of a summer-long ban on filling pools.

If you possibly can you should have holding tanks for water, and these should be sunk into the ground, otherwise you *will* need permission from the *comune*. Any tank within 400 metres of a dwelling must have a cover. This is more honoured in the breach than in the observance and it is relatively unusual to see lids for these cisterns. Likewise with a well, the law requires that all wells are covered, locked and inaccessible to children, *even those trespassing on your land*. If you have to have a visible holding tank or cistern on your land you must ask permission of your local *comune*. These tanks come in brilliant electric blue, scarlet, yellow, turquoise green or brown. Strictly speaking they should be painted to blend in with the local scenery, but it is unusual to see such care taken, more's the pity.

Ideally, if you have more than 2000 sq. metres of garden you should have a separate contract for the garden only. If this is not possible you will have to resort to holding tanks which should be filled in winter when you use less water anyway. Count 100 litres daily per 2000 sq. metres of land as a minimum. If you have a pool you must have a separate water contract, even though you may not change the water in the pool from one year to the next. Of course if you have a well or a spring on your property your problems are solved, but do make sure you have a well or spring which is active all year round.

Those living in Piedmont or the alpine regions do not usually have water problems though the Po Plain can dry up sufficiently to cause rationing. Those in Tuscany and further south often have specially constructed tanks under the house holding up to 500,000 litres of water for summer use. Yes, that is half a million litres of water and obviously this sort of storage is not possible without a spring or water source on your land and moreover one that you can be sure of from year to year.

If you buy a country property and want a garden, make sure of the water situation first since it is unlikely it can be altered later except at very great cost. Enquire of the local *comune* and/or the local *acquedotto* people and try and get an answer in writing, though this may be difficult knowing how unwilling the local officials are to commit themselves on paper.

Lawns, which all northern Europeans seem to want, are not always easy to grow. In central and southern Italy many resort to paved areas and/or Bermuda grass as a substitute. If you have a cold winter, do not use *dichondra repens* – it turns to brown slime at the first frost. *Lolium perenne*, known as *loietto* in Italian, is common ryegrass and a native to Italy. It is probably the best bet for a lawn, although a really good mixture of bents and fescues can work well north of the Po.

Finally, avoid tropical and sub-tropical trees and shrubs which require a lot of water such as avocado trees which need 40 to 50 litres a day, quite a price to pay in metred water for a daily avocado! Be wary of Brazilian, East African or equatorial natives unless you have unlimited water.

Italy can be roughly divided into seven gardening zones which are shown on the map on page 235. These are:

1. Alpine Italy which is sub-divided into north and south zones by a line going from Ivrea, just north of Turin, in the west, across the plain just north of Milan to Lake Garda which has a micro climate of its own to Vittorio Veneto and Udine in the east. The southern part of this region is further sub-divided into the Langhiano Hills and the province of Asti near Turin and the karst district (*carso* in Italian) in the extreme east.

2. The Lombardy-Po Plain (*La Pianura Padana*) is the richest agricultural region in Italy and its biggest stretch of flat land. It follows the Po River from the east near Turin to the Adriatic and includes the areas around Milan, Verona and Venice.
3. The Western Adriatic. (*Adriatico occidentale*) covers the area from Rovigo down the coast to the heel of Italy. On the west it is bounded by the Apennines. It is sub-divided into the Marches-Abruzzo Sector (*Settore Marchilgiano-Abruzzese*) the Apulo-Saltentino Sector and the very special Gargano Peninsular Sector (*Distretto Garganico*).
4. West Coasts of Italy sub-divided into Liguria in the north, Tuscany in the centre and Campania-Calabria in the south.
5. Sicily.
6. Sardinia.
7. The mountainous regions of the Apennines with Perugia at their centre.

Alpine Italy

The northern sector of alpine Italy, which includes the Dolomites, the Carnic and Julian alps, is very richly endowed botanically but is a hard area for the gardener. Although there is a spring, it comes late and summer follows swiftly. Nothing tender should be put out before June, but if you can provide protection with cloches or plastic tunnels this is enough. All this region has a high snowfall, and as a result much of the soil around the area of the lakes is acid. Within sight of limestone alps heather, rhododendrons and camellias can be seen and blueberries are common in the Val d'Aosta. As altitude can change soil type, it is well worth testing various parts of your garden in the first instance to see what can and cannot be grown.

Although winters are cold, summer and autumn are long and the sun can be terribly hot, so protection should be provided for roses and flowering shrubs or otherwise their glory will be over by lunchtime. Until you are at 1000 metres altitude, most new trees, shrubs and roses need no protection but above that line climbers on walls and roses tend to get damaged and roses can be very late in getting going again. Wind can be a problem and you should lightly prune in November or December to prevent wind rock and follow this by the final pruning in late February or early March. Never, ever prune too hard too early since a very cold wind could dry up much of the plant and you will have very little or nothing to prune back to.

Some of Italy's best wines are produced in this region and there is no reason why you should not plant vines where little else will grow. They are attractive to look at most of the year and, depending on the variety you plant, you will have grapes for wine or to eat – or both – at the end of the season. It takes a great deal to kill off a vine. Disease is a far more likely cause of death but there are many cures on the market. The main problem is diagnosing the disease in order to get the right cure. This is also the main region for fruit growing, particularly apples, pears and cherries all of which do remarkably well.

The Lombardy-Po Plain

This area is given over to arable and animal farming and, near the cities, industry. Virtually anything can be grown but protection from mid-summer sun must be given. Before planting flowers, roses and vegetables you should think about planting trees to give light shade. *Robinia pseudoacacia* (false acacia), *Carpinus* (hornbeam), poplar windbreaks, and if you don't have very cold winters *Albizzia julibrissin* (the silk floss tree) all provide the right sort of shade, i.e. they dry quickly after rain and don't drip all over your plantings. Be prudent when planting poplar though.

Water is not a great problem here and almost certainly you will be able to get a garden contract for summer use. Lawns of coarse grasses are possible but do not expect Cumberland turf. *Dichondra* or *cynodon dactylon* can be used but, in winter, mud in the house can be a problem if you have pets. Think seriously about planting lots of shade trees and shrubs and paving central and much used areas.

Of course there are parts of this region where the soil is very poor, such as around the lagoons in Venice and the tracts of sandy soil around Brescia, but by digging in plenty of purchased soil or better still home-made compost you can improve the soil greatly.

To the north of this region, where it borders Alpine Italy, is the *Distretto Insubrico* which takes in all the northern lakes. The soil is mostly acid, the rainfall is rather high and many of Italy's most famous gardens such as Villa Taranto at Pallanza on Lake Maggiore, the Giardino Hruska at Gardone Riviera, Isola Bella, and Parco Burcina at Biella are in this area.

The Western Adriatic

This sector begins at Rimini in the north and follows a narrow coastal strip down to the Gargano Peninsula. Immediately after

Gargano the strip widens to include half the foot of Italy and the whole of the heel. The part north of Gargano is a fertile region and enjoys a goodish climate, neither too hot nor too cold but very subject to storms due to its position between the mountains and the sea. The coastal strip can be said to enjoy a sort of Mediterranean climate which gets a bit too cold in winter for citrus to survive. Most shrubs need protection more against the wind than against cold.

The Gargano Peninsula is interesting for two reason. The first is that, geologically speaking, it still belongs to Dalmatia across the water and the second is that, from a botanical point of view, it is packed with endemic plants, one of the best known being *Campanula garganica*. A lawn of coarse rye-grass will stand up to the depredations of winter and summer in this region. Well worth a detour, as the Michelin Guide says.

Below this peninsula is Apulia where, as you go south, the climate becomes hotter and hotter and certainly drier. The olive, and to a certain extent, citrus fruits, are the main crops here. The oil is heavy, rich and fruity and not to everyone's taste but good with bean salads. Anything you plant should be able to take an occasional buffeting of wind but otherwise you can grow most things, other than a conventional lawn. Indeed, even a lawn of *dichondra* or Bermuda grass is not going to live up to expectations. Plant for shade and have paving, pots and more pots.

The West Coasts of Italy

The Ligurian coast round to La Spezia presents no problem as far as climate is concerned except that inland – and, therefore, upland – the winters can become rather cold and typical Mediterranean plants will freeze to death. There is a general water-shortage, though strangely this has lessened in the last few years due to organizing its distribution more logically. It is extremely expensive – among the most expensive in Italy. Really nice lawns are not possible without a great deal of time and trouble but, that said, shade planting can help matters. As elsewhere, you cannot plant too many trees and shrubs. Citrus will grow on the coast and so will *jacaranda, mandevilla* and the various fragile South American creepers. Olive groves abound, but the olives are mostly for the deliciously light olive oil, *Taggiasco*, and it is difficult to find eating-olives in the area. I waited two years to get plants of the olive *Ascolana*, which has almost inch long fruit, and had to import them from the other side of Italy. Vines are grown on terraces and much of the local wine is badly made and expensive because its care and harvesting are not mechanized.

Tuscany's main crops are the olive and the vine, and both are more carefully grown than in Liguria. Gardeners should follow suit and also plant roses since Tuscany's soil is either clayey or sandy and in the latter *rugosas* do wonderfully. Keep feeding both types of soil with plenty of organic manure and plenty of peat, home-made compost or coco fibre. Such treatment will work wonders in the end, though incorporation can be back breaking.

Campania and Calabria are naturally barren parts of Italy but amazing things can be done if you choose the right plants and have a certain amount of water and luck. Much of the barren landscape is due to man, who cut down local forests during the last century. The greatest enemy here is the sun which has a truly relentless quality in this region. However, *robinia,* or false acacia, eucalyptus pines, the Persian lilac (*Melia azerdarach*), also pepper trees (*Schinus molle*) and oleanders will all grow easily and rapidly. The carob tree (*ceratonia*) also will give an enviable amount of shade. Pergolas festooned with *bougainvillea, plumbago, mandevilla,* jasmine or passion flower, patios with citrus trees in octagonal pots, hidden gardens with fountains (using the same two litres of water unceasingly) should be the order of the day. When losing heart in the heat of Calabria try to remember what the Israelis made of the desert. Remember that not all succulents have spines. Yuccas, *euphorbias* and *agaves* can be the backbone of a truly dry garden. There are wonderful dark black *jojarbs* from Morocco, glaucous blue *crassulas*, vivid green jade plants (another *crassula*) and pale grey *tradescantia* which go wonderfully with the Mexican purple-heart plant which is also a *tradescantia. Irisine* is brilliant red, tender but an ideal plant for a pot in a Calabrian garden.

Never throw any water away which you can put on the land. Construct underground tanks if you can before you buy shrubs. Alternatively have several large cisterns, covered against breeding mosquitoes in summer, and hide them behind a rendered white wall which you cover in *plumbago* or a white bougainvillea or both. Avoid the magenta sort which is not a peaceful colour to be with on a daily basis.

Sicily and Sardinia

Although very different from each other in that Sardinia frequently has freezing temperatures in winter and Sicily does not, except at altitude, they both have the problem of very poor soil. Sicily has a justly famous citrus-fruit industry, as well as a large, but not always very well thought of, wine industry. However, since most of the white wine drunk as an aperitif in the north is Sicilian this is not very kind. It also has a long tradition of gardens going back to the time of the Greek occupation. Rainfall is almost non-existent in large areas of Sicily and in Sardinia falls mostly in the autumn and winter. Little is done to store it for a sunny day. A lawn is simply not possible, although in some areas Bermuda grass may work. Paved areas and patios are a better bet and much, much less heartache. Unless you are farming or wine growing, there is no possibility of purchasing water for anything. However, you can grow such things as *hardenbergia, iochroma, jacaranda* (with a certain amount of water) and all the West Indian bougainvillea and even frangipani, though these need a little liquid help on occasion.

Central Apenine Italy

Strangely for a mountainous country, most people do not live at altitude and this area is dotted with medium-sized towns such as Arezzo (still in Tuscany), Perugia, Urbino, Orvieto and Spoleto and many more, all soaked in history and endowed with beautiful archi-tecture. It is also well endowed with rivers and although some of these dry up in high summer, most of them keep going throughout the year. Water is not a desperate problem and can usually be purchased for garden use. Summers are hot and dry but winters are cold and sometimes even freezingly so. Good pears can be grown here, as in the north of Italy, as well as cherries, peaches and apri-cots. What else can be grown in this region depends entirely on the altitude of the individual garden and its aspect. Extremes of climate are not uncommon, therefore not only hardy shrubs and trees should be chosen but also those which can stand up to a summer's baking.

Most of the area has alkaline soil but towards the south, around Monte Terminilli, there are outcrops of acid soil where heather grows spontaneously. One of Italy's most famous National Parks, the Gran Sasso, is in the south of this region and is well worth a visit even if you do not live nearby. For the sybaritic there is a luxury hotel there where Mussolini was kept prisoner and 'rescued' by the Nazis as well as several others of a more modest sort.

If you enjoy gardening, you will find it rather more dramatic in Italy: your successes will be absolute knockouts and your failures, usually due to no fault on your part, will make you want to weep.

If you don't particularly like gardening, then most parts of Italy will cure you of any residual interest once and for all. Most people, even enthusiasts, find they have to quit the gardening scene in summer by eleven o'clock at the latest because it becomes far too hot to work. There is a saying in Italy about the soil – '*Sessanta per cento argila e quaranta per cento miseria*' sixty per cent clay and forty per cent misery. Equally, there is something extremely satisfying in turning stodgy clay into garden loam, once it happens; and eventually, with hard work, it does.

I'd recommend two books on Mediterranean gardening, both difficult to get: one is Hugo Latymer's *The Mediterranean Gardener* and the other is my own *Mediterranean Gardening*. The first goes into design far more deeply than the second, which is more of a practical handbook.

Below is a list of some of the better-known horticultural concerns. It is by no means exhaustive but should be a help to the newcomers. Readers who find good nurseries could spread the good news by writing to me for the next edition.

Allavena, via Arziglia, 18012 Bordighera (IM). Succulents and cactus only.
Alpiflora, San Giovanni di Bellagio (CO).
Ansaloni, via Emilia 253, San Lazzarao di Savena (BO).
Vivaio Anselmo, Strada Nuova 15, 18000 Imperia. Palms.
Az. Ag. Aschieri, via del Cristo, 17031 Albenga. Famous for their *anthemis* and *pelargoniums*.
Asteggiano, Corso Casale 2893, Turin.
Az.Ag. Villa Borromeo, Oreno (MI).
Az.Ag. Buriani, via Ca' Rossa 15, Fossanova San Marco (FI).
Vivaio Carbone, via Carbone 17, 16021 Bargagli (GE).
Comaschi, via Leoni 13, Como.
Co-op. Flor del Lazio, via Appia Antica, Rome. Conifers and trees.
Del Bianco Ivo, via a Saffi 35, 47046 Misano Adriatico (FO).
De Luca, via Capodimonte 19 bis, 80100 Naples. Ficus specialist.
Eurafrican Plants, Lungotevere dei Mellini 45,00100 Rome. General Mediterranean trees, shrubs and plants.
Fumagalli e Ronchi, via Regina Giovanna 42 Milan.
Flli. Gabiragi, via Alcide de Gasperi 20, Omate (MI).
Gardesign, via B. Colombo 17, Somma Lombarda, (VA).
Flli. Ghiradelli, via Alcide de Gasperi 2, Omate (MI).
Hobby Garden, Piazza Colombo 32 – 34 18038 Sanremo (IM).
Flli. Ingegelloni, Corsdo Buenos Aires 54, Milan.
Marai Vivai, via Campeggio 16, Foro Illatico, 00100 Rome.

Flli. Margheriti, Monte San Paolo, 53043 Chiusi (SI). One of the largest selections in the country but no mail order.

Noaro Luciano, via Vittorio Emanuele 18033 Camporosso (IM). Large selection of local Mediterranean plants and will take special orders.

Az. Ag. Nespoli, via Garibaldi 25, Carugo (CO).

Paghera, Lomato (BS) Very innovative garden design and good conifers and shrubs. One of the most upmarket concerns in Italy.

Pallanca, Cornice di due Golfi. 18038 Bordighera (IM.) Near the Grand Hotel del Mare. Vast range of succulents and cactus. Show garden.

Pamparino, via Capprazoppa, 17024 Finale Ligure (IM).

H. Peer Vivaio. via San Mamolo 34, 40100 Bologna. Aquatic plants only.

Porcella Vivaio, via Nazionale 57, 17037 Ortovera (SV).

Pugliafito Carmelo, via Garissi 48, 98051 Barcellona Pozzo di Gotto (ME).

Rose & Rose Emporium. Contrada Fossalto 9, Fabro (TR). More than 500 roses on offer at various prices. Delivery from end November to end February throughout Italy. Expensive. Contact Tel: (0763) 828.12 Fax. (0763) 82 828.

Sgarvatti Mediterraneana, Km 14 S.S.195, Capoterra (CT). Mediterranean shrubs and trees.

Vivaio Torsanlorenzo, via Campo di Carne 51, 00040 Ardea (Roma).

Valco Orchidee, Regione Posillico 3, 17031 Albenga (IM) *Ficus* orchid and *aralia* specialist.

Vanin Vivai, via Noalese 27, Quito di Treviso (TV).

Villa Galanta S.a.s., Frazione Brocca di Campi, via San Romolo. 18030 Perinaldo (IM). Over 300 bare-root old-fashioned and modern shrub roses by mail between Christmas and end March; largest collection in Italy of *ceanothus* spp. Tel (0184) 67.22.09. Fax: (0184) 67.24.79.

Walter Branchi Rose. Corbara 55, 05019 Orvieto (TR). Around 125 roses – old fashioned and/or rare or re-discovered. Tel. and Fax:(0763) 30.41.54. Expensive, but excellent for rare roses unavailable elsewhere.

15
Food, Wine and Shopping

From being one of the cheapest countries in Europe for food and restaurants, Italy has become one of the most expensive, if not the most expensive, when one considers some of the prices one pays for very so-so food. Those spoilt by good London restaurants will be appalled at the average meal given by certain quite expensive Italian restaurants.

There used to be good Italian desserts, such as home-made tiramisu, zabaglione and brilliant *crostate*. These were based on items such as quality marsala, fresh thick cream and fresh fruits; today, these are things of the past except in the very best restaurants. Nowadays you are more likely to get something resembling Angel's Delight for zabaglione, frozen tiramisu which must make the older Venetians throw up their hands in horror, and fruit tarts made from pastry which has had nothing to do with butter and little to do with fresh fruit. However, the good news is that you can still eat well in much of Piedmont, much of Tuscany and Lombardy and in the Veneto. With rare exceptions you have never been able to eat really well in Venice, Florence or other well-trodden tourist centres.

Italian restaurants start off quite well with *antipasti* which are usually good, though items like industrial *mortadella* (bleached rubber) and Russian salad from a can are appearing more and more frequently.

The usual offering for the meat course is veal in town and rabbit in the country – and the rabbit is always better. Only the pasta course can be relied upon almost throughout Italy. Fish requires a bank loan both in the market and in restaurants. No wonder the Italians pour over the Austrian, Swiss and French frontiers for Sunday lunch.

Some years ago the Government of the day imposed a tax on what they considered luxury seafood. Today, only sardines and squid seem to have escaped, though in fact this is not the case. Lobster, prawns, even mussels and John Dory all carry an extra tax.

Even when a particular fish is not taxed its price makes it appear as though it is. Short of having a copy of the Act with one at the time of purchase it is difficult to know just what is and what is not carrying a luxury tax since, though much has been exempted, the restaurants and fishmongers have not necessarily reduced their prices. The price of red mullet in Italy, which is commonly featured in the Italian kitchen, has to be seen to be believed.

Near the French frontier, cheese is often served before the dessert but this is not common in the rest of Italy where cheese frequently appears as an hors d'oeuvre or *antipasti*. This can be in the form of thin slices of parmesan cheese served with Parma ham or *mozzarella in carrozza* which is delicious on a cold wintry day, *mozzarella* again but served with a tomato and basil salad and cheese filled tartlets of puff pastry.

As mentioned before, dessert can be a bit of a deception in many restaurants. However, one is still fairly safe in ordering ice-cream or sorbet (*gelato o sorbete*), and even the industrially produced ice-cream is of good quality. Italy must be one of the few countries in Europe where Haagen Dazs has not made inroads simply because the market has been catered for by the Italians themselves for many, many years.

One of the most irritating things the newcomer to Italy encounters is that anything Italian with an international reputation is seldom any cheaper in its country of origin. Alfa-Romeo cars, Parma and San Daniele ham, balsamic vinegar, *mostarda di Cremona*, Chianti, Prosecco, milk-fed veal and all their cheeses are all as expensive, or more so, as abroad.

Fresh milk is difficult to get, as is non UHT cream (usually this is from Bavaria); butter, unless it is Danish, appears to taste rather cheesey or is simply pale, tasteless and rich. Yet, I remember thirty years ago when there were beautiful butters, creams and rich cheeses available in the Bologna and Milan markets. Now, in common with the rest of the world, everything is pre-packed and much of it is tasteless.

After that long and heartfelt moan perhaps it would be kind to mention some of the things which have not changed for the worse in Italy. Their pasta which at most levels is still superb, Arborio rice, their game, their mushrooms which come in all shapes and sizes (and prices), their white truffles in early October, their *funghi porcini*, their buffalo *mozzarella* which is as different from the product you have on your pizza as champagne is from lemonade, most gorgonzola, most *pecorino* cheese, most of their Parmesan cheese, their salamis, their San Daniele *prosciutto*, their macaroons particularly from Isaia, and most of all their wines from as far apart as the Friuli and Sicily. Italy's aperitifs such as Martini, Carpano and Campari are rightly world famous and cannot be bettered by any country in the world. Most Italian residents have been fortunate enough to have meals both in restaurants and private houses which have restored their faith in the real Italy where the quality of the ingredients as well as the talent of the cook, to say nothing of the wine cellar, all recall a considerably less hurried way of life. Italians have a gift for presentation of food which is second to none.

For the average Italian, the day begins with a light breakfast, known as *la prima collazione* or *collazione* for short. Often this is taken in a bar on the way to work. My husband swears by the quality of the coffee in the Ventimiglia Station Buffet, for instance. At home, alas, it is often last night's coffee heated up with or without milk. The espresso machine though is much more common in Italian homes than in other countries. Bread or brioche (*brioss* in Italian) comes with jam or marmalade which is nothing like English orange marmalade. Health fiends have many fruit juices to choose from, orange, pineapple, grape, passion fruit, grapefruit, guava, banana or raspberry, and as well as juices there are fruit nectars which contain some of the pulp to make the drink more substantial and better tasting.

In all but the very large cities, lunch or *pranzo* is the main meal of the day and usually consists of a *primo piatto* which is always some form of pasta or rice followed by meat or fish, with or without potatoes. On Sundays and holidays this is preceded by *antipasti* or hors d'oeuvres, which in parts of Italy can be a meal in itself. Although canelloni and lasagne are pasta dishes they are frequently eaten as a main course even in Italy, and especially by women, followed or accompanied by a green salad.

Except at the weekend the Italians are not great pudding-eaters and tend to reach for the fruit bowl at the end of a meal rather than indulge in chocolate mousse, spotted dick or raspberry tart.

The evening meal is usually a light affair unless they are going out to friends or to a restaurant. Unless it is the main meal of the day, it usually comprises something like cannelloni and a salad, cold meats or a piece of grilled fish and salad.

For a country which is the biggest wine-producer in the world (some of it truly terrible), the natives are not great drinkers. The further south one goes the less alcohol is drunk, until in Sicily one glass with a meal and no aperitif seems to be the norm. In the mountainous regions of the north the men can put down quite a lot of the local *acquavite* or *grappa* but hardly touch the excellent wine.

Whenever Italians are confronted with some new food they immediately wonder how it would go with pasta. Even dogs have pasta instead of the English bread or French rice. Good pasta is what an Italian abroad misses most; not because it isn't imported, but because foreigners tend to overcook it. Depending on where you come from in Italy, you cook pasta more or less *al dente*; but never as so many restaurants do, by cooking it in advance then heating it up by passing a sieveful through a tank of boiling water. I know of a restaurant in London which charges more for *al dente* pasta or pasta for Italians than for 'ordinary' pasta. When I questioned the logic of this since *al dente* pasta took less time I was told it took more because someone had to stand, watch and time it exactly. Hence the extra price.

Pasta can be divided into three groups: often (but not always) made at home, when it is known as *pasta fatta in casa* or *pasta casalinga*; *pasta all'uovo* which can contain anything up to six eggs per kilo of pasta (yolks only since the whites do nothing); and *pasta asciutta*. Alas, not all *pasta fresca* is better than *pasta all'uovo*, particularly if it has been manufactured by one of the pasta giants such as da Ceccho, Barilla, Agnesi, Panzani and so on. It is essential to stick to such names for *pasta asciutta* since they use only the finest quality durum wheat.

The shape of the pasta matters. Although made from identical ingredients macaroni tastes very different from spaghetti or *farfelle*. Certain southern pasta dishes, such as *spaghetti all'Amatriciana* (from Amatrice in the Abruzzo) or *spaghetti alla carbonara*, taste far better made from *pasta asciutta* than from *pasta all'uovo* – indeed the latter would be horribly rich made with egg pasta. Typically though, fresh pasta calls for rich sauces, eggs, cream, ham and fresh herbs; whereas the southerner would reach for olive oil, bacon or *coppa*, tomatoes and sometimes very hot peppers.

It is worth remembering that in Italy the standard pasta-dish which you can usually get anywhere is not *spaghetti alla bolognese* but *spaghetti alle vongole* or *con vongole*. Almost any adult Italian can cook spaghetti and the ingredients for the *vongole* are to hand either fresh or frozen, which is almost as good as fresh or from a jar. A *ragù bolognese* is an expensive sauce, to be made in largish quanties using the best beef and not just any old mince, chicken livers, ham, tomatoes and cream. The quality of the sauce diminishes in direct proportion to its distance from Bologna, as anyone who has had the real thing will know all too well.

If you are a pasta buff then get yourself a pasta making machine. The prices run from as little as 25,000 to 250,000 lire. They vary in type from the machine into which you insert your already prepared dough and turn a handle to get thinner and thinner dough to the sort you throw the ingredients into and sit back and wait for results. In comparative terms they go from the wooden washing board to the most modern Miele electronic washing machine. Pasta machines produce thinner pasta than is possible by hand.

Not all Italy eats pasta however. The country can be divided into rice and polenta eaters, mostly in the north; ribbon pasta eaters, mostly in the north and central part; bean eaters in Tuscany, Umbria and parts of the mezzogiorno; *pasta asciutta* eaters mostly in the south, though the sheer convenience of this product ensures its appearance throughout Italy. *Pasta asciutta* is probably the ultimate in wholesome fast food. It is a slow starch. It is quick to cook and the ingredients for saucing it are nearly always to hand. Pizza is considerably more complicated to produce unless you buy it ready-made and anyway its fat-count can be terrifyingly high. Students in Italy live on *pasta asciutta* with tomato sauce and lashings of parmesan cheese or, in Liguria and Sardinia, *pecorino* cheese.

Rice as a staple is common in the north from Piedmont to Venice, though it is not the rice which you serve dry and fluffy – for that you must purchase the almost ubiquitous Uncle Ben's. Italian *arborio* rice never becomes totally soft but appears to have a capacity for absorbing flavours not given to other sorts. Designed for risotto, it often takes the place of pasta and always has the ingredients incorporated into it and is never served as an accompaniment, except in the case of *osso bucco* where the *risotto alla milanese* is made with butter, white wine and saffron.

On all the coasts of Italy there are thousands of restaurants producing *risotto di frutta di mare* superb, good, bad and indifferent. It is such an elastic dish that it can be expanded or contracted according to what you have in the house or what is available in the market. The really good *risotti* are worth journeying for. The main joy of Italian rice, as with chick peas, another Italian favourite, is that you virtually cannot overcook it. *Riso arborio* is the type to look for when planning a risotto.

In the north, the eating of polenta dates back to Roman times, though the cereal was different then – usually millet or buckwheat. Today, all polenta is made of maize usually grown in Italy where it is known as *grano turco*, though it first came from the Americas and not from Turkey. Polenta comes in various qualities from quite coarse to very fine and there is an instant polenta which should be avoided at all costs – it tastes appalling. Cooking polenta is easy. You boil a good litre of water and throw in 250 grammes of the grain. The coarser the polenta the more water it will take up. Allow approximately twenty minutes, stirring all the time. After being badly scalded once I now wear rubber gloves when stirring boiling polenta which can produce exploding bubbles of scalding cereal that stick to any part of you they touch – so be warned. Once cooked it can be eaten as it is, which is not a great gourmet treat, even with cheese or a tomato sauce to help it down. Normally it is poured into a shallow, wetted metal tray and allowed to get cold. It should never be less than half an inch thick and never more than an inch. This should be cut into small squares, rounds or lozenges. These are then shallow fried in butter in Milan, in lard in Rome, in olive oil elsewhere. Venice cannot make up its mind what to fry them in and you get it in all sorts of guises from shallow to deep fried in oil, lard, butter, olive oil or even chicken fat – this last is very indigestible. The Venetians also have white polenta which, although in no way related, tastes like fried semolina. They are very fond of this, proud of it even, and serve it, baked in the oven with butter, for breakfast with milky coffee. Otherwise it is baked in a hot oven for serving under roast birds such as quail and partridge. Certainly polenta has an affinity with rich, heavy, wintry sauces and is probably best like this. Like pasta, the Italians rightly reckon it has no place in salads. Most of the time it is rather stodgy and uninteresting. Milan has a famous pie, called *pasticiatta*, of layered polenta, mushrooms, cream and sometimes seafood. You need to be a teenager or tremendously hungry to really enjoy something so unbelievably rich and stodgy.

Gnocchi is another *primo piatto* served in Italy. Home-made it can be delicious, but I have never come across restaurants which are known for the excellence of their *gnocchi*. These *gnocchi* are based on a choux pastry mixture to which very dry, plain, unsalted mashed potato is added. They tend to become less slimy when cooked in simmering water.

Fruit and vegetables are excellent throughout Italy and the country is more or less self-sufficient in this domain with the exception of exotic fruit including bananas and grapefruit which are imported from Central and South America rather than from the West Indies. Artichokes tend to be smaller than the French and Spanish type, pointed in the north and the centre of Italy and rounded in the south. They are frequently eaten raw, sliced and with a vinaigrette.

The Italians appear to have a penchant for bitter things such as all forms of endive, chicory, *catalogna* (a boring bitter green vegetable) and various forms of bitter lettuce and *radicchio*. This last comes in two forms, long and pointed from Treviso and round like a large, red Brussels sprout from Choggia south of Venice. Needless to say, partisans of each are daggers drawn. The Chioggia sort is slightly more bitter. Lambs lettuce is one of the many winter salads available, as well as Belgian endive. *Lollo rosso* is far less common in Italy than in the UK.

There is not a great deal to say about Italian fish except that its distribution is usually only local and that it is of excellent quality, as is virtually all the frozen fish. It is uniformly expensive throughout Italy, even at the seaside itself. Adriatic fish are considered better tasting than fish from the other coasts of Italy, though whether this is really true is doubtful. Certainly scampi are better from the Adriatic and the sole from that part is considerably bigger and more succulent than from the rest of the Mediterranean. This is probably something to do with the Adriatic becoming quite cold in winter. Sardinia is justly famous for its fish and most of the larger coastal towns and cities boast a particular fish dish or soup. Incidentally, all restaurants are obliged to say on their menus whether or not their fish, meat or vegetables have been frozen.

Much of the meat for sale in Italy has been imported. The best *vitello* is usually imported from the Netherlands. *Vitellone*, however, is always home produced. The Italians are realists – keeping steers on pasture to make beef animals is an expensive process for which they will not get the right amount of profit. Thus steers are killed young – between veal and beef stages – and sold as such. The only place you will get real beef is in Tuscany and nearby since most of the best grazing is found in Tuscany and due north. Nevertheless, even the best Florentine T-bone steak, excellent as it may be, does not resemble Aberdeen-Angus beef.

Lamb is mostly produced in mountainous areas such as Piedmont and central Italy, and much of it is killed so young that it is rather tasteless with a leg feeding at the most two people. Otherwise it is killed too late and has far too much taste. Frozen New Zealand lamb is imported, but only in certain joints which the bigger supermarkets often have on special offer.

Provided the animal is not too big, most pork in Italy is excellent, though the really superb animals go to the ham and salami manufacturers. Often in the various famous ham districts such as Piedmont, Friuli and Parma, the non-leg parts of the pig either go to butchers or to salami makers. These pigs have been fed on what amounts to a luxury diet all their short lives.

Although kid is an expensive and delicious dish, and almost mandatory at Easter, goat is not much eaten except in ready-made (frozen) sauces for pasta. A gourmet experience to be missed in my opinion.

Most of the chicken and poultry farms are found on the Po Plain, many round Verona, though some of the best free-range chickens and rabbits come from Piedmont. Free-range chickens command at least half as much again as run-of-the-mill chickens and are available in good markets and in the various *pollerie* to be found in many towns. These sell everything to do with poultry from eggs to boiling hens. By tradition, the best chickens come from Emilia-Romagna and Tuscany though not many of their free-range birds are available out of their immediate area. Duck is not commonly eaten in Italy and the *canard de Barbarie* which produces the *magret* breast is virtually unknown though much bought by Italians coming to France. The average duck in Italy is about 60 per cent fat, 20 per cent bone and only 20 per cent eatable flesh so one can understand why it is not popular. Turkeys on the other hand are considered very *signorili* for a dinner party and the average turkey, free range, will feed eight. They are not bought with a view to eating them cold later.

It is a sad fact of life that Italian hunters will shoot anything that moves anywhere. Birds in particular are very popular and include pigeon (*piccione*), very expensive, partridge (*pernice*), pheasant (*fagiano*), thrushes (*tordi*), larks (*allodole*), blackbirds (*merli*) and figpeckers (*beccafichi*). Skewers of miserably small birds are sold for grilling to be consumed bones and all, and are hardly worth the cartridge, each one killed to provide a mere mouthful. Of the farm-bred birds the most commonly seen are quail (*quaglie)* and guinea-fowl *(faraona)*.

Hare is seen sometimes in the winter markets and there are many Italian recipes for cooking it, one of which includes chocolate to darken the sauce. Wild boar (*cinghiale*) is seen more often, but it is always from an older animal since anything under 30 kilos is safe from the human predator. Think in terms of six to seven hours of slow cooking to tenderize wild boar and put in two or three *unshelled* walnuts to counteract the gamey taste. The shells absorb much of it.

One of the glories of Italian produce is *prosciutto crudo* or raw ham, whether it comes from Parma which is the main centre of production, San Daniele in the Friuli, or the Langhiano and the Val de Susa (for the famous San Giuliano ham) which are both in Piedmont. The most expensive is San Daniele since the production is also the smallest. Parma ham is said to be made from pigs fed on the whey from Parma cheese-making, though whether this makes it better is a matter of debate. Certainly the actual manufacture is important and the more humans are involved, rather than machines, the better the end product. Credit-card thin is the byword for serving slices of this ham, and to keep it is better to lay it flat on sheets of aluminium foil and freeze until a quarter of an hour before serving than to leave it wrapped up in its greaseproof or wax paper packet. Serve with slices of melon or fresh figs or, in winter, shavings of new Parmesan cheese. A potato peeler stands in well for a cheese shaver.

Salami is another well-known Italian export and not always the best is exported. Again, sliced salami (but *not* mortadella and cooked sausages) stores better in the freezer than in the refrigerator. This was told to me by a well-known Torinese restaurant owner who reckons three hours is the maximum for keeping sliced salami or ham before eating it. The finest and best-known salami is Felino from near Parma made by Luigi Bischi. Other names to look for are Galbani (the cheese people), Vismara, Citerio, Zibello, and Busseto. There are also excellent *salami artigiani* and any good Italian delicatessen will allow you to taste.

Although you will see the word bacon on packets in various Italian supermarkets it bears little resemblance to the British product. The nearest is *pancetta* which is belly of pork, very salty, but excellent for wrapping up birds (do not add any salt) around terrines, etc. Although there is a lean *speck*, sometimes spelt *spech*, *spek*, it is rarely seen and most are about 90 per cent pure pig fat and constitute a heart attack on a plate. Also, modern eating has ensured that most of western Europe no longer has a taste for such high-calorie food. This product usually comes from the mountainous regions where the winter cold gives one an appetite for this sort of thing.

Another Italian glory is cheese. Although most Italian cheese is exported, certain are actually made abroad, so *ricotta*, for instance, made in France or England will taste very different from the Italian version. Ditto mozzarella made from cows' milk. It is not good. Even in Italy the average mozzarella must be eaten for texture rather than taste. Real mozzarella was, and is still, made from buffalo milk and the difference is a gastronomic revelation.

Parmesan cheese is not much made out of Italy though plenty of hard *grana* cheese is. Parmesan is always called just *grana* by the Italians, though there are three sorts of *grana* the name of which comes from the grain of the ripened cheese. This name leads to confusion since there is *grana Ferrarese* from Ferrara, *grana Reggiana* from Reggio Emilia and *grana Modenese* from Modena and so on as well as the classic *grana Parmigiano*. The difference between these cheeses is slight to the non-expert though Parma swears its own is the finest, if only because it is fit to be sold very young and served in shaved curls with the local ham. And very good it is too. Otherwise, for all the others, none is sold at under two years of age. Improvement and strength of flavour comes with age and so does a reduction in weight, hence the increase in price. The gradations are *vecchio*, *stravecchio* and *stravecchione* at five years old when the price becomes astronomical. Ready-grated parmesan tastes soapy and is not worth buying. A food processor or a cheesemouli are the best bet and the resulting grated cheese will keep for a couple of days if covered with cling film.

There is not much to say for *Bel Paese*, a modern cheese invented by Galbani in 1928. It is soft, rich and rather tasteless and much eaten by children and the toothless in Italy – the equivalent of St. Ivel or Baby Bel. Ditto *cacciocavallo* which is a southern cheese and rich but rather bland. *Ricotta*, as its name suggests, is twice cooked and used for tarts, puddings and often eaten with stewed fruit or with cinnamon and sugar. Italians copy two Swiss cheeses, Gruyere and Emmenthal, and the Swiss do not worry. *Groviera* is the Italian word for the worst copy of this cheese on the market and the Emmenthal is no better. *Fontina* is a Piedmont cheese very rich and melts easily. It is used for a type of 'fondue' and is excellent for toasted cheese and ham sandwiches.

Pizza uses mozzarella and the generally received idea is that *mozzarella di buffala* is too expensive to put on a pizza so only the cows' milk version is used. However, a really well-made Neapolitan version using buffalo milk is quite an eye opener. *Mozzarella di buffala* served with a tomato salad with plenty of basil is a common light lunch in summer in Italy. *Provolone* is another cheese which comes in these two versions.

As in France, some of the best cheeses come from sheeps' milk: *pecorino* from Sardinia and Liguria is well known. It is a vital ingredient of the true pesto sauce. In commerce, this sauce contains all sorts of things it should not, such as cashew nuts, presumably because they are cheaper than pine nuts or almonds. The ingredients are: a large bunch of fresh basil, a coffee cup of best olive oil, some pine nuts or two tablespoons of ground almonds, the same coffee cup this time full of grated *pecorino* cheese. You need no salt because of the cheese and no pepper because of the basil. Whizz the whole lot up in a mixer or food processor or failing that with a pestle (whence pesto) and mortar. Using Parmesan cheese makes it a little milder. Add more olive oil if needed. Enough for four on gnocchi or pasta.

Talleggio and *Tallegino*, *Robiola* and *Robialina* are very rich, creamy cheeses. The addition of the letters *-ino* to the name of a cheese indicates age and depth of flavour. *Asiago* is a delicious cheese but can be bitter – try a piece before buying.

Apart from Parmesan the most famous Italian cheese must be *Gorgonzola* from Lombardy. It comes in several versions ranging from the strong, Bergarder type to a mild *dolcelatte*. There is a white version of *Gorgonzola*, obtainable only in Lombardy, called *Pannerone*. The largest maker (and exporter, for that matter) is Galbani and this company has invented and commercialized the combination of *Gorgonzola* and *Mascarpone* (sometimes spelt *Mascherpone*). It has a striped appearance, is packed in large plastic boxes and appears to answer a need for those who find *Gorgonzola* pure too strong. It now accounts for some 60 per cent of export sales.

Most Alpine and mountain markets will have some form of *Tome* cheese – most of which are very good. They are usually called *tomma di . . . .* and are rather similar to the French *Tôme de Savoie*.

To see an Italian market in late autumn with the stalls piled high with every sort of mushroom is a breathtaking experience. The mushroom most favoured in Italy is the *Boletus edulis* or *porcini*. Although wild, all mushrooms on sale to the public have been passed by the local health authority so no danger is involved. Every decent town hall has its resident mycologist. Not so, neces- sarily, with your friends. The newspapers are full of mishaps since Italians are avid mushroom-hunters and it is a popular dawn pastime. However, because the mushroom population is dwin- dling this mushrooming is usually highly controlled and permits are required. It is always best to contact the local *comune* before picking.

Italians grill, bake, fry in batter, and stuff mushrooms, and they are particularly fond of them raw in salads with a little olive oil, balsamic vinegar and parsley. I remember, years ago seeing an Italian in a Swiss train restaurant-car remonstrating with a waiter over creamed mushrooms on toast. 'What a thing to do to a mush- room!' he wailed. 'Well, at least try it,' cajoled the waiter, 'you've paid for it and there's no other first course.' This economic argu- ment struck a chord and he picked up his knife and fork and demolished the lot, I think with enjoyment.

The most famous *funghi* of all are, of course, truffles. The best come from Piedmont around Alba and command a fortune. They are also found in Tuscany and Emilia-Romagna but the taste is not so fine or subtle. In both Piedmont and Bologna they appear in cheese and egg dishes. When served on pasta it is always the home made sort dressed with butter or cream.

Surprisingly, the Italians do not use a great deal of herbs in their cooking. Certainly those they do use they use to the point of bore- dom. Occasionally it is pleasant to have a tomato salad with parsley or marjoram instead of the eternal basil. Sage is used with a heavy hand and, like basil, is not to everyone's taste. Although thyme is all over the Italian hills from top to bottom it is not much used; the bouquet garni is practically unknown, and the use of the bayleaf seems restricted to Bologna, as tarragon is to Siena.

Abroad, oregano is a well-known herb. It varies tremendously from one end of the country to the other. In the north, when it is fresh and green, it is almost indistinguishable from its cousin marjoram, whilst in the south it becomes strong and rather stale-tasting. It needs to be used with considerably more discretion than most Italians accord it. One of the nicest but least used herbs of all is myrtle, which seems restricted to Sardinia where a still-hot cooked joint of kid or lamb is put on a bed of myrtle leaves to absorb the perfume. Like so many mountain people, Sardinians are not mad about piping-hot food. You could do the same thing by wrapping up a joint or a chicken and the myrtle in aluminium foil for twenty minutes or so. Alternatively, roasting the meat in a roasting bag with the myrtle would give a similar result.

Anyone living in Italy will tell you that the two most used spices are industrial (as opposed to natural) vanilla and nutmeg. Much of Italy's buns, biscuits, brioches and *pannetone* are ruined by a heavy hand with the vanilla essence. Not so nutmeg, which is used with a much lighter hand in such things as béchamel sauce, spinach, ravioli stuffing, chicken liver and aubergines. Cinnamon and anise are spices much used in the south where they also occasionally use cardamom in baking. Saffron is used for certain fish soups and stews, as well as for the Milanese risotto which goes with *osso bucco* of veal. In the Abruzzo and Apulia, along with certain other parts of the south, much use is made of very small hot peppers which come as a dreadful shock to any visitor.

Much of the north cooks with butter and sometimes butter and sunflower oil, though in Liguria olive oil is used rather more than in Lombardy and Piedmont. Around Rome, *strutto* or lard is used on an equal footing with oil. There are several oils – sunflower or *olio di girasole*, peanut or *olio di arachide*, colza or *olio di semi*, maize oil or *olio di mais*. Olive oil, except by those who grow olives, is seldom used for cooking except for frying fish and then usually that is reserved for serving it later with a vinaigrette. It is nicer than it sounds. Often, by the thrifty, olive oil is mixed with sunflower oil in salads and mayonnaises.

What olive oil to use is very much a matter of personal taste. There are many non-Italians who absolutely hate olive oil because they have only had heavy versions of it or, at the other end of the spectrum, over-refined olive oil which is very nasty.

The really heavy and fruity oils from Apulia are fine for a bean salad or spaghetti but spell death to any mayonnaise. Lucca in Tuscany is world-renowned for its oil, but there are just as good oils from around Florence, Siena, Massa Carrara although less well known. The oil of Liguria is the lightest of all oils and can be used on its own or in a mayonnaise. Alas, because of two successive bad winters in 1985 and 1986, Ligurian oil is among the most expensive there is. Sardinia is also famous for its oil, particularly around Sassari, but it is stronger than Ligurian oil.

A law of the 13th November 1960 governs everything to do with Italian olive oil. The official classifications are as follows:

Extra-vergine has no chemicals used in its manufacture and has only one per cent acidity.

Soprafino vergine as above but 1.5 per cent acidity.

Olio vergine di oliva has no chemicals but the oil is extracted by using cold water and centrifuging. Three per cent acidity.

Olio vergine di olio di oliva is a mixture of rectified olive oil (tasteless due to the rectification, usually from the south) and *olio extra vergine* for taste and it has 1.5 per cent acidity.

Olio di oliva pura is usually the result of pressing with hot water. Ideal if you want to fry with olive oil.

To make matters more complicated, some of the larger firms now blend their olive oil by homogenizing, centrifuging, etc., to obtain a standard product year in year out. This can be good enough for salads and certainly is excellent for frying. Only trial and error will tell if it can stand up to being used for mayonnaise. Eggs potentiate both the good and the bad points of olive oil.

The colour of the olive oil is a measure of its flavour and possibly of the treatment it has undergone. The dark green oils are usually much stronger than the pale straw coloured oils of Tuscany and Liguria.

Good everyday names to look out for are Sasso, Berrio, Calvi, Carpelli, Ranieri, Fratelli Carli, Gianni and Arduino. Several of the Chianti-growers also produce olive oil, at a price which ranges from 12,000 to 55,000 lire a litre, though the average price is around 20 or 25,000 lire a litre which is the price of Antinori and Badia e Colti Buono. Some of the larger towns in olive-growing areas specialize in selling local produce and often really excellent olive oil can be bought from them at around 7,000 or 8,000 lire a litre. This untreated olive oil can sometimes throw a sediment which should not be used as it is usually unpleasantly bitter.

Wine

The Italians have an easy approach to wine. If they like it they drink it. Luckily there is still a great deal of relatively fairly cheap wine on the market which makes 'research' inexpensive. Although it is unlikely that you will ever find an Italian chucking a couple of ice cubes into a glass of Barolo, there is never any pretentiousness about wine. That said, it must be admitted that there are now some incredibly expensive wines in Italy that require quite a recommendation before the public is going to buy them. Chianti is one of the worst offenders in this; a good *DOCG* Chianti can cost the same in Italy as at Harrods in London. On the other hand, there are literally dozens of growers in Tuscany who produce excellent *vino da tavola* containing the same ingredients as Chianti in the same proportions for something like a third of the price. Most foreigners know little of this and most Italians know a lot. Therefore, it pays to be guided by Italian friends, always provided you have enjoyed the wine with them. Tuscany is fashionable and is cashing in on the fact and there are many other wine-producing areas in Italy doing the same thing to a greater or lesser degree of success.

Strictly speaking it is not quite true about the pretentiousness bit, since any foreigner who has been a short time in Italy soon gets invited to some sort of reception where tiny glasses of spumante (often quite warm) are offered in such minute champagne-flutes that at least fifteen servings can be obtained from a bottle. The idea is that you should think the drink is considerably more expensive and exclusive than it is. Paintings, books, sculpture, all sorts of exhibitions are launched in this manner. Often the food offered is of the same tiny size but, considerably more often, it is in the form of ludicrously large chunks of pizza, usually excellent, which the guests fall upon like ravening wolves for want of something better to drink. At home or at wedding receptions, Italians become excellent hosts.

Italy is the largest wine producer in the world and is probably responsible for much of the wine lake the European Union moans about. It is quite obvious that none of this lake is made up of premium wine. Today, the whole wine-industry, for that is what we are talking about, is undergoing an enormous change with modern California-style wineries, Australian wine-makers, American marketing-men, entering the world market with the intention of becoming world leaders against such competition as California, Australia, South Africa, New Zealand, Chile and, above all, France, whose very poor opinion of Italian wine is based on received prejudice dating back at least as far as their grandmothers' generation. The Italians are succeeding beyond their wildest dreams and the people at home can often only get a look in by paying overseas prices for the wine they always used to drink. The wine industry in Italy has been divided into two: the industrially produced (and for once this is not a pejorative term) and the *vino artigiano*. This latter can be one of three things: utter rubbish and suitable only for sale to vermouth and aperitif makers; average wine for local consumption; and well-made wine in small quantity. It is this last you should concentrate on if you want to get value for money. Only research will tell you whether the Valpolicella from a small vineyard or from Pasqua or similar large concerns is better – and probably it differs from year to year. All I know is that I can buy this type of wine cheaper and better in France and yet they have to pay to transport it from what is virtually easternmost Italy. Certain parts of Italy have only relatively small vineyards such as the Trentino and the Friuli, rather like Burgundy, and they produce excellent wine, though not on a worldwide scale – as yet. Certain of their white wines are becoming well known out of Italy, which only betokens a price rise. Other wines, such as many of those produced in Liguria will end up being drunk only by the locals and then on a special occasion since they are not mechanized in the vineyard itself and therefore the bottle price includes the cost of hand-picking, hand-weeding and above all, hand-digging. A bottle of Cinqueterre Vermentino can cost up to 15,000 lire and it really isn't any better than a 6,000 bottle of similar wine from the Piedmont. Practically every vineyard is going over to what the Americans term varietal wines, i.e. Sauvignon, Pinot Bianco, Pinot Grigio, Chenin Blanc, Cabernet Sauvignon, Chardonnay and Riesling. Those coming from the north-east of Italy are infinitely better than those from Liguria which are double the price.

One great help to the beleaguered Italian wine-grower is that, apart from the vermouth producers, foreign wine-makers import vast quantities of their wine for blending with their own rather inadequate amounts. Sometimes it is for the actual liquid but mostly it is to increase the alcoholic content. Austria, Switzerland, Germany and even France all import bulk Italian wine. Much of the French cheap 'fizz' is based on cheap Italian white Trebbiano.

Italian wine is divided into three categories which in a way are meaningless, as so many things are in Italy, but still need to be explained.

DOC: Denominazione de Origine, which is roughly equivalent to the French AOC. Because the Italians, and particularly the Government, regard the *DOC* merely as a statement of where the wine comes from and the grapes it was made from and not of the quality there is now another category:

DOCG: Denominazione de Origine Controllata Garantita, and so far very few wines have obtained this coveted label. The wines are

Chianti Classico (other Chianti is merely *DOC* or even *Vino da Tavola Controllato*), Barolo, Barbaresco, Brunello and Vino Nobile de Montepulciano. A few years ago the *DOCG* label was extended to a very ordinary white wine called Albana di Romagna, from an area not known for high quality wines, Ronco del Re, a Sauvignon blanc from Casteluccio in the same region as the Albana is a better wine and cheaper because it's only a *vino da tavola*.

It is said that giving a *DOCG* to such a wine was a deliberate political move to bring the *DOCG* label into disrepute. To date, ten years later, nobody has offered a good reason for anyone wanting to do this.

Suffice to say that a *DOCG* label together with the name of a good producer such as Antinori, Badia e Colti Buono, Frescobaldi or Ricasoli will provide an excellent bottle of wine. All *DOCG* Chianti bottles also carry the black cockerel logo.

Vino da Tavola: The majority of Italian wine is sold under this label but that is not to say it is any less good than *DOC* which, alas, is not always a guarantee of quality. It is nothing more than a specification of place and the grapes used. However, even on a *vino da tavola* bottle label there are often indications of the quality of the wine. The words *superiore* or *classico* indicate superior quality and sometimes increased alcoholic content. The name on the bottle can be important, although much excellent wine is made by the *consorzi* who are very fussy about what they bottle. Such names as Ricasoli, Stella and Mosca, Angoris, Frescobaldi, Santa Margarita, Pasqua, Antinori, to name but a few, are well known for their quality. A numbered bottle used to be a sign of quality but nowadays it is done purely for VAT purposes.

In Italy you get what you pay for and the secret is not to over-pay. Cheap wine such as is sold in supermarkets like la Standa and called names like Merlot del Veneto or simply Vino San Giovese are designed to be drunk immediately. Most wines under 5,000 lire a bottle have a tendency to oxidize very quickly.

The best Italian wines are, without a doubt, red. Barolo, 'the king of wines and the wine of kings' as the saying goes, comes from Piedmont and is world famous. Its near neighbour, also from the Nebbiolo grape, Barbaresco is less so but still excellent. However, English speakers often confuse it with Barbera, which to their great shock and sorrow is coarse, harsh wine. Also from Piedmont are the red Dolcetto which usually comes from Asti but also from Ovada and simply *di Piemonte*. Known as the three Gs to Italians the wines of Gattinara, Ghemme and Gavi are well known and appreciated, though Gavi, a delicious white from Piedmont, can be ridiculously highly priced. A pleasant weekend can be spent around Alba and Asti trying out various wines both white and red. The hotels are inexpensive and the food is some of the best in Italy.

More and more Italian wine is being made from a single or two grapes. Pinot Bianco, Pinot Grigio, Pinot Nero, Tocai (no relation of the Hungarian Tokay), Chardonnay, Sauvignon, Chenin Blanc and Riesling and the best all come from the Trentino and the Friuli. The most well-known wines from further south are Soave, Orvieto from Umbria which comes in three types, *secco, amabile* and *abbocato*, i.e. dry, medium and sweet. The *amabile* is usually quite sweet enough for most tastes and it makes an excellent aperitif wine. Verdicchio, particularly when it comes from a single vineyard as opposed to a large producer, is an excellent summer white wine. Look for *dei Castelli Jesi* on the label. Frascati and Marino are the Roman white wines, pleasant but nothing to write home about.

Tuscany produces the two sorts of Chianti, *classico*, easily recognizable from the black cockerel on the label, or simply *DOC* or *vino da tavola* from Chianti. What is interesting is that Antinori produce a wine made from Chianti grapes and aged for several years in Bordeaux barrels. It has a simple *vino da tavola* label and costs a fortune. It is called Tignanello and tastes like first-class claret. You can get it at Harrods, Berry Brothers and Rudd etc.

The most famous wine of Emilia-Romagna is Lambrusco, a sparkling red which is said to go well with the Bolognese rich cooking. It comes crisp and dry or rather sweet and tacky. I find the idea of fizzy red wine abhorrent but there are greater connoisseurs than me who think otherwise.

The best whites in this region are made from the Trebbiano grape and it is significant that much of this is exported for blending purposes. Most of the reds are made from the San Giovese grape – they are very drinkable but hardly memorable. They are, together with Merlot, the supermarkets' biggest sellers.

From Naples downwards, the wine gets steadily worse and the price drops, until you get to Sicily where, surprisingly to the foreigner, there are some truly excellent wines. The best wine on the island is produced by the Duke of Salaparuta. Its classification is only *vino da tavola* but both the red and the white Corvo are superb. There are other producers of Corvo on the island which are not nearly so good so it pays to read the label and pay rather more.

Sardinia, too, produces good wine which is often sold under the Stella and Mosca label, and there is a dry Malvasia which is interesting if only as a change from the excruciatingly sweet variety.

They also produce a famous Vernaccia wine which most foreigners find is an acquired taste.

From wine to vermouth and every Italian has his favourite *amaro* or bitter. The big names are Cinzano, Martini and Rossi, Cora, Riccadonna, Campari and Carpano. Carpano was the first to make vermouth in Turin during the eighteenth century. Today this company's main sales come from its Punt e Mes vermouth (Turin dialect for a point and a half – of bitterness) though the original Carpano Carpano as it is known in Italy is still the most popular *amaro* in its home town. Davide Campari have been producing Milan and Lombardy's favourite *amaro* for a similar time though for others it can be an acquired taste. However, once acquired, its admirers remain faithful for life. Several companies produce Campari soda in bottles, including Campari itself. It cannot be compared with the real thing, which is sometimes quite difficult to get when the ready-made stuff is stocked. This is presumably because it's easier and faster for the waiters to serve and it's difficult to cheat on measures. There are many herbal alcoholic drinks which are usually drunk after a meal though some do double duty as an aperitif as well. They range from the very bitter Fernet Branca, which must be the nastiest popular drink on earth, to Averna, which boasts over forty herbs in its making and is surprisingly gentle. Cynar is another strange *amaro* based on artichokes. It is amazingly popular in Italy but, much as I adore artichokes, this is one form I can't manage to swallow.

Italian brandy is nothing like cognac and as long as one accepts that fact from the start the disappointment will be considerably less. It is more like Spanish and, to a degree, Portuguese brandy. The best makes are Stock from Trieste, *Carta Nera* fron Vecchia Romagna and Florio's *Brandy Mediterraneo* from the South.

Grappa is rather similar to French *marc* and is made more or less in the same way from the detritus of wine-making. Some very superior *grappa* is made by using only the crushed grapes without any of the stalks or other bits and pieces. It commands a higher price naturally. Many of the big wine-houses also make a *grappa* from their own wine-making. It should be aged for quite a long time to remove the harshness normal in young *grappa* which can leave the average drinker quite breathless.

Acquavite are made from various fruits and are not at all sweet though quite potent from an alcoholic viewpoint. They are made from plums (*prugne*), cherries (*ciliegie*), pears (*pere*), more rarely from apricots (*albicocche*) and raspberries (*lamponi*). More or less any fruit which can be distilled is made into *acquavite* but some are considerably better than others. For instance, the *prugne* is quite like the Yugoslav slivovitz and both the cherry and the pear *acqua-vite* tend to resemble the Swiss *poire* and *kirsch* rather than the French variety. Among the best producers are Psenner, particularly for pear and Aquivelia of Udine who make an excellent plum *acqua-vite*.

Probably the most famous Italian after-dinner drink is Maraschino which is made from the Marasca cherry and comes in a square, straw-covered bottle. It is a product of what was Italian, or rather Venetian, Dalmatia and still, today, the best is produced in what is now Croatia. The Italians also do a good one in both sweet and dry versions – the latter is best for drinking and the first for cheering up a fruit salad or any cherry dessert. Stock do a cherry liqueur, known as Cherry Stock, something like Cherry Heering and they also do a brilliant and cheap answer to Grand Marnier called Orange Stock which is still under five pounds a bottle and wonderful value for money.

Italy has a fantastic variety of Scotch and Irish whiskies the price of which goes up each month, though they are still cheaper than in any of Italy's neighbours. Irish is ousting Scotch as the really smart drink – they know nothing about how to drink it and pour it over ice like the Americans. They do the same with single malt Scotch. Gin and vodka are still the cheapest spirits and a great number of very ordinary *grappe* are considerably more expensive.

Champagne, incidentally, carries a punitive tax presumably in order to featherbed the spumante industry. As a result there is a tremendous cachet attached to the French product.

Cleaning

Most of the soap powders in Italy are the products of the detergent giants and if you don't know the names then look for the manufacturer's name which you will immediately recognize. For washing clothes by hand, use a packet marked *buccato a mano* and you will be safe. Naturally, this must never be used in a washing machine or the froth will block everything up and the machine will flood. Italians like a lot of suds when washing by hand so use as little powder as possible. Bleach is generally sold under the name of ACE but is never as gentle as the British publicity says for that article.

There is spray starch and even Fabulon in Italy but finding ordinary laundry starch can be a problem. Most branches of la Standa supermarket have it. *Amido*, as it is called, is used, incredibly, to bathe babies and the elderly. The idea is that it softens the water and leaves a film on the skin. Tiny beads of starch are placed in the bath and hot water is then poured on and you rinse yourself off with the shower – or you don't, according to personal taste. That is why, if all else fails, you can find starch in the chemist. Having got your starch you mix it up in the same way – two or three tablespoons to a litre of water, of which you have kept a little back to mix down the powder, and the rest you pour on boiling. Look carefully as the result may need sieving. According to whether you are doing shirts or table cloths and napkins you use more or less powder. Instant or cold-water starch is instant disaster.

Many floors are made of marble or marble chip tiles and are in fact very delicate. They should be washed in hot soapy water which contains no alkali, acid or ammonia, which are present in many excellent cleaning fluids such as Ajax. Such liquids will break down the surface of the floor and make it porous, after which it will quickly and permanently discolour. One of the best things is to purchase pure liquid soap or bring out a bar of Sunlight soap. You can also get pure liquid soap at Italian chemists; it is called *sapone liquida*. An alternative, much used by Italian maids when there were such creatures, was to use methylated spirits or white spirit known as *acquaraggia*. Both have a penetrating smell and clean very well although you should wear gloves. If all else fails with an old, damaged marble floor then a professional clean and polish by a specialist cleaner should do the trick. These are known as *imprese di pulizia* and they will give you a quote (*un preventivo*) for the work. Granite, which is much used, is definitely less delicate but is often more expensive. Even granite will show marks from harsh treatment and although there are no heat problems, within reason, ice-cream, wine glass and water glass stains can prove stubborn.

Tiles can be a problem since if they do not respond to a normal stripping off of the old polish you will need to consult a specialist cleaning firm. They will almost certainly tell you to have a new lot of tiles. Granite is frequently used for worktops in Italian kitchens but you should read above for the possible problems. Often, with the pattern, you cannot tell whether your surface is clean or dirty which can be an advantage or disadvantage according to your personality. Also, never, ever forget the weight of marble and granite and be very circumspect about what you put in a flat. The ground floor of a house causes no problems but a fourth floor apartment can end up on the third or even the second as happened to a friend of mine in Milan.

Much used in Italy are *cotto* unglazed tiles which are made from the same clay as terracotta pots. Depending on the medium used to lay them more or less efflorescence appears, usually in white patches. There are several treatments for this problem ranging from cold water (useless) to neat vinegar (always works, but sometimes the efflorescence comes back) to diesel fuel and the removal of its excess with sawdust. Do not put this on the compost heap, but do burn it – it is a very dangerous compound to leave around. Whatever you do, do not try to polish *cotto* since this will interfere with drainage and you will have puddles of water lying around for long intervals. The same goes for any offered waterproofing treatment. *Cotto* is meant to be absorbent and there are a whole lot of people who feel that the more stained and patchy the *cotto* is the better it looks. If you are a neat, tidy person *cotto* is not for you; on the other hand, if you like a back-to-nature feel for your house it is ideal.

Shopping

Italy is a country where every region has its own special handicrafts, porcelain, pottery, leatherwork, copper, glass, basketware, furniture, fabrics, lace etc. Leather is probably Italy's most famous product and although there is some nasty cheap-looking leather in the weekly markets, the shops still represent to the rest of Europe incredible bargains.

Otherwise Italy is no longer a cheap country for high fashion but a pair of shoes, a handbag or a beautiful sweater will still cost less than elsewhere. Gold jewellery is still a bargain and they will copy anything – often from a photograph in a magazine. A 'Byzantine' gold ring set with emeralds, sapphires and pearls costs a third of its London counterpart and plain gold necklaces, bracelets etc. are almost cheap. All are in 18 carat gold. Perhaps the stones are not the finest you can buy, but pretty rings or brooches are not necessarily chosen for investment. Provided you do not go to the top jewellers in Rome, Florence, Turin or Venice you should be pleasantly surprised.

Remember that virtually every gold chain on sale abroad has been made in Italy. There are factories turning out millions of gold chains in 9, 14, 18, 19 (for Portugal) and 22 carat for the world market. There are thousands of goldsmiths who will happily remodel your aunt's favourite bangle or a hideous snake bracelet.

Italy is a pleasant place to shop in. There are still few department stores or supermarkets so you tend to get personal attention. Italians are mad about discount stores and these should be avoided unless you are after a particular bargain. It is not the country to buy antiques in – they command incredible prices but the owners are happy to let you browse without pressing you to buy.

Finally a word of warning. In the country, the village shop is useful but this is because it has to give credit. In fact Italians give credit all too easily. This, along with the almost daily deliveries the owner has to make from the nearest town, is reflected in the price of their goods. Thus, the prices in a village shop about 15 km from the nearest town are usually on a par with the most exclusive grocer in that town. It certainly pays to think in advance and do the main shopping in town, leaving the village shop for daily bread and real emergencies. Virtually all villages have a weekly market and all towns have a municipal market, often on Sunday mornings as well. It is a *sine qua non* that market day in a biggish town increases the prices by between ten and twenty per cent. A foreign accent doesn't help matters – I was once complimented on my Italian but firmly told that until I could speak the local dialect I was going to be charged as the foreigner I was. So there.

16
Education

Over the past twenty years or so the Italian educational system has changed from top to bottom. Part of this has been due to the higher expectations of parents so that nursery education from a very early age is common throughout the north and centre of Italy and a far higher percentage of pupils go on to higher education than previously.

The basic minimum is ten years of formal schooling, from six to sixteen. This will not get you to university but it will teach you to read and write and get you into various technical colleges or on apprenticeship schemes.

The system is longer and slower than many other countries in Europe but the student gets there in the end and is very well qualified, albeit at around twenty-four or twenty-five, when he is ready to look for a job. Some of the disciplines demand a very long study period, such as law, most engineering degree courses, architecture and medicine.

For the English-speaking resident in Italy, a choice has to be made. There are plenty of good private schools near the large cities but most are Catholic run so are not to everyone's taste. Many are run by the Jesuits which for some can be even worse. Private schools are expensive as anywhere else, but a lot of people feel it is worth making the sacrifice. In any event, boarding schools, which do exist, are few and far between but those living in deep country sometimes feel they have no alternative. Although most of these boarding schools are Catholic there is no obligation for any people to be Catholic. There is also a social aspect to private education, as in the UK, and many Italians prefer the manners of privately educated children. The erudition of the teachers in these schools is something which makes money for the Church and proselytizing is most unusual these days.

For those parents living and working in Italy, a great deal of heart-searching must be done to decide whether to educate their childen in the Italian system or in that of their own country. The financial side is not the least of these considerations.

Until the child is ten or eleven an Italian education can prove only beneficial since, with the minimum of parental or ouside tuition, the child will be able to read, write and express himself in two languages. At eleven a decision must be taken. Unless the family has strong and almost permanent ties with Italy then a British education will probably serve the family purposes better than having an odd man out speaking mostly Italian, knowing mainly Italian literature and history, and learning all the sciences and foreign languages from an Italian base.

Some large cities such as Rome and Milan have French lycées where the pupil becomes truly international, speaking English at home, French in the classroom and Italian in the playground. Both these cities also have International Schools where the pupils can study for the Italian Maturità or British GCSEs or the American exams. They are all rather expensive and educating your child at a British prep or public school plus airfares would probably represent better value, though he would not remain bilingual. Although Italian learnt painlessly in childhood can be kept up in the holidays it is not always an ideal way of remaining bilingual – children don't come home in the holidays to have more lessons.

The cheapest solution is to keep your children with you, put them into the Italian state system and let them have extra coaching. This is particularly appropriate if you live in one of the larger cities in a good area where your child will meet people of similar background.

Another point in favour of the UK solution is that a child will not only be at university sooner and for a shorter time than in Italy but that he will be doing his studies in the most important language in the world which alas, beautiful as it may be, Italian is not. Those who can afford this option should take advantage of it though some private coaching may be needed to get the child through the requisite entrance examinations.

In principle, education should be the same from one end of Italy to the other. Alas, this is not the case. What is available in the large cities in the north and centre of Italy such as Florence, Bologna, Turin, Genoa, Milan, Trieste and Venice is very different from what is on offer in Bari, Foggia, Cosenza or even Naples. Teachers from the north and even those from the south or central Italy do not want to work in the south and, anyway, teaching is not a particularly well paid profession at any level. The south does not have a great pool of well-educated highly motivated people to draw on. Those southerners who are well educated usually do not want to teach. Then there is the long-entrenched southern tradition of children helping the family finances from an early age. The law notwithstanding, there are still children who quit school at eleven or twelve to go to work instead. The figures for Italian literacy in general are around 85 per cent but in fact there are considerably more people in the deep south who cannot read or write than this remaining 15 per cent. In the north it is rare to come across natives who cannot read and write. Indeed, the high literacy figure of the north tends to hide the true situation in the south.

The Italian school year, as elsewhere in Europe, runs from September to the following June and there are minimal holidays at All Saints' Day, Christmas, New Year, Epiphany and Easter.

Children can start in an *asilo nido* or kindergarten as young as three. These institutions are either private (and therefore you have to pay) or run by the local *comune* and of course they are not compulsory. Italian children are well behaved, gregarious little people largely due to these institutions and, like nursery schools all over the world, they teach them how to be sociable and how to behave with others.

The next stop is *scuola elementare* to which the child goes immediately after its sixth birthday and stays for five years. Foreign children are accepted easily in these schools but frequently extra coaching is required in Italian, particularly for writing the language. There is absolutely no problem finding a professional teacher for these lessons since most teachers 'moonlight'. The watershed age for learning a language in six to nine months appears to be around eleven or twelve, which also happens to be an age when most children no longer wish to conform.

Scuola media is started when the child is eleven. As these schools exist only in towns, children living in the country are bussed to one of them in the nearest catchment area. There is no such problem in the large cities. This middle school lasts three years. School textbooks and stationery have to be supplied by the parents. Private schools supply books but the terms' bills reflect this. All books including textbooks are expensive in Italy but sometimes they can be obtained second-hand. You must be sure that the book requirements have not changed from the previous year. Rather than endeavouring to purchase the second-hand books from the bookshop (which is more interested in selling new ones) try to purchase from a child who spent the last year in the class to which your child is moving. Some Italian schools have a market for second-hand books and clothes at the end of the school year and this can offer great savings. Sad to say, but no surprise, the school year rarely starts with everyone having obtained the entire booklist.

At the end of the period in *scuola media* a *diploma di licenza media* is given to those who have passed the necessary examination.

Throughout this period the child must average 60 per cent marks in order to move up to the next class. This assessment is done by the form teacher and headmaster (or headmistress) coupled with examination results. Those who do not make it can retake their annual examination in whole or in part in the September. If they fail again it is a case of *respinto* and the whole year has to be done again.

It is at this age, fourteen or fifteen, that most of the school leaving is done. This is almost invariably confined to the very rural south, but occasionally it happens in the very industrialized cities in the north when boys want to start earning as soon as possible. With so much unemployment this is becoming rarer and rarer since the jobs are not available.

Otherwise normal pupils take the most important examination of their lives so far. The academic types go on to *liceo*, either *scientifico* or *classico*, in order to get to a university later on. Five years is the length of the course. Others may go to one of the technical institutes where they receive a diploma which is a professional qualification, whereas the *liceo* gives an all-round education whilst preparing the pupil for university. It is worth noting also that many of the diplomas obtained from these institutes are qualifications also for entering university and many people do go on to study their chosen subject more profoundly.

Those wishing to teach start either early in a *scuola magistrale* which turns out schoolteachers (and where the diploma as opposed to the *maturità* does not give them entrance to a university) or go to an *istituto magistrale* which prepares elementary school teachers who get a *maturità* at the end of the four-year course at the age of eighteen or so.

Students remaining in a *liceo* will study for their *diploma di maturità* which is roughly equivalent to A levels and obtained at about eighteen after five years of study. The *esame di maturità* comprises two written examinations and one oral known as a *colloquio*. A *maturità* examination can be taken in the following fields:

Science:	Diploma di maturita scientifica
Technical:	Diploma di maturita tecnico
Classics:	Diploma di maturita classico
	(which includes language and literature)
Art:	Diploma di maturita artistico
Teaching:	Diploma di maturita magistrale

The minimum passmark is 36 out of 60 or 60 per cent – the same magic figure that has dogged the pupil since *scuola media*.

Since the subject for one of the essays is known on the 15th April prior the pupil has six weeks to bone up on his chosen subject. Two modern languages, at least, are taken throughout the period and the choice is usually from English, French and German. No student is allowed to sit the examination if his teachers feel he is not up to scratch academically.

The *maturità* allows entrance to any Italian university – in principle. Naturally there are universities who are in a position to pick and choose good students and thus maintain their already high rating in the academic world. Strangely, you are at total liberty to study what you like at university, irrespective of the type of *maturità* you have passed.

Although there are not enough universities in Italy to satisfy the demand, not all of them are of superb quality. They are also expensive. Boys going to university tend to finish their degree and then do their military service, usually as an officer, rather than have a gap of almost two years. It is now that most UK nationals tend to think in terms of a British university which, although fee-paying to students who have not passed the previous three years in the UK (and this may shortly apply to those who have), often offer a better and quicker degree than Italy.

The private universities are considered better than the state with certain exceptions. These are:

Milan:	Libera Università Cattolica del S.Cuore
	Libero Istituto Universitario di Lingue Moderne
	Universita L. Bocconi (Economics)
	Politecnico di Milano
Naples:	Istituto Universitario Navale
Urbino:	Libera Università
Turin:	Politecnico
Venice:	Istituto Universitario di Architettura
Rome:	Libera Università Internazionale degli Studi Sociali

There are thirty-nine state universities as follows: Ancona, Bari, Bergamo, Bologna, Brescia, Camerino, Campobasso, Cassino, Catania, Chieti, Cosenza, Ferrara, Florence, Genoa, Aquila, Lecce, Macerata, Messina, Milan, Modena, Naples, Padua, Palermo, Parma, Pavia, Perugia, Pisa, Reggio Calabria, Rome – La Sapienza, Rome – La Seconda, Salerno, Sassari, Siena, Turin, Trento, Trieste, Udine, Venice and Viterbo.

The famous Catholic university in Milan (for which you do not have to be a Catholic) has branches in Brescia, Piacenza and Rome.

Some of the state universities have branches elsewhere such as that of Siena in Arezzo, both Parma and Pavia have branches in Cremona, Turin University has a branch in Novara and Vercelli, Chieti University has branches in both Pescara and Teramo.

It is impossible to give a rundown on all the universities in Italy, both state and private, but it should be remembered that Bologna is the oldest university in Europe, Naples has the Orientale which is the oldest faculty of Oriental Languages in Europe and Pisa has one of the toughest entrance requirements in the country. The Bocconi University in Milan has an enviable reputation in Europe on a par with Harvard Business School, with which it competes. Still in Milan, their Politecnico has turned out some of Italy's most brilliant engineers.

Scholarships are possible but few and far between. State universities also cost but are means-tested. Italians marry quite late and quite a few fathers become *coltivatori diretti*, i.e. go back to the land, if only on paper, to get their child's university education free, an option which is not open to the average foreign resident. A degree cannot be taken in less than four years, the first year being a foundation year. However, the final examinations can be delayed and delayed and it is not unknown for students to be over forty before they finally make it.

17
Utilities

As with the rest of the European Union, most of the utility concerns in Italy have either been privatized or are in the process of being de-nationalized, for want of a better expression. This has not always brought large benefits, particularly as far as water is concerned, but in most other cases it has to be said that privatization has improved the service. Telecom Italia, which has taken over from SIP, has discovered that the cheaper a call is the more people use the telephone and most peoples' bills have halved in the last two years in spite of the increase in rental charges.

Water

Water is supplied either by your local *comune* or *città*, or by a more or less local Società d'Acquedotto. I say more or less local since many of these companies operate outside their own provinces and there is a thriving take-over trade at the moment in Italy of various water-supply companies. Each take-over results in a certain percentage increase in the price of the water. If you have had a contract for many years and are paying a very low rate you will hardly notice it, but newcomers can scarcely believe some of the prices they are being charged, even in Northern Italy where there is little water shortage. There is no logic, beyond profit, to the price of water and it varies from one part of the country to the other.

Depending on your locality you will either be given a water allowance or simply allowed to use as much as you can pay for. Tuscany for instance is very short of water not so much because of the long, dry summers as the total absence of any method of stocking water, i.e. no reservoirs. This predicament worsens the further south you go until in the deep south you end up purchasing water brought in by tanker. This last will not affect many readers of this book, thank goodness, but it is worth considering when you find you are not allowed to water your garden at all.

In many districts you will find that with over 1500 or 2000 square metres of land you will be required to have a second 'garden' contract known as *uso vario* and pay for a separate water meter.

Naturally, with all these changes virtually the whole of Italy is now on metered water. It is metered in a clever way. You are asked how much you think you need and figures are quoted to you. Even though you know that a cubic metre is 1000 litres you cannot imagine you will use more than say, 300 cubic metres over the year. The man agrees with you and writes the contract accordingly and you are caught. Certainly you will not be using more than 300 cubic metres a year but when it is divided into four quarters you will find that in spring and winter you will not use nearly 75 cubic metres and in summer and autumn that amount will go nowhere and you will use more and pay a penal rate for every litre over 75 cubic metres. When you go to re-negotiate your contract it will be done but at the new and more expensive rate. The answer is to have a seasonal contract from the start for at least 100 cubic metres for a couple on their own and even as much as 150 cubic metres (i.e. 600 cubic metres a year) if you are a couple with two children. Bear in mind a washing machine can use 80 litres, as can a dishwasher and these are far more frequently used than people realize. Watering a 1500 square metre garden can easily use 1000 litres a day – a reason for automating your irrigation if possible. You may find that you are not permitted to have more than a certain amount, in which case the foregoing becomes of purely academic interest.

It would be pleasant if the water supplied at these new, high prices were clear, bright, pleasant-tasting and healthy but all too frequently this is not the case. Italians tend not to fluoridize their water but they pour vast quantities of what is nothing more nor less than common bleach into the system in the earnest hope that anything nasty will be killed. This is probably so and whilst most Italian water is 'clean' it tastes quite dreadful. Nitrates abound.

In the country where the water is supplied from various *vasche* the news is less good. For some reason the filters are either in a very poor state or are too widely meshed or are not there at all. The result is that every time there is heavy rain the water is almost dark brown with mud. The only answer, if you live in the country and have suffered or will suffer this problem, is to fit your own filter which, incidentally, must also be supplied with a non-return valve. The water company will not tolerate a return of their own dirty water. In fact, the valve is an EU requirement. This is a small price to pay for clean water and a further filter, such as Britta obtainable in the UK and Italy (it is German), will solve all problems except for a baby's bottle. Do not economize on the main filter since there are filters on the market at 15,000 lire which, being made of nylon mesh, last about a week before a hole is torn in them. The filter should be made of stainless steel and be in a special type of bottle. It needs looking at about once a month and cleaning at least every three months. You will be surprised at what you get out. Hot detergent water is best and then it should be well rinsed. Dishwasher detergent is best but Ariel works well also: though it is more difficult to neutralize.

It is as well to remember that many places, if not most, in northern Italy have cold to extremely cold winters and pipes should be lagged inside the house and out. In any event, pipes in the country should be well lagged and put at least 30 cm underground and 50 cm is better. Italian insurance companies do not pay out for burst pipes except on a third-party basis. As you drive around Italy you will see water pipes snaking their way in the most out of the way places. None is lagged. In the bitter winter of 1986, I was the only person with lagged pipes and the only person with water to give my neighbours. Still they insisted that insulation *'serve a niente, Signora. Lei era fortunata'*: 'That serves no purpose, you were fortunate.' Italians are traditionally conservative and very fatalistic.

Gas

Most of the larger towns in Italy have town gas, called *gas di città* which is supplied by Italgas. There are other private companies but Italgas is the biggest and the most seen. Methane gas is also commonly used in many towns. It is known as *il gas azzuro*, presumably from the colour they have dyed it – methane is colourless, and slight adjustments have to be made to various appliances. Methane gas is also supplied in large gas-tanks but, at present, is not used in too many homes. There are no limits on how much gas you can have and there are no shortages. Gas central heating is possible and is considerably cheaper than with propane or butane.

All gas appliances sold in Italy, unless sold specifically for bottled gas, have been approved by Italgas. Persons coming from abroad must have their gas appliances checked and approved by the local gas authority before linking them up to the gas system. Prices for town gas are relatively moderate compared with other utilities in Italy but without a Residence Certificate, i.e. for a holiday or temporary home, you will pay a higher rate than normal.

Rural Italy lives on bottled gas. If you intend to run your central heating on gas then you should arrange a contract with one of the major gas and oil companies such as AGIP, BP, MonteShell, IP, Elf who will lend you a large holding-tank, known in Italian as a *bombolone*. You sign a contract, usually for ten years (but selling the house breaks it), promising to spend at least a million or a million and a half lire's worth of gas a year; alas, it is not difficult to achieve this minimum. You must provide a suitable site for the holding tank and the company will furnish you with a diagram of what to do and where to do it. They will, for a fee, also get clearance from the local *Vigili di Fuoco* or Fire Brigade. You can do this yourself via a *geometrà* but it is never any cheaper and occasionally more expensive. Strictly speaking, you should have a fire extinguisher near the tank to put out any fires. I have had two stolen and no longer do this. In any event, if there is a fire the last thing I am going to do is station myself near a gas tank.

Bomboloni can also be put underground in special containers which hold 500 or 1000 litres maximum. The generic name is a *bombolone Amico*. It has the great advantage of being more or less hidden. These *bomboloni* have had teething problems (from which I suffered, due entirely to a bulldozer sitting on top of one). This type of container costs you between 500,000 and 600,000 lire because it is not something which can be picked up and taken away, again as I know to my cost when I had to have a new one. If you sell the house and your contract is broken the *bombolone* can do for the next person. In any event, the various supply companies annually examine these containers to make sure they are not leaking in any way (unlikely) and that the various pressure gauges are functioning properly. Whilst the company will fit everything to do with the *bombolone* itself, you are responsible for the piping which carries the gas to the house and boiler. This must go underground at least 50 cm deep and be in a standard brilliant yellow sheathing. It is preferable to cement it below, and pour cement on top so it can't move or suffer damage from a pickaxe or spade.

It should be remembered that only in exceptional circumstances can a gas central-heating boiler or a water heater be put indoors and never in a basement, particularly when butane or propane gas is being used. There are very strict rules about chimneys etc. and you would be wise to use a proper heating engineer rather than just the builder constructing or restoring your house. Equally strict rules apply to the running of copper pipes under the floor: they must go from each radiator in one unsoldered piece and must be lagged and the radiators must be at least 10 cm off the floor. The tendency in Italy is to put in too small a boiler for the house which then not only heats inefficiently but also costs considerably more over the years than paying a little more for a bigger boiler. Italian boilers are excellent and very advanced in both heat conservation and gas saving.

However, the Italians love selling German boilers which, all too often, they do not install properly.

Electricity

Electricity is supplied by several companies, the largest of which is ENEL SpA. which is the privatized form of the old ENEL, standing for *Ente Nazionale per l'Energia Eletrica* and this is the most commonly seen. Italy has few raw materials such as coal, iron or hydro-electricity so most of the power is purchased from abroad, notably France followed by Switzerland and Austria. By choice it has no nuclear power stations and the country's constant lament is that France made illegal inroads on her westernmost frontier with a view to getting the three important power stations. This is quite true and it was absolutely monstrous behaviour on the part of the French. However, it was over fifty years ago when this happened and little can, or will, be done to change matters; the Italians should now regard this action as part of their less fortunate history and get on with building new power stations. It is said that with the privatization of ENEL, much-needed capital will be poured into the energy market, but so far all one has seen is a plethora of new pylons and supply lines dotting the countryside. You can still wait eighteen months for an electric line to your house. You must pay in advance or you will wait even longer and in the end pay far more.

Throughout Italy the maximum power allowed per household is 3 kilowatts. The minimum is 1.5 kilowatts which can only be of academic interest to those coming from other parts of Europe. There are two sorts of contract: resident and non-resident. You will need to produce a Residence Certificate from the local *comune*, not less than a month old if you want electricity at the cheaper resident rate. If your house or apartment is a secondary residence and not, as the Italians arrange matters, in the name of the wife (the wife taking her residence in the country or seaside property and the husband having his in the city) then you will pay non-resident rates which are virtually double those for the resident. There are times when consumers feel that ENEL and the other utility companies (they are in this together) just think of a number and double it for non-resident rates. Then there are local taxes, provincial taxes, IVA etc. to add, and it comes to a tidy sum in spite of only having 3 kilowatts.

You can have more electricity if you wish to pay heavily for it. It can go up by increments of kilowatts but in no circumstances can you do this on any but a non-resident basis, even if you have been and still are a bona fide resident of the place. Moreover, not only will you pay non-resident rates but you will also be charged a *sopratassa* on the entire number of kilowatt hours used.

One way round this with a new or a restored house is to have each floor individually wired and have a contract as though they were separate flats. The husband and wife have the ground floor for instance, a son the first floor and a daughter the top floor. That way, by thinking ahead you can have, at best, 9 kilowatts at the standard resident-rate though you would be paying three standing charges (not onerous), and at worst, 9 kilowatts at the ordinary non-resident rate without paying the *sopratassa*, though, again, three standing charges would be due. Even so, this is cheaper than paying the *sopratassa* on 9 kilowatts. This applies only to those who are resident – for non-residents it is not really a viable proposition. Also, it is not open to those who buy an ordinary apartment or an already finished house, except at great cost.

Occasionally, property purchasers come across houses which still have old contracts at 6 or even 9 and 12 kilowatts and a deal is quickly done to keep it in the vendor's name and let things remain as they are since the moment a new contract is arranged it will be done at 3 kilowatts. Strictly speaking, this is illegal but ENEL tend not to ask questions. Naturally, you cannot pay this directly from your bank and would have to pay each bill as it came in at the post office. This is often done by landlords who do not want the Revenue to know they are letting an apartment; absolutely everything is kept in their own name, all at non-resident rate. Anyone who has paid bills at non-resident rates whilst being a bona fide resident will know how infuriating it is.

It is surprising how quickly you get used to having such a small amount of electricity and how you always think before you put on a dishwasher or washing machine. For ages, having changed over to gas in a new house, I kept forgetting my oven has nothing to do with the electricity supply so ingrained was the habit of thinking before switching on. Alas, there is always a weak point and with most British, and me, it is the electric kettle which I frequently switch on without thinking.

It is possible in Italy to purchase gadgets which will give certain machines, such as televisions or ovens in particular, priority over others. It is something worth considering, particularly if you let your apartment or house. Timers are part and parcel of Italian life and are cheaper purchased in any other country – most are made in the UK, Austria or Germany anyway.

This means an immersion heater which comes on at night is a possibility. There is no such thing as white metre or reduced night-rates in Italy – you are discouraged from using electricity at all.

ENEL and all utility companies like to be paid by direct debit from your bank. This is called *domicilazione* and your bank will arrange it for you. The first account rendered under any contract can be paid by you only in the normal way, via the post office or via your bank who will debit the sum to your current account or any other account for that matter. Thereafter, the direct debit comes into play. You will still get a copy of the bill for your records. It is impossible to pay the bill on this copy – it is carefully marked to stop you doing so.

ENEL are quick to cut you off if you don't pay, though they have to give you at least fourteen days' notice, which will come by registered letter. Neither they nor any other Italian concern, both private and state, is particularly careful about their dates and you may well find you have only a very few days to pay a bill which should allow a fortnight if not a month for payment. ENEL sent me a registered letter saying I had failed to pay the two previous bills, neither of which I had even received. It seemed unlikely they would let several hundreds of thousands of lire hang fire for two months without complaining by registered letter. You always have to go to their office in person if you want anything done. Apparently the computer, as in any other country, said that they had sent out these bills and that they were not paid. All this was very true but the first time I had these bills was with the registered letter and it was only the date which appeared on the computer screen beside the two bills' expedition which gave me the clue. Telecom Italia, who normally are not too bad, managed to send me a bill for payment the next day – the *Poste Italiane* helping in its late delivery. When I remonstrated I was told that it was enough that it arrived the day before it was due. '*Basta, il giorno prima, Signora.*' Part and parcel of Italian life are long queues of people in the various utilities' offices moaning about wrong or late bills.

Six bills come every two months, of which four are based on estimates. Each June and December they actually read the meter and send you a nasty surprise in the form of a *congualio* or final adjustment which, if you have it paid by direct debit, can do a great deal of damage to your bank balance. The way to avoid this is to read the meter yourself. In the front of every telephone directory is the *Numero Verde* for *ENEL-Lettura*. Suppose you receive a bill which is, you know, far too small and will later lead to an enormous payment at *congualio* time. On it you will see the date for the next reading (estimated or otherwise), called *prossima lettura*. Not more than three working days before this reading is due you ring the *Numero Verde* which will ask for your client number – *numero cliente* – you tap this in on your telephone buttons, then you are asked for your latest reading and you tap that in. This is all done by computer and synthesized voices. You will either get the answer that your reading has been registered, *la sua lettura è stata registrata*, or a voice saying it cannot accept your figure. In this case you must ring your local ENEL number to be found on the account slip who will send you a form on which you can fill in the number. Once your readings are accepted you will find the payments are far more equalized over six periods than if you have a *congualio* twice a year. On the other hand it is sometimes a help to have a very low bill. Nowadays, it is your choice.

Site electricity is available on a special contract and you must supply the wiring to and from the mains which can often be quite a long way from the site as well as the earth trip. Again 3 kilowatts is the maximum allowed and your bills must be paid immediately they arrive or ENEL cut you off without demur – no warnings at all. It costs the non-resident rate on the basis that you can't *live* on a building site.

Italy boasts, quite literally, the most sensitive circuit breakers in the world. Consequently, the slightest clap of thunder or spark of lightning can put out all the lights. This can be a disaster with freezers and there is no freezer-insurance in Italy. The earth trip is usually at the gate of your property and woe betide if you have a long drive – it usually happens when it rains. If you live in a block of flats and there are more than four apartments then you have it by the front door, otherwise it seems as far away as possible. If it is a holiday home it is a good idea to have someone who can go into the house or flat from time to time, but particularly after a storm or after they themselves have had an electricity cut, in order to put all the items back on. Most freezers have between 48 and 72 hours before the food begins to defrost. When putting it on again, use the 'super' button if there is one.

Every new electrical installation in Italy must be done by a qualified person who can issue the necessary *Certificato di Conformità*. In the case of old installations, you may well find that certain things have become illegal. As a new owner but not as a lessee, it is your duty to ensure that the electrical installation is up to scratch – *l'impianto eletrico è a norme di legge*. Failure to do so can result in a whopping fine. The way to go about it is to get in a qualified electrician who will tell you what has to be done to bring it up to date and will supply you with a certificate stating that it is a *norma di legge*. This can be quite difficult because most electricians do not want to guarantee, in writing, the work of others; he will undoubtedly find something that should be done to make it worth his while. In any case, most foreigners find there are far too few wall plugs in Italy. Alternatively, if you are sure the electrical installation is in good condition, you can call in ENEL for a small fee who will pass it or condemn it as they consider fit.

Telephone

It has to be said that even in the days of the old SIP the Italian telephone operators and engineers must have been the most polite in the world, notwithstanding the false sincerity of the Americans. SIP has turned into Telecom Italia and the people remain the same but the service is infinitely better and considerably cheaper. 'The cost of calling keeps on falling' could also be the motto of Telecom Italia.

The cost of calling may have fallen but the monthly rentals have gone up considerably and commercial lines are very expensive by comparison with private lines. Although they have got rid of the stupidities such as not being able to have a cordless telephone or fax or mobile which was not supplied by SIP, they have clung to others, the most important of which is that you cannot have telephone extensions in your house unless it is a commercial line. No TI engineer will do it for you, but a good electrician who also does telephones can remove the privacy piece in the wiring and thus you can listen to your children from your bedroom whilst your spouse is doing the same thing from his or her study.

Telecom Italia have discovered that there is a vast market in selling all sorts of extras to the public, such as answering machines, fax machines, Videotel – which is connected to the European Videotext network, a dedicated Videotel Channel for doctors who can get information on various specializations such as cardiology, neurology, obstetrics, etc., modern PBXs, telephone traffic recorders (useful with children or guests in your house) and many, many others.

With the purchase or rental of these various items comes the possibility of having a maintenance contract which can cost quite a lot. The only thing that can be said is that Telecom Italia's service personnel arrive very quickly after your complaint and if they cannot mend it on the spot you will get a replacement on loan. Overall their service is considerably better than normal commercial after-sales service.

A list of useful as well as some strange numbers in Italy appears in Appendix H.

Rubbish Disposal

Once you own a house or apartment or become a tenant you are obliged by law to declare yourself at the local town to be assessed for rates. The assessment is based on how many cubic metres you inhabit and how many persons there are in the household. Bills for rubbish disposal come once or twice a year, around the same time as a demand for ICI, *Imposta Comunale Immobiliere*. Depending on where you live and on the season of the year, rubbish is collected from large bins supplied by the *comune*, up to five or six times a week, obviously more in summer than in winter. Each of these bins carries a message about depositing your rubbish between six and eight in the evening – a time at which most people are either eating or relaxing in front of the box. Nothing metallic should be put in; there are either special bins for this or certain designated places for putting things like refrigerators, old railings, saucepans, washing machines etc. If you can't manage to get these items to the dump they can be collected – at a price.

Occasionally in very smart blocks of flats (which are so expensive that the owners would have servants anyway) part of the condominium charges are for rubbish disposal. In fact this simply means that a porter or some other person takes the rubbish to the nearest local bin. Thus such persons pay twice for the service. Included in rubbish disposal is the sweeping of the street and even the smallest village in Italy has its resident street-sweeper. Italians are not very civic-minded and chuck everything on to the street for him to sweep up, yet usually their own apartment is spic and span.

18
Restoring Property

The Italians are remarkably good at restoring old property and many appear to have a real feel for the past. That said, do not think it is necessarily cheaper than starting from scratch. Always be guided by a qualified architect or a *geometrà* who can show you several samples of his work in this field.

All too often you will find that your ruin is under the thumb of the Beni Ambientali. This is not so bad as it sounds since they will ensure that your renovations, particularly outside, are in accordance with their requirements. For instance, if you purchase in the historic centre of a town or even village you will not be allowed to use metal windows or metal shutters. You may be limited to certain paint colours, roof tiles or types of facing stone. Most foreigners' gripe is that the B.A. are not strict enough and allow people to get away with murder, particularly *coltivatori diretti*, who, because they are in agriculture, reckon they can put up any sort of shed, greenhouse, water butt in bright blue or scarlet plastic simply on the grounds that earning their crust requires it. In my own village we have a superb mediaeval view absolutely ruined by three electric blue water butts. All the local *comune* will say is that not everyone's car colour is pleasant either.

Newcomers to Italy are always appalled at how the Italians have ruined the outskirts of their big cities and how ghastly their modern architecture is. They therefore plump for the better design or the seventeenth, eighteenth or even nineteenth century. In some places they can purchase houses older than that and all the time they comfort themselves with the idea that they can arrange the inside as they want. It is not as simple as that. All too frequently people want to change the inside of a house in such a way that the old outside walls will not support the new structure. Be guided by an architect or *geometrà* who has had experience (preferably a nasty one) in this field and won't encourage you in what can be absolute madness without your realizing it.

Get your priorities right: the first is the cost of the ruin added to the cost of restoring it plus a percentage for administration, the architect and unforeseen hiccups. You will soon see that you can buy something ready-made just as cheaply. If the roof is in good condition and already insulated this will reduce the cost quite a bit. So will already fitted windows since all carpentry and wood in Italy are expensive. Count at least one and a half million lire per square metre of house and you should be fairly safe, though sometimes, in certain cases such as town houses in resorts or seaside towns, the price can rise to two and a half million lire. Depending on the location, you can count on every lire you spend being worth around half as much again when the house is finished – and you will have earned this profit, no doubt about it.

One of the reasons rather nice farmhouses are for sale in Tuscany, Umbria and Latina is that people nowadays do not relish the hard work involved in running a farm in what is a very dry area in summer. You will not, for instance, find cheap farmhouses where there is good water-supply – they will still be used as farmhouses. Therefore, think of putting in water tanks, either under the house if this is at all possible, or, failing that, immediately next to the house but underground, or near the house in individual containers of 1000 or 2000 litres a time, again if possible sunk into the ground – water tanks are extraordinarily ugly. Virtually the whole of Italy is on metred water now and the idea is that you fill up your tanks in autumn, winter and early spring for the dry weather to come. Half a million litres does not go very far for a family of four with a garden in a hot, dry summer. Household use will account for a cubic metre a day, i.e. 1000 litres with baths at 80 litres a time, washing machines at 40 or 50 litres etc. Washing lettuce for a salad takes almost 20 litres. The garden will easily take half that amount if there is a lawn. One and a half cubic metres a day over the summer amounts to at least 150 cubic metres.

Make enquiries at the local *municipio* offices together with the local water-board. Find out if you can have what is known as agricultural water, i.e. not filtered or treated. The connection charge is around one and a half million lire but the water is relatively inexpensive. The cost of water is going up all the time and the big companies, such as Italgas, are now buying the small privatized water-companies and *acquedotti* run by the local authorities and charging what they like – and not always for very wonderful water.

Alternatively, find out if you have water under your land. A water diviner in Italian is a *rab-dovante*, which you won't find in every English–Italian dictionary, or less commonly and less specifically, *un'indovino*. However, before going to such expense establish whether you will be allowed to drill a well on your land since in some areas it is expressly forbidden. Ask your *geometrà* or architect to get the permission *in writing* before calling in the water diviner. Water-divining in fact is quite scientific and there are expensive modern instruments which will achieve the same results but at greater cost, always supposing you can lay your hands on someone who has them. A good water-diviner will be well known in his district and you may well have to wait for his services. You may need to go down as much as 50 or 60 metres before you find water and the cost of this drilling can be expensive. Always add at least one third onto the estimated depth so as not to have any nasty surprises later on.

Central heating is expensive and radiators are not always suitable for an old country house. If you are not living in the house all year round, consider a wood-burning stove or even stoves, provided you know you can obtain wood and get it delivered. The logs used must not be too large as the stoves, mostly Scandinavian, only take small amounts. They also take compressed sawdust 'logs' made specifically for this purpose. You will find this option cheaper than gas- or oil-fired central heating, unless you are in a town where methane gas is available. The stoves come at all sorts of prices but I know of a house on the outskirts of a largish village which heats with two Swedish Jøtul stoves fuelled with sawdust logs. They have just under 100 sq. metres of space, a stove upstairs and one in the living room. The house is always as warm as toast in the winter. The only drawback is that it will need refuelling every six or seven hours unless it is gas- or oil-fired. Compared with aluminium radiators they are extremely efficient.

For lovers of open fires (i.e. without an insert which immediately makes a fireplace more efficient but rather ugly) there is a new gadget in Italy called a 'Caldofa' which costs around half a million lire and basically sucks cold air in from the room which is then heated by the open fire's heat and delivered by a fan via a filter back into the room. You need to be careful about the very dry atmosphere it creates and probably humidifiers are necessary.

Electricity is of prime importance and your local electricity company (not always ENEL though that is the most common) will give you a written estimate of what it will cost to join your house up. In most places you will need to provide them with a *Certificato di Conformità* stating that the installation has been carried out by qualified personnel in accordance with current practice. If you need more than two poles to connect your house think in terms of at least two million lire. You may wish to generate the electricity yourself with the new Japanese generators which work both on diesel and ordinary petrol. Most of the modern sort have an automatic start-up device. They can be noisy if not muffled and are best stored in an outhouse if you have one. Down in the basement is not always the best place, as you may well learn to your cost. Generating your own electricity can have certain drawbacks and you should make a thorough investigation before embarking on such an undertaking.

The most important parts of the building are its basic structure, the roof, how watertight it is, the windows and the floors and of course the staircase. After that comes the plumbing, the central heating (or not) the kitchen and the decoration. In an old house you should paint the whole place out in a pale paint and wait twelve months to see if there are any leaks before investing in expensive wallpaper or fabric.

If you think there is the slightest chance you may have central heating then at least have the plumbing for it so that all you need to buy later on are the radiators and the boiler. If you fail to put the copper piping in at your re-building stage you will find later it will prove either ugly because it will all be apparent or, worse still, not insulated. If you have central heating and are away quite a lot then aluminium radiators are better than the cast iron sort which can burst in very cold weather.

Before laying a single brick you will need permission from either your local *comune* and/or the Beni Ambientali and/or the Region. No matter if you are an architect or a surveyor yourself, you will need to employ one of these people. THERE IS NO WAY YOU CAN MANAGE ON YOUR OWN.

You need to know your way round the Italian legislation concerning building and restoring property and moreover you will need a superb command of the language to argue for what you want. A *geometrà* can sometimes be marginally cheaper in restoring property than an architect. Indeed, if you are an artistic person yourself with plenty of imagination (don't look for imagination or artistry in the average *geometrà*) then a *geometrà* is a better bet for you.

Italian legislation requires a ceiling height of a minimum 2.75 metres. If you buy an old two-storey cottage you may well find you have to raise the roof and/or excavate the ground floor to obtain this height. Either way, this can be expensive which is why it is some-times cheaper to buy a *casa padronale* in the village of your choice, than the charming but low rustico going for 50 or 60 million less. Certain Italiam *comuni* insist that you change no windows (they can be very poky), no entrances (except to renew the door), no stair-cases (which can be death traps), and build no garden walls (everyone comes and helps themselves). This can mean that in parts of the Veneto or Lombardy you cannot have double-glazed windows which are vital for comfort and fuel saving. You must find out about these things before purchasing otherwise you will end up with inefficient inferior double-glazing. Beauty notwithstanding, there seems to be no *comune* which will stop you putting up a wire mesh fence which, in my humble opinion, must be one of the ugliest things ever invented by man. It can, I know, be covered with variegated ivy, *trachelospermum*, jasmine or, in certain parts, *Clematis cirrhosa* which is evergreen, but it remains ugly for a long time. If you think you will want garden walls, get permission at the time of doing the main restoration – never leave it until the last minute.

A vendor will know that getting permission takes time and cannot expect you to purchase until you have the *licenza* in your hand. After all, he would certainly have to wait for an Italian to do the same thing. If you want to keep him quiet then you can sign a contract with *the provision that your purchase is dependent on your getting planning permission.* Occasionally, you will be offered the property with a project already passed. This is the province of the *geometrà* or architect who can arrange for the permission to be transferred to you with your alterations. A planning permission given to someone else, sometime before, is not always able to be taken up by a successor in title, so do check. In any event, check the dates – it should have at least two years to run.

You will need a builder who specializes in restoring houses, not just any old builder. Look at work he has done; he should be proud of it. Fierce penalty-clauses should be in the contract which itself should be several pages long and cover everything from plumbing, plastering and electricity to tiling, carpentry and kitchen fitting.

Insist on paying the full price with IVA. Otherwise you will find you have saved 19 per cent IVA (VAT) only to pay 30 per cent INVIM which is a type of capital gains tax on all sales of property. The builder is not worried about the VAT – after all he only passes it on – but fifty million lire black is fifty million not declared and therefore income-tax free. The builder should be paid by the architect or *geometrà* who passes the work – you never pay direct.

It is probably cheaper to put carpet upstairs in the bedrooms and even cheaper to bring carpet from the UK. If it is strictly for your own holiday use and not for all-year-round living or for letting, then Italian moquette is satisfactory. However, it is nothing like so easy to clean as British wool or wool-and-nylon carpet, and this will be particularly important if you let the property.

Having finished your house you will need a professional valuation for insurance purposes. Someone from the company may visit the property. Bearing in mind that Italian policies are often for *ten* years (unless you watch very carefully what you are signing), you may prefer to cover directly with Lloyds. Some may give cover for earthquake which no Italian cover ever does. See the chapter on Insurance for more details.

Grants do exist, but your architect or *geometrà* will probably burst into laughter if you mention such a thing. If you are fortunate enough to get financial help with your historic monument, it will be so hedged around with various recondite requirements you will almost certainly end up wishing you had never asked in the first place. As an Italian friend who works in Hamburg, once said to me, 'In other countries they give you grants and advice, here they just fine you.' There is more than a grain of truth in that remark and the worst thing is that you cannot immediately undo your wrong and avoid the fine – you pay and then you undo the damage. Perhaps this is due to what the northerners call the *mentalità borbonica* which loves complications and has more than a whiff of the Spanish Inquisition about it. Personally, I think it is entirely to do with the percentage of the fine which goes to the policeman who makes out the ticket.

19
Building

This chapter is written from the heart. We have twice built a new house in Italy. The first time we waited almost two years before we could move in due to having originally said we were not in a hurry – fatal words. The builder left it so long he could not complete the house with the specified materials because they had all greatly increased in price. So he used 'seconds' throughout and we both ended up at our lawyers.

The second time was even more disastrous. We had the building plot, we had a perfect architect with whom we are still friends, we had permission and we thought we had enough money. At which point the Tangentopoli scandal broke and the *Mani Pulite* campaign began. We were 'blocked' for almost three years due to our *comune* having issued building licences without first going to the Beni Ambientali for their prior approval. There are many parts of Italy which require this sort of permission from what is more or less the equivalent of English Heritage; indeed, almost anywhere which is rather beautiful and/or has a number of old buildings and churches will be subject to this authority. The local provincial police keep tabs on all building and restoration sites on behalf of the regional Beni Ambientali. We only managed to start building by presenting a medical certificate. To all the other costs we had to add three years' exorbitant rent for a squalid little house we had thought of using for a mere nine months. As if that were not enough, virtually all our stored furniture, paintings and prints were ruined by mildew and required expensive restoration, replacement or throwing away. On the subject of mildew more anon.

The contract between you and the builder should be long, otherwise it cannot possibly cover all eventualities. Make out a list of things which are important to you. Discuss it with the architect or *geometrà*. The contract should not be less than ten full sides of single-spaced A4 paper for a normal three-bedroomed house. If you happen to have a tame Italian lawyer show him the contract before signing. It does no harm to show the builder you are a serious, careful person. Too many British leave their brains in the English Channel on the way to Italy. Do not listen to any *geometrà* who tells you a short written contract is enough because he, himself, will be in control of the builders. It may well be you will change builders and *geometrà* in between times.

Before even thinking about building your own house there are two most important things to remember. Firstly, the administrative side costs an absolute fortune. On a house costing 300 million lire it will be about 15 per cent. The larger the house the less it costs. This is made up of the cost of the building permit (*licenza*), the cost of getting clearance from the sanitary department of the local health authority, the cost of registering your new house at the local Land Registry (*Catasto*), the cost of the engineer who 'designs' the reinforced concrete structure of the property and provides the specification, the cost of another civil engineer coming to examine the reinforced concrete once it has been completed, the cost of connecting up to water and fitting a filter, the enormous cost of connecting electricity, the cost of running in a telephone line, the cost of an architect, the cost of a *direttore dei lavori* and finally the cost of organizing the absolutely ruined land around your house. This last item, quite separate from administrative matters, can cost up to sixty million lire, especially if you need to truck in earth.

Secondly, you will almost certainly have to build in the local style. Do not think you can put up a Scandinavian chalet-type house near Sorrento or in Tuscany, although you might get away with it in the mountainous part of the Friuli in north-eastern Italy.

Italian law requires that you have a clerk of works (*il direttore dei lavori*) for any undertaking that requires permission from the *comune* and/or the Beni Ambientali. The Italians tend to use a qualified *geometrà* to do this and often they have used the same person to design the house from scratch or map out the restoration programme. However, talented professionals they may be, but *geometri* are *not* architects. Most of them have none of the imagination of an architect and are not internationally minded. They are purely and simply Italian in outlook and a great deal of the time this does not suit the foreigner. For a start, the Italians seem to love lots of little rooms, perhaps so they can say they have a twelve-roomed house when really it is only six or seven. They like small windows; this is something traditional stemming from the days when windows were very expensive and let in far too much sun. Quite often local ordinances control the size of windows and doors. Often shutters can only be made of wood and in the local style. This can be quite expensive if they are *alla genovese* which are louvred with both the upper and lower portions able to be opened separately.

An architect is a far better proposition since he can usually do a *geometrà*'s work rather better than a *geometrà* can do his. Often his 6 or 7 per cent will include being *direttore dei lavori*, as opposed to around 5 per cent for a *geometrà* plus the architect's fees. The fees of a *geometrà* are all set out by their governing body. They rarely abide by them and usually charge between 3 and 4 per cent, minimum, on the entire cost of the house. You can make a contract for a given sum, set by the *geometrà* of course, which usually ends up cheaper. Even items you purchase yourself such as bathroom fittings, bookcases, internal shutters etc. all go on the cost of the house bill as far as he is concerned, where you might well think such things were decoration. Perhaps it is as well to mention here that your architect, whatever his or her nationality, must be qualified to work in Italy and be registered to work as an architect otherwise he will not be able to present any project to the local *comune* nor will he be able to oversee the building. Incidentally, most professionals, such as lawyers, architects and certain engineers are required to add around 2 per cent, to their final bill which is paid into their pension fund. It is not insurance, which is quite separate and paid by the individual.

Assuming that your architect has obtained the necessary permission you will find you have to pay an urbanization fee plus a another fee which depends on how many cubic metres you intend building. How many cubic feet you are allowed will depend entirely on how much land you own and its density value. Usually one pays two thirds of the fee when the *comune* gives the *licenza* and the other third once the house is finished.

Every piece of land in your particular *comune* has a description as to how much can be built on it and whether the buildings are for civil or agricultural use. It also clearly states the density, i.e. how many cubic metres can be built for how many square metres of land. Other land, often not even neighbouring, can be used to increase the size of the house. My own *comune* does not allow any but contiguous land to be used for this purpose. In the country, there is nearly always a strip of land which is deemed to be agricultural land and cannot be used in the computation. Moreover, in the country, but not in the town, you must build at least 10 or 11 metres back from the road. This is important because in hilly or mountainous areas it can mean you will have to excavate at great expense, re-build terraces, and then purchase expensive top soil to fill in the huge gaps. There are masses of excavating firms who make a fortune transporting away soil they will later sell back to the house-owner. It is essential when excavating to have a *geometrà* or engineer on site to oversee the work. Otherwise unnecessary and expensive excavations can take place.

The architect or *geometrà* then officially informs the *comune* of the date on which the work starts and puts up a large notice in a prominent place on the site stating the landowner's name, the architect's name, the number of the building permit and its date. This must stay up until you move in and start clearing up the site. He will also attend to your application to pay Italian VAT (normally at 19 per cent) only at 4 per cent on all building costs. However, his fees are charged at 19 per cent. Whatever the builder says refuse to cheat on this since 4 per cent is ridiculously cheap and all the builder is trying to do is reduce his income-tax bill. You won't succeed totally but, since you will have odd jobs to be done on which VAT will not be charged, there is no reason to cheat with someone or a company within the VAT system.

Ideally, you should build in an area where, within the next five or ten years, you are fairly sure the density regulation will increase so that you have the possibility of extending the property should you or your successor wish to do so. You will have to re-apply for permission if you want to make alterations and also for walling in your property if this was not applied for at the time the building permission was granted. Building in town is less likely to carry with it the possibility of extensions being made later on but in the country it is quite common.

There comes a point, however, where a house in the country can often become too big for the resale market. Italians love the country but not to live in as their permanent or only home. The general consensus is that the countryside is primarily for peasants. Tuscany and Umbria are among the first places to offer a wide range of country houses, mostly re-done or restored by the English.

There are certain standard oddities about Italian houses. The bedrooms are often unbelievably small, this in a country where a standard double bed is at least 1.6 metres or 5 feet wide minimum. Recently I came across a single bedroom which was a mere 2.38 metres by 2.60. The owner registered my shock as approbation and explained that her husband was a naval architect, used to working with small spaces.

The bathrooms are not always en suite, even to the extent of forcing the occupants of the master bedroom to go out into the corridor to get to their bathroom. This is because many provinces do not allow a water-closet to give on to a living room or bedroom. A straightforward bathroom comprising bath, shower and wash-basin can be made to go off a bedroom. As it is pleasanter not to have a loo in the bathroom, it is worth either making this convenience totally separate or better still, putting a water-closet and bidet in another small room 1 by 3 metres which gives off the bathroom thus circumventing the planning difficulty. The whole idea is ridiculous because practically every modern Italian hotel has a normal bathroom or shower room off the bedroom. On the plus side you will find that Italian bathroom fitments and taps are second to none as is their bathroom design. Marble, an almost unheard of luxury in the rest of Europe, is common in Italy and often cheaper than tiles. It has the great advantage of being unaffected by mildew whereas the grouting around tiles can become badly affected.

North of Rome, and certainly north of Bologna, plump for double glazing. If using metal windows such as those made of aluminium, get the anti-condensation sort. The extra cost is a long-term economy and your expensive wallpaper or curtain fabric will not be ruined. Alternatively, make sure that the framework of the window is at least 2 to 3 centimetres proud of the wall which means your curtains are not sticking to the windows. Italians do have sash windows, known as *alla guillotina*, which need to be put in by a specialist firm. If you are in a Beni Ambientali zone you will probably be restricted as to the sort of windows and shutters you can have. In any event, most Italian casement windows open inwards, which can be a wretched nuisance.

Wooden windows which fit and do not let heavy rain or snow enter are rather rare in Italy and I know quite a few people who are compelled to close their shutters in a heavy rainstorm. It is perfectly possible to find windows that fit but do not leave the matter to your builder or joiner unless you are certain you are of a like mind. A whole section of Italian society has a somewhat fatalistic attitude to life and accepts badly fitting windows and doors, poor or total lack of insulation and cracking plaster as part and parcel of everyday life. On the other hand, the Italians produce wonderful windows which incorporate mosquito screens and shutters. Shutters are absolutely essential in virtually every part of Italy and they are very expensive and difficult to fit afterwards, as many northern Europeans have found out to their great chagrin. Whilst roll-up shutters may well be allowed on blocks of flats you could find they are forbidden on houses in your area. Your architect or *geometrà* will know the local requirements.

It is easy to read the word *intonaco* and imagine it means plaster. It does not. It means the walls will be rendered, possibly with two coats, one coarse and one fine. To get a really smooth finish you must have '*l'intonaco comune (grigio) con rifinitura in gesso lisciato di circa 1cm*'. This means ordinary grey rendering with a final finish of smooth plaster. There are also many proprietary finishes in Italy, most of which are excellent, which do a similar job to ordinary *gesso lisciato* as well as the French type of *crépi* but above all, remember to avoid *scagliola* which is also based on *gesso* but which cracks in both heat and cold and collects damp and mildew like a sponge. If you do not specify a plaster finish you will find you will be left with merely rendered walls – smooth if you are lucky.

When rendering the walls, put in at least two air bricks per room since there are three causes of humidity. One is damp weather, the second is poor insulation and therefore condensation, and the third is poor air-circulation. The Italians accept mildew as a fact of life, even as an act of God. It need not be thus. Provided your roof is well insulated you will not get condensation from hot air in the room meeting a very cold ceiling under an uninsulated roof. Still on the subject of air circulation, those who have lived in the tropics often have ceiling fans, which in high summer can be very useful in the hottest regions of Italy, and in winter they reverse the direction of the blades, thus not only circulating the air but bringing down the hot air which has risen to ceiling level. The fan should be on at the slowest speed and it appears to solve a lot of circulation and mildew problems. Certainly if you already have a fan fitted it is worth trying this in winter. It is very important though to pay attention to the direction of the blades.

Each concrete pilaster should be clad in thin brick before rendering so that the thermal values are the same for all parts of the wall and room, otherwise you are likely to collect mildew on the pilasters, particularly those in a corner. Finally a good air-circulation, of any sort, without causing a draught, does wonders against mildew. If all else fails, particularly in bathrooms and closed cupboards, then use an anti-mildew paint made by Max Meyer, an Austrian manufacturer who guarantees no mildew for three years. Other companies make anti-mildew and/or anti-condensation paint, but no one gives such a long guarantee as Max Meyer. Bleach is a good temporary cure but cannot be used for long. The secret is to stop mildew appearing in the first place. I once sat at a dinner table where the ten of us all had mildew tales to tell. The Italians fondly believe 'Great Britain is much drier than Italy' and also, their greatest compliment and throwaway line in one, 'much more organized against mildew and that sort of thing than we are.'

Wood is expensive in Italy and often not of very good quality. Nor are the carpenters of very good quality. The best wood is reserved for furniture making and somehow does not seem to come on to the general market. Nor do the good joiners employed by the furniture makers. The Italians are rather laid back about treating

wood against fungus and insects so it is as well for you or the architect to check on this. I once saw a new extension being built on to
a house without using treated wood. When I mentioned this to the
owner she said airily that it was all right since the roof space was
closed and there were no windows for the insects to come through!
Doors in Italy come in two qualities only: rubbish and superb. The
latter cost something like five hundred pounds apiece and are
factory lacquered with superlative door furniture of heavy brass and
brilliant design. I brought mine from London at a fraction of the
price demanded for a poor quality sort and had them shipped over.
However, another thing to watch is the positioning of door handles,
which is normally 3 ft or 90 cm in the UK and between 108 and
110 cm in Italy. This height looks ridiculous on an average English
door and particularly on eighteenth-century doors commonly on
sale in the UK. It is also infuriating since it seems to catch sleeves,
hit backs of hands and generally irritate. I have used copies of late
eighteenth century six-panelled English doors with hardboard
fronts. They come primed and paint up superbly – to such an extent
that you would not know they were not solid wood. They excite
many compliments from Italians and one joinery shop I know now
imports them from London. Wooden floors are prohibitively
expensive throughout Italy, except for the regions of Aosta and
Friuli-Venezia-Giulia where they have the material on the spot. Tiles
are usually relatively inexpensive and long-lasting, and tilers are not
expensive. A good tiler works fast and charges around 10–15,000
lire a square metre, including laying material on a large job such as
a whole house. I have noticed good tilers use purchased plastic
'spacers' between tiles whereas the average builder doing a bit of
tiling tends to do without and produces a less good finish. Tilers
abound and it's worth asking for a specialist, especially if you are
using expensive tiles such as Brunelleschi or Cotto Veneto. Non-
Italians are tempted by unglazed terracotta but it can be a mistake
if you are in a frost area, and it stains very easily. For some this is
part of the charm, particularly in a garden, but for others it's the
last straw. Keep to paleish, neutral colours you will not get tired of,
or alternatively rich browns – leather-coloured tiles can be wonderful. Above all, avoid marble effect tiles which seem to be designed
to attract the dirt, particularly in pale colours.

Carpets are usually synthetic or wool/synthetic, nearly always in
4 metre broadloom and foam backed. The British are almost always
appalled at the price/quality ratio. Underlay, such as Duralay or
similar is unknown and the felt is thin and expensive. Therefore,
read the next paragraph carefully if you have more than 75 sq.
metres of good carpet to fit.

Peter Jones (of the John Lewis Partnership) of Sloane Square, London SW1 (telephone: 0171 730 3434) will organize delivery of their carpet and underlay (you having sent the plans beforehand) and send a man (or men) out to lay them. Even with the airfare, delivery cost works out cheaper, particularly from the choice and quality viewpoint. Having paid more than five hundred pounds to fit just two bedroom carpets (i.e. around twelve pounds per square metre), I regret greatly not having known of this before, particularly as the carpets in question came from Peter Jones. They often supply workmen such as carpenters and plumbers, though these last are not such a good idea since certificates have to be given for the plumbing installation and only a qualified Italian plumber can do that at the moment. But carpenters are another matter.

Do make sure that insulation is mentioned in your contract. Insulation is a knotty problem in Italy, though admittedly less knotty in the north of Italy where the cold is better understood. It is against the law to have a radiator less than 10 cm off the floor, to have unlagged pipes to feed the radiator (though not to feed your bath or wash-basin for some reason). Connections between the radiator and heating boiler must be made of a *single* copper tube without any joints. Strangely, there is no legal requirement to put a thermostat on each radiator and this you must do for yourself or get the plumber to fix them for you. They cost rather less than 35,000 lire each and he will charge you at least 70,000 each if he supplies and fits them. The law notwithstanding, you will get, if you or your architect are not vigilant, unlagged pipes all over the house, cemented into walls and running under the tiles, dispersing, at vast cost, useless heat. I have a gas counter and was surprised to find that with all the radiators switched off the feed pipes under the floor were heated and that they cost me over a cubic metre of gas a day to heat, uselessly. That may not sound much but if the situation is left thus it would mean some 125 litres of propane gas per month just wasted at a cost of well over 100,000 lire. Therefore, when you don't need the central heating turn it off at the boiler and not at the radiators. No pipes should go under the floor, along the walls or in the walls, hot or cold, without insulation, but you will have to fight for this and watch it is used.

There are thousands of types of insulation, from extruded poly-styrene to rock wall, or from glass wool to foam. In the roof it is probably best to use a mixture of rock wool or glass wool and poly-styrene boards. Glass wool used in walls tends after a time to fall in a heap at the bottom, or so I found when taking down an outside wall to build an extension on one occasion. 'Polipan' is one of the most commonly used materials in Italy and 6 to 8 cm in the wall cavity is not too much. However, it must be actually fixed to the wall nearest to the house. Italian builders are inclined to simply bung it in the middle of the cavity which is tantamount to having a door but leaving it ajar.

Except in the hottest parts of Italy, you should always install at least a basic central-heating system, even if you do not put in the boiler or radiators. It will cost considerably more later on and you will have all the pipes showing. It will cost around one and a half to two million lire to put in the copper pipes (copper being almost the price of gold in Italy) and stopcocks for a three-bedroomed house. Even without the radiators and boiler, you must get a certificate for their installation, *a norme di legge*, since no other plumber later on will wish to give one on someone else's work.

The best boilers in Italy tend to be German: Vaillant is a good make but not as high on technology as, say, Weisshaupt. For years I had a Beretta in London, which I found excellent, and many of their models have heat exchangers. Very often a plumber is not a heating engineer and where a largish house is concerned it is as well to go to a specialist. I speak from experience: we once employed a builder who put in an excellent Vaillant boiler and thought that was enough; it turned out that we had the wrong boiler, in the wrong place, the wrong size with the wrong connections. Nothing about it was *a norme di legge* and we had to pay for the expensive modifications.

Central heating boilers need a pump and a pump needs electricity – so indeed do most forms of hot water, including gas-heated. If you use an electric immersion-heater it is best to do so at night by using a programmer – there is no cheaper electricity at night in Italy but at least it is unlikely that other appliances are being used. Water-heater jackets are unknown in Italy and much admired. It makes a wonderful present for someone with what amounts to an unlagged immersion-heater. There is initially a tiny amount of felt insulation, but the extra jacket saves thousands of lire.

The electrical installation will be inspected by ENEL (or whatever other supplier of electricity you have in your area) in the absence of a conformity certificate. This is issued by the electrician and states that the work has been carried out according to the latest requirements. That means no plugs near baths, wash-basins etc., proper and special cables for electrical appliances, a properly earthed installation with earth trips as well as a minimum of 6-8 mm cable bringing the mains electricity to the house. Finally, make sure the electrical installation charge in the contract includes connection to the electric meter outside the house. Often it does not and you need to count at least one and a half million lire for this vital extra.

Unless your house has to be faced in stone, as is sometimes the case, it will probably have rendered and painted walls. Do not be tempted to leave it unpainted as cement is sponge-like and winter or rain will give you a very damp house and the dreaded mildew. Once the walls are dry, paint by using first a waterproofer, known as *impregnante*, followed by one or two coats of top-quality plasticized paint. It is a strange fact that the Italians make the finest marine paints yet their ordinary household sort are of rather ordinary quality. Your architect will advise you of the best quality and you will find it will probably be foreign: German, French or Dutch and occasionally English. There is nothing to stop you bringing over English outside paint and, provided you have a large car, it is considerably cheaper. Make sure you have some over for touch-ups, and also make sure that all angles on your houses and/or arches are slightly rounded to avoid chipping the rendering.

If you have obtained a loan or mortgage to build or restore your house, the architect or *geometrà* will give the necessary certificates to the bank for stage payments to be made. They may well send their own valuer/engineer/*geometrà* to the site to look at the work himself. It wouldn't be the first time in Italy that a builder and/or owner was pulling a fast one on the banks or mortgage company. Needless to say, the cost of this visit and report will be paid by you. (See also Chapter 11 Banking.)

When all the work is finished the architect or *geometrà* issues a certificate to that effect and takes down the sign. Thereafter, permission will be required for all but the most minor work; it is always wise to ask first in order to avoid what could be a swingeing fine. Your original building permission will state a date for finishing the work and this can be extended by application to the *comune*. It is always best not to be too quick about getting your End of Works Certificate.

Once this has been issued and you can show a Conformity Certificate from both the plumber and the electrician, you will be entitled to a Habitation Certificate – that is when you have paid your last tranche to the *comune*.

There will be moments when you will feel at a very low ebb, convinced you will be bankrupt or pushing up daisies before the house is finished, but such feelings are only transient. One gets a compensatory lift almost at each stage payment, as if to mitigate that particular horror. The most exciting moments are when the roof goes on, when the brick walls are put in between the concrete pilasters, when the windows are fitted, when the final plastering is done, when the floors are tiled and, finally, when you can and *must* lock all entrances to the house.

A *geometrà* once told me that someone who builds a house can immediately expect two lire for every one he has spent. With the administrative costs this is manifestly not so. However, it is undoubtedly slightly cheaper and, if you are lucky, you do get what you want and not someone else's idea of elegant living. Nevertheless, you need courage and I still remember realizing with horror that everything we owned seemed to be invested in a rubble-strewn building site on which there was little more than a reinforced concrete structure with a roof, but no walls, worth not much more than twenty thousand pounds, always supposing we could have found a buyer. Italy abounds in quarter- and half-finished houses where the owner has run out of money or has built illegally and then been 'blocked' for ever. One of the secrets is to find a builder with a long history of successful house-building who can show you his work. The other is to work out a tight contract with him as to price and finishing times. With this achieved you are more than halfway to success.

Ending on a realistic note, it must be said that no matter how punishing your penalty clauses may be, it takes almost two years to get to court and a great deal of cost to go there. The best judges in Italy are in the penal courts dealing with murder, the Mafia and drugs. The civil courts tend to get the dross so far as judges are concerned, so it pays to settle or cut your losses. As in the UK, lawyers prefer to settle and so should you if possible.

Appendix A
Embassies and Consulates

Her Britannic Majesty's Embassy Via XX Settembre 80a 00187 Roma	Tel. 06 482 5551 Fax. 06 70 47 54 67

Consulates

Florence/Firenze
British Consulate   Tel.   055 28 41 33
Lungarno Corsini 2
50123 Firenz

Genoa/Genova
British Consulate   Tel.   010 56 48 33/6
Via Ottobre 2
16121 Genova

Milan/Milano
British Consulate   Tel.   02 80 34 42
Via San Paulo   86 24 90
20121 Milano   86 24 92
                                 Fax. 02 72 02 01 53

Naples/Napoli
British Consulate   Tel.   081 66 33 20
Via Francesco Crispi   66 35 11
80112 Napoli

Rome/Roma
British Consulate   Tel.   06 475 5441/6
Via XX Settembre 80a   475 5551/6
00187 Roma

Venice/Venezia
British Vice-Consulate   Tel.   041 522 72 02
Palazzo Querino   Fax.   041 522 26 17
Accademia 1051 – Dorsoduro
Venezia

Italian Embassy
14 Three Kings Yard   Tel. 0171 312 2200
London W1Y 2EH

Consulates General

38, Eaton Place   Tel. 0171 235 9371
London SW1X 8AN

32 Melville Street   Tel. 0141 226 3631
Edinburgh EH3 7PG

111 Piccadilly   Tel. 0161 236 9024
Manchester M1 2HY

Vice-Consulate

7/9, Greyfriars   Tel. 01234 356647
Bedford MK40 1HJ

Appendix B
Citizenship

There are two kinds of British citizenship – 'otherwise than by descent' and 'by descent'. Both types of citizenship confer an automatic right of abode in the UK. The philosophy behind the distinction is that a British citizen 'otherwise than by descent' passes on that citizenship to his children but a citizenship 'by descent' does not. In general terms, a person is a British citizen 'otherwise than by descent' if he was born or adopted in the UK or obtained British citizenship by naturalization or registration in the UK.

A child born out of the UK after the beginning of 1983 (subject to certain transitional provisions until the end of 1987), to parents neither of whom is a British citizen 'otherwise than by descent', does not therefore, except in special circumstances, acquire automatic British citizenship but may become a British citizen by registration. Registration will, depending on the circumstances, give one or other of the two types of citizenship, and if it is that of a British citizen by descent, it must be made within twelve months of birth. Exceptions to this rule are children one of whose parents, although a British citizen by descent, was employed out of (but recruited in) the UK in certain UK government or EEC services; such children born out of the UK will acquire automatic British citizenship otherwise than by descent as though their parent had had that citizenship.

The above is the briefest outline of the very complex rules in the British Nationality Act 1981. If you are going to have a child out of the UK, you would do well to get the leaflet *British citizenship. Children born abroad*, which is issued by the Home Office and is obtainable from Consulates, where you will be able to get the necessary elaboration to fit the terms of your case.

Quite apart from consideration of British citizenship problems, you should always register the birth of a child at your local British

198

Consulate, since this will provide you with a 'British' birth certificate which will be much more useful in the future than the Italian birth certificate you will obtain in any event.

Appendix C
Places of Worship

Church of England

Since many churches have restricted services and some are even in the process of closing down, do please telephone or make enquiries before banking on going to a particular service. Where the number has not been given in this list it will be found in the local telephone directory or, if that fails to elicit anything, via the local *municipio* or town hall. Telecom Italia seems to have no compunction in arbitrarily changing telephone numbers, but those given here are up to date as at August 1998. Almost certainly the entry will be under *Chiesa Anglicana* rather than the actual name of the church.

Alassio	Served from Genova. St. John's Church, via Cardellino, 21.
Assisi	Services at Chiesa di San Gregorio al Mango.
Bari	Served from Naples Christ Church.
Capri	Served from Naples Christ Church.
Florence (Firenze)	St. Mark's Church, via 1° Maggio 16, Tel: 055 29 47 64.
Genoa (Genova)	Church of the Holy Ghost, Piazza Marsala.
Milan (Milano)	All Saints' Church, via Solferino, 17, Tel: 02 655 2258.
Naples (Napoli)	Christ Church, via S. Pasquale a Chaiai, Tel: 081 41 18 42.
Palermo	Church of the Holy Cross, via Mariano Stabile.
Rome (Roma)	All Saints' Church, via del Babuino, Piazza di Spagna, Tel: 06 36 00 18 81.
San Remo	Served from Menton, France. All Saints' Church, Corso Matuzia, 1, Tel: 00 33 4 93 57 20 25
Siena	Served from Florence. St. Peter's Church.
Sorrento	Served from Naples in the summer only.
Taormina	St. George's Church, via Pindarello, 10.

Trieste	Served from Venice. Church of St. Anastasio, via Manna, 6.
Varese	Served from Milan. Evangelical Church, via Verdi.
Venice (Venezia)	St. George's Church, Campo San Vio 30123, Tel: 041 520 0571

Roman Catholic

The following are English-speaking Roman Catholic churches in Rome. Many are run by the Irish. In many large cities, such as Milan, Venice and Florence, confessions can be heard in English and there are usually notices to this effect on the notice board just inside the church.

Sant'Agata dei Goti, via Mazzarino
San Clement, via San Giovanni in Laterano
St. Patrick's Church, via Boncompagni
San Silvestro, Piazza San Silvestro
Sam Tommaso di Canterbury, via Monserrato

Church of Scotland

| Rome (Roma) | St. Andrew's Church, via XX Settembre. |

American Episcopal Church

| Rome (Roma) | St. Paul's Church, via Napoli, 58. |
| Florence (Firenze) | St. James's Church, via Bernardo Rucellai, 13. |

Synagogues

To contact any synagogue or Rabbi you should look under the entry: Comunita Ebraica di——. The telephone numbers given here are up to date as at August 1998.

| Alessandria | via Milano, 5/7 Tel: 0131 26 22 24 |
| Ancona | via Manfredo Fanti, 2bs Tel: 071 20 26 38 |

Casale Monferrato	Vicolo Salomone Olper, 44
	Tel: 0142 71807
Ferrara	via Mazzini, 95
	Tel: 0532 24 70 04
Florence (Firenze)	via Farini, 4
Genoa (Genova)	via G. Bertora, 6
	Tel: 010 846 1006 (includes fax)
Leghorn (Livorno)	via del Tempio, 3
	Tel: 0586 89 62 90
Mantua (Mantova)	via G. Govim, 11
Merano	via Schiller, 14
	Tel: 0473 23 49 99
Milan (Milano)	via Guastella, 19
	Tel: 02 483 02806
Modena	Piazza Mazzini
	Tel: 059 22 39 78
Naples (Napoli)	via Cappella Vecchia, 31
	Tel: 081 764 3480
Padua (Padova)	via San Maratino e Solferino, 5
	Tel: 049 875 1106
Parma	vicolo Cervi, 4
	Tel: 0521 20 02 43
Pisa	via Palestro, 24
	Tel: 050 54 25 80
Rome (Roma)	Ashkenazi: Lungotevere Cenci, 24
	Tel: 06 687 5051
	Sephardi: via Catalena
Turin (Torino)	Piazzetta Primo Levi, 12
	(formerly via San Pio, 12)
	Tel: 011 65 85 85
Trieste	via San Francesco, 18
	Tel: 040 37 14 66
Venice (Venezia)	Ghetto Vecchio, 1189
	Tel: 041 71 51 18
	Ghetto Nuovo, 2899
	Tel: 041 71 50 12
Verona	via Portici, 3
	Tel: 045 800 7112

Appendix D
Dangers

Mosquitoes

Italian *Zanzara* – *pl. Zanzare*. The best thing is to prevent their entry – a counsel of perfection, but mosquito screens, known as *zanzariere*, pastilles which are burned at night by plugging in an inexpensive appliance to any electric socket, and ointments to protect the skin all help. Babies and small children can safely be protected by an ointment known as *Autan*. There are those who disapprove of breathing in chemicals for eight hours on end, as is the case with burning pastilles, but taken overall, it is probably less dangerous than getting bitten to bits each night. The appliance is known as a *Zanzarefuge*.

Cover all rain-water tanks etc. (swimming-pools, because of the chemicals used to clean them, do not attract mosquitoes) to avoid breeding grounds for these insects.

Once bitten, put on any of the following ointments obtainable from an Italian chemist – *Ultralan, Ecoval* or *Fargan*, which will reduce the itching and reduce the swelling.

Mosquitoes in Italy are not malarial.

Vipers

It is most unusual for people to be bitten by vipers or any other of the very few poisonous snakes found in Europe, and this minimal risk is even further lessened by keeping one's garden free of large clumps of undergrowth. However, domestic animals in the country sometimes do get bitten. In any event, you should always have anti-venin in your refrigerator. The pack comes complete with a syringe and is good for twelve to eighteen months. Thereafter you should buy a new pack. Even old anti-venin is better than none but, of course, less potent in its neutralizing action. This anti-venin is known in Italian as *Serio Antifidico Purificato Tetravalente* and neutralizes the poison of the *Vipera aspis*, *Berus* and *Ammodytes*, which are the only poisonous snakes in Europe. The 5 ml syringe comes ready for use. If you can inject it within twenty minutes of the bite, do so at or as near as possible to the site of the wound. After a greater lapse of time, it can be injected anywhere in the body but the lower abdomen is the best place. Irrespective of the size of the person or animal, you inject the whole 5 ml dose. Then get the patient to a doctor or vet as soon as possible, taking with you the empty syringe to show him the dosage you have injected. The serum can be kept out of a refrigerator for about eight weeks provided it is kept in the shade and at a temperature of less than 25°C (77°F) but after such a lapse of time it should be thrown away and a new supply bought.

On no account cut or cauterize a snake bite – that only compounds the problem. If you understand the principle of the tourniquet, a moderately tied one can retard the diffusion of the poison but an overtight tourniquet, or one which is not for a few moments every five or so minutes slackened off, can be as danger-ous as the bite itself.

Dogs and cats which are bitten by vipers and which survive as a result of an injection of anti-venin become very subdued and off their food for several weeks after the event.

People who are allergic to anti-tetanus injections or who are asthmatic or are liable to skin rashes may react badly to anti-venin, and it could be worth their while undergoing a desensitization treat-ment during the winter. This is something to be discussed with one's doctor.

Scorpions

Italian *Scorpioni*. Frightening but harmless, scorpions tend to live under stones, tubs etc, so care is needed when moving piles of stones or heaps of rubbish. The Italian scorpion, *Euroscopius itali-cus*, is equipped with a poison sac in its tail. One of the most common ways of being stung is to put on a shoe without first look-ing inside. Except for the extremely sensitive, a scorpion sting can be compared with that of a wasp or at worst a hornet. It can be very painful and causes swelling and a numbness verging on local paral-ysis but the effects disappear within an hour or so. Disinfect the area and apply liberally any anti-histamine ointment such as the

Italian *Trimenton* or *Polaramine* and take an analgesic by mouth such as aspirin, paracetamol or the Italian *Novalgina*. Take also plenty of fluids but not alcohol.

Dogs are very sensitive to scorpion poison but it is not likely that any lasting harm will be done. Cats play with scorpions and tend to get stung from time to time. The only answer is to spray weekly all likely hide-outs and crevices with a specific spray. Bayer and Ciba both do a spray against insects which have a thick carapace, and most anti-ant formulae will also work against scorpions.

Wasp, Bee and Hornet Stings

Italian *Punture di vespa, di ape e di calabrone*. The most common time to get stung by a bee or wasp is in the late autumn when they are sleepy or even half-dead and unsuspectingly you put your hand or foot on one. The first thing is to remove the sting. Particularly in the case of a bee sting, do not try to remove it with tweezers because you will simply be compressing the poison sac deeper into the wound. The sting is barbed and there are muscles in the poison sac which continue to pump in poison for anything up to a quarter of an hour. The best method is to take a small tea or dessert knife (or even use your thumbnail) and scrape back the sting *in the direction in which it entered*. This requires quite a bit of pressure on a very sore place. Cover the area liberally with an anti-histamine cream. The swelling and itching can last a couple of days and are usually more irritating than the sting itself. Again, unless you are one of those rare ultra-sensitive persons, a bee or wasp sting should do no harm. Hornets should be treated as bigger wasps; their stings are more painful but potentially no more dangerous.

Jellyfish

Italian *Medusa*. Very painful and the first thing to do is to keep the person who has been stung out of the sun. Anti-histamines by mouth as well as on the body if the damage is widespread will help, and get medical attention if necessary. As jellyfish poison is largely nullified by application of heat, it is a good idea to get the patient into a hot bath – though at the seaside this is not very easy. Local application of hot cloths to the affected part can help. *Trimenton* and *Polaramine* are both good and are available both in ointment form and for oral use.

Weever Fish

Italian *Tracina*. It has a spine on both the gill cover and the dorsal fin which can inflict a painful wound. The venom is not considered dangerous except to the most sensitive and can usually be neutralized by immersing the damaged part in very hot water or by using a hot compress. Some swelling is to be expected. It is best to consult a doctor.

Moray Eel

Italian *Murena*. Those who go underwater fishing run a slight risk of being bitten by this fish but not if they keep away from underwater caves. In the Mediterranean, this bite is never fatal, but in addition to the bite itself, poison is also injected. You should allow the patient to bleed a bit to ensure that some of the venom runs out. Thereafter, urgent medical attention is required, preferably in a hospital if there are any breathing difficulties. The pain is intense, and often analgesics such as Nisidina or Novalgina or even morphia are given by the injection but analgesics taken orally will also help to a certain extent.

Harvest Mites

It is strange that the harvest mite, or chigger as it is known in the United States, has not featured in this line-up of dangers before this edition since many fair-haired people suffer horribly from its bites in late summer and early autumn. It is a small insect, related to spiders (as are all mites and ticks), barely visible to the naked eye (indeed, I have never once seen the offender), and it lives in grassy places or in the undergrowth. When biting, it appears to inject a certain amount of local anaesthetic so that the bite is small and at first not at all painful. However, the poison it injects must be terribly potent given the pain and damage it eventually does. The limb, for it is usually a limb, swells up within 24 hours and over a period of three or four days becomes extremely painful. This condition appears to have no palliatives or cures once this stage has been reached and, therefore, it is essential to remove the poison as soon as possible. (See below for the method.)

Harvest mites or chiggers hate citronella, Autan and most of the commercial insect repellents so it is common sense to use them. They bite through nylon stockings or tights. Apparently they do not transport any disease through their bite other than localized swelling and intense pain.

Be warned, they can lodge in clothing and if you have been badly bitten remove everything and wash yourself and the clothing well. Also they lodge in bedding, particularly in sleeping bags.

There is on the market in all countries which have problems with snakes, scorpions and similar charmers, a small gadget for siphoning out the poison which can prove extremely useful. For instance, a hornet sting once extracted together with the poison becomes no more trouble than a mosquito bite. These kits are common in France and available in virtually every chemist. They are called *aspivenin*. Not so in Italy and you will have to search for it. It is known as an *aspira-veleno* and comes, usually, with three or four sizes of sucker and a large syringe. With certain bites it is as well to make the wound bleed, a little only, in order to ensure the poison is coming out. Allow at least one minute for such things as hornet stings, harvest-mite bites and scorpion stings. The longer you can siphon the better, though never exceed more than three or four minutes. Usually the box of rigid plastic has a relief design of a scorpion, a serpent, a wasp and a spider. I have never used it for weever-fish damage and have never come across a moray eel, but I imagine it would work in such cases also. *What it will not do is help with jellyfish stings; indeed it may exacerbate the problem.* It is absolutely invaluable for those who have been bitten by harvest mites or chiggers. Dark-haired and olive-complexioned people tend to be of little interest to harvest mites. It's the red-heads and Scandinavian blondes they are after.

Appendix E
Anti-poison Centres

If you think you have been accidentally poisoned or if your child has licked the top of a pot of lead paint (children do incredible things, as do small puppies and kittens), you should immediately contact the local hospital or the Red Cross for an ambulance (or the nearest vet if this is more appropriate). Most doctors and vets in Italy have paging machines. Alternatively, if there is a doctor nearby, you should contact him. In any event take the offending item with you so they can see what they have to work against.

In the case of a viper bite use anti-venin which you should always have in your refrigerator – then call the doctor and show him the anti-venin you have injected. If necessary, the doctor will put you in contact with the local anti-poison centre. Unfortunately, there are few of these and most are in the big cities. If all else fails, contact the nearest centre yourself. The telephone numbers are given in local telephone directories and are free. Where there is no proper anti-poison centre, the local hospital will usually have someone on duty who can help.

Casena (Province of Forlì)
Ospedale Maurizio Bufalini,
viale Ghirotti, 286,
Cesena

Genoa/Genova
Ospedali Civili di Genova,
San Martino,
Via Benedetto XV,
Genova 10

la Spezia
Ospedale Civile della Spezia,
Sant'Andrea, Servizio Rianimazione,
la Spezia

Lecce
Ospedale Generale Regionale,
Vito Fazzi,
Piazzetta Bottazzi, 6,
Lecce

Messina
Università di Messina
Facoltà di Farmacia,
Villagio Annunziata,
Messina

Milan/Milano
Ospedale Miguarda,
Cà Grande,
Centro Antiveleni,
Piazza Ospedale Maggiore, 3,
Milano

Naples/Napoli
Ospedali Riuniti,
Centro Anativeleni,
via Cardarelli, 9.

Padua/Padova
Università di Padova,
Istitute di Farmacologia – Centro Antiveleni,
Largo Egidio Meneghetti, 2,
Padova

Rome/Roma
Università Cattolica S. Cuore,
Centro Antiveleni,
Largo A. Gemelli, 8,
Roma

Università di Roma,
Policlinico Umberto 1,
viale del Policlinico,
Roma

Turin/Torino
Università di Torino,
Centro Antiveleni,
Corso Polonia 14,
Torino

Trieste
Istituto per l'Infanzia,
via dell'Istria, 65/1,
Trieste

Vicenza (Serves Provinces of Venice, Vicenza, Treviso,
  Pordenone, Verone and Belluno)
Ospedale Civile,
Dipart. Rianimazione. Servizio Informazione
  Tossicologica,
Vicenza

Appendix F
Broadcasting

Anyone who has lived abroad, for even a short period, quickly realizes that the dissemination of news as done by the BBC World Service is probably second to none.

British newspapers, excellent as they may be, are expensive abroad, often arrive late and usually are obtainable only in large towns. Therefore, British broadcasting and television become all the more precious, particularly after seeing what is on offer locally.

Listening to the BBC overseas service is the cheapest way of keeping in touch with Great Britain. The BBC World Service on television tends to be considerably less parochial and far more international, to the point where one becomes better informed about Ghana or Tibet than about the Thames Valley.

You do not need to invest in an expensive radio but it is as well to know a few basic facts. A small portable radio will do; it should show wavelengths in metres and in kHz or mHz; your set should cover at least 16–29 metres or 6–18 mHz as this will enable you to receive broadcasts not only from the BBC but also from other countries' radio stations. Choose a receiver which is easy to tune with a broad tuning-scale and, if possible, at least one bandspread for shortwave. Avoid in particular a receiver which has the whole range mentioned above packed into one single scale only, since the best reception often requires very fine tuning.

Sets with these facilities are easy to come by and are relatively inexpensive. Most have telescopic aerials which are usually sufficient, but these can be extended by adding a piece of wire which you then wrap round a kitchen-towel cardboard roll and hang the rest of the wire out of the window. Usually this is only necessary in large blocks of flats with a great deal of steel in their construction.

By day, reception is best on higher frequencies 15–21 mHz and at night the lower frequencies are best around 6–7 mHz. At dusk and dawn, the middle bands are best 9–11 mHz. If you have problems it is best to get in touch with the overseas service of the BBC at Bush House, London WC2 4PH.

The BBC also have a World Service television channel which is principally for news and information programmes though there are occasional 'specials'. This is not an encrypted service and it costs nothing beyond getting the correct box to decode it. The same decoder however unlocks BBC Prime which is devoted to mostly less than 10-year-old comedy programmes and documentaries. This is quite an achievement when one considers Sky Broadcasting puts out Morecambe and Wise shows made in 1973! This service is encrypted and you pay a subscription to the BBC for it. Details from Bush House as above.

Because of copyright reasons Sky Broadcasting, which includes Granada TV, cannot broadcast abroad except for the news and related programmes which are not encrypted. There are many channels all of which are open to those with an address in the UK and a British bank account from which BSkyB can be paid direct each month. There are many who have Sky Broadcasting in Italy but it is illegal. If you are caught by Sky with one of their cards abroad it is said they can zap it from their satellite to ensure you will no longer see their programmes.

For those living near the French border it is best to have a television which can get both the PAL and Secam systems. Italy is on the same standard as the UK and most of Europe. The same goes for French videos – they will be black and white if you do not have a dual standard television.

Italian television leaves a great deal to be desired since, for many years, this is all they have had; most seem content with the mixture of quiz games, old American soaps, awful musical shows and similar rubbish. Occasionally there are good programmes but they are rare. The impresario and one-time Prime Minister of Italy, Silvio Berlusconi, owns three private TV stations and commands 50 per cent of Italy's viewing every evening, which is rather frightening when you consider his political aspirations.

The less said about Italian radio the better. It seems to be designed for less intelligent housewives, and there is far too much advertising.

The main Italian state television stations are:

RAI Uno – Controlled more or less by the Christian Democrats, though this is played down now. Has the best news – 8 p.m. is the main news time.

RAI Due – controlled by the Socialists.

RAI Tre   – controlled by what was the former Communist Party.
It has the best music programmes.

It is not that any of these stations is overtly political; it is simply
another area for political preferment; to work in one of these
stations, even as a secretary, you need to have party affiliations.
    How very different from the BBC or even Sky.

Appendix G
Metric Equivalents

Length

1 cm = 0.394 inches
1 m = 39.5 inches or 3.28 feet or 1.094 yards
1 km = 0.621 miles

1 inch = 2.54 cm
1 foot = 30.48 cm
1 yard = 91.4 cm
1 mile = 1.690 km

kilometre = *chilometro*
inch   = *pollice*, pl. *pollici*
foot   = *piede*, pl. *piedi*
yard   = *iarda*, pl. *iarde*
mile   = *miglio*, pl. *miglia*

Capacity

1 litre (*litro*) = 1.760 pints or 0.88 quarts or 0.22 gallons
1 pint   = 0.568 *litri*
1 quart   = 1.136 *litri*
1 gallon   = 4.546 *litri*
1 cubic metre = 1,000 litres
pint   = *pinta*, pl. *pinte*
quart   = *quarto*, pl. *quarti*
gallon   = *gallone*, pl. *galloni*

Weight

100 gr   = 3.5 oz = 1 *etto*, pl. *etti*
250 gr   = 8.75 oz
500 gr   = 1lb 1½ oz
1 kilo   = 2.205 lbs
1 metric ton = 1,000 kilos = 0.984 long tons

214

1 oz	= 28.35 gr
1 lb	= 454 gr
1 cwt	= 50.802 kilos
1 long ton	= 1.016 metric tons

ounce	= *oncia*, pl. *oncie*
pound	= *libbra*, pl. *libbre*

The Italians have no word for the avoirdupois 'stone' and are incapable of understanding the reason for its use.

Surface

1 sq. m	= 10.76 sq. feet = 1.19 sq. yards
1 hectare	= 2.47 acres
1 sq. foot	= 0.093 sq. m.
1 sq. yard	= 0.836 sq. m.
1 acre	= 0.405 hectares
hectare	= *ettaro*, pl. *ettari*

Volume

1 cu. cm	= 0.06 cu. inches
1 cu. m.	= 35.32 cu. feet = 1.131 cu. yards
1 cu. inch	= 16.39 cu. cms
1 cu. foot	= 0.028 cu. m.
1 cu. yard	= 0.764 cu. m.

Temperature (approximate conversions)

F	C	
32	0	
40	5	
50	10	
60	16	
90	32	
98.4	37.6	body temperature
100	38	
212	100	

C	F
0	32
5	41
10	50

15	59
20	64
25	77
30	86
35	94
37.6	98.4 body temperature
40	104
100	212

Oven Temperatures

Most gas ovens are supplied with a temperature chart which gives equivalent for the dial numbers. Electric ovens are often fan-assisted, and usually you can cook at a slightly lower temperature and for less time than with a conventional electric cooker. The Italians, like the Spaniards, tend to cook at hotter temperatures than the rest of Europe. Solid-fuel cookers are uncommon in Italy though by no means unknown. An 'Aga' is a status symbol.

240–300 F = 115–150°C   310–375 F = 155–195°C
380–410 F = 195–210°C   420–450 F = 215–235°C
450–500 F = 235–255°C

Shoes and Clothes

Shoe sizes vary so much in Italy from maker to maker that one person can have a spread of 1½ sizes or three sizes over various ranges. Generally sizes are in centimetres but British sizes are also used. However, all Italian shoe shops will measure your feet before trying on shoes. Sizing in ladies' clothes is different in Italy from other European countries. The better the maker, the more generously cut the garment, but the following is a rough guide.

UK	USA	Italy
8	6	40
10	8	42
12	10	44
14	12	46
16	14	48
18	16	50
20	18	52

Shirt sizes (collars) are as follows:

UK and USA	Italy
14	36
14½	37
15	38
15½	39
16	40
16½	41
17	42

Appendix H
Useful Telephone Numbers

113 – EMERGENCIES: Equivalent to a 999 call; you state the service you need.

112 – CARABINIERI: Be circumspect about calling them on this number for an accident since they do not usually come out unless there are injuries. On the other hand this is a better number to call than 113 since they will ensure you get the right service for your particular emergency.

12 – DIRECTORY ENQUIRIES (ITALY ONLY): This service will provide you with telephone numbers and postal codes of telephone subscribers. You state first the city or province and town then the name and address.

1412 – A little known service: if you have a telephone number, you can ring this number and, following their instructions, obtain the subscribers' name, address and post code.

182 – TELEPHONE ENGINEERS: *Servizio di Guasto*. You use this number when there is a breakdown, obviously from somebody else's number. Follow the instructions given and your breakdown is automatically registered.

183 – TELEPHONE ENGINEERS: For faxes and other similar equipment which are under a maintenance contract with Telecom Italia.

115 – FIRE BRIGADE: *Vigili di Fuoco*

116 – BREAKDOWN SERVICE ON ROADS AND MOTOR-WAYS: mostly run by ACI.

117 – GUARDIA DI FINANZIA: only in Italy would one want to call the Tax Police and Customs urgently.

118 – HEALTH EMERGENCIES: such as dangerous spillage after an accident, dangerous fires, and drownings not already reported to the *carabinieri*.

110 – OPENING HOURS: Of museums, galleries, shops and religious services in many cities. Its cost is minimal.

114 – ALARM CALL: Using the 24-hour clock, you simply key in the four digits of the hour you wish to be wakened. The rest is done automatically.

119 – SERVIZIO TIM: TIM stands for Telecom Italia Mobile and concerns mobile telephones which you can have under contract with this arm of TI. They will also deal with problems of service, breakdown and can even be contacted from abroad by dialling 00 39 3399 119. It is operational 24 hours a day and costs the price of an ordinary or international mobile telephone call.

161 – SPEAKING CLOCK (in Italian).

186 – TELEGRAM SERVICE: It costs around 1,000 to 2,000 lire extra to dictate a telegram (in more or less any common language) plus the cost of the telegram itself. This cost is automatically debited to the subscriber so if it is not your telephone you will have to make your peace with this person. The same number for national and international telegrams.

187 – This is a free line to request a telephone line, a second telephone line, fax line or fax etc.

170 – BOOKING A CALL (ABROAD): This is considerably more expensive than direct dialling but useful if you want to telephone somewhere which does not have an international dialling code.

176 – Furnishes information on foreign telephone numbers, worldwide, 24 hours a day and politely. Each search is debited at 6 scatti.

1795 – Among other things, does reverse-charge calls, but nationally only. If you want to know the cost and duration of such a call this is the number to dial. Operates 24 hours a day.

188 – CUSTOMER COMPLAINTS: A number to ring when you want to complain about your telephone bill and/or certain calls. Not all Italy has electronic exchanges and therefore not everyone can have a detailed bill. However, this is becoming more and more common. Although the service is free it only functions during normal Italian office hours (8.30–12.00 & 2.30–4.30 p.m.).

16488 – HELPLINE: For when you cannot for a variety of reasons pay your telephone bill on time. You or an Italian-speaking friend explain the reasons and offer a date or method of payment and get a response – not necessarily what you had hoped for.

1331 – If you are about to excavate, re-design your garden or entrance and you think there may be telephone wires underneath the ground then telephone this number. You should be armed with accurate plans of the land concerned before calling this number. The service is free.

197 – URGENT CALLS: This is the number you ring when you have not succeeded in obtaining a number. You dial 197 then on the spoken request you dial your wanted number without hanging up. Your correspondent's call is interrupted by TI telling him or her there is an urgent call. The results are not always what you want but the service can be useful.

19696 – FREE HELPLINE FOR CHILDREN: Whenever I have called to find out what exactly it is, the number is either engaged or the woman's voice is so soft you can't hear what she is saying. At least it's free. The service is called Telefono Azurro.

Appendix I
The Media

The two most important newspapers in Italy, both of world renown, are *Corriere della Sera* (which has both a morning and evening edition) and *La Stampa*. The latter is partially owned and certainly controlled by the Agnelli family of Fiat fame. There is an evening edition called *Stampa Sera*. This paper is probably of better quality than the former but, as with so much in Italy, it is also a question of politics. Also, because of some rather strange payment rules, journalists are obliged to move around from paper to paper and magazine to magazine in order to get salary increases. Their readers often follow them.

Other famous newspapers are: *Il Giornale* which is probably the most intelligent right-wing paper at a national level; at the other end of the scale is *l'Unità* which is the mouthpiece of the Communist Party (known as *Il Partito Democratico della Sinistrà*), *la Repubblica* which is an independent national daily, *la Padania* which is the mouthpiece of Lega Nord and its leader Umberto Bossi and offers morning balm for all northerners who believe Italy should be split in two. Of the more local papers there are: *Il Gazzettino* (Venice and the Veneto), *Il Mattino* (Naples and Campania), *La Nazione* (Florence, Tuscany), *Il Secolo XIX* (Genoa, Liguria and Southern Piedmont), *l'Osservatore Romano* (the Vatican paper), and *Il Messagero* (very left-wing and Roman). Perhaps the most interestingly named paper is *Il Resto di Carlino* of Bologna, which may sound amateurish but isn't. A *carlino* is a French pug.

There must be a greater number of rubbishy magazines on sale in Italy than anywhere else in the world – and they also import the same type of thing from France, Germany, Austria and America. They can easily be recognized not only by the come-hither photograph on the front cover but by the inner contents of supposition, scandal and soft porn. There is little to choose between any of them.

There are, however, some excellent magazines on sale in Italy including Italian editions of *House and Garden*, *Vogue* and *Architectural Digest*. Mondadori produce *l'Airone* and *Gardenia* which is the only proper gardening magazine in the whole of Italy, and *Gente* Magazine also do travel and other specialist magazines from time to time. *Dimore/Homes & Villas of Italy* is a bi-lingual magazine which features prestigious houses and apartments for sale and to let. It is laughingly easy to distinguish the good from the rubbish.

Books are expensive in Italy, the main reason being that not a great number of people speak Italian compared with English, Russian, Spanish and Portuguese. Moreover, the Italians in general are not great readers. The late Peter Nichols, who was a British journalist and correspondent married to an Italian, once reported hearing an Italian woman saying, 'No I haven't read the book but a friend of mine read me the review over the telephone.'

Only the very best Italian authors are translated into English such as Primo Levi, Giorgio Bassani and Umberto Eco; asking for English versions of Italians will ensure good reading. Alas, this is not the case the other way round. Some truly terrible 'airport' books are translated into Italian and a lot of the good stuff coming from England remains untranslated. Muriel Spark, who won the Italia Prize, has many of her books not yet translated, as have authors like Elizabeth Jane Howard, Bill Bryson, Martin Amis or even Nancy Mitford. Danielle Steele and Catherine Cookson are widely available in Italian, though what an Italian from Venice makes of life in the north-east of England I cannot imagine.

Appendix J
The Provinces of Italy and Their Abbreviations

AG = Agrigento
AL = Alessandria
AV = Avellino
AN = Ancona
AO = Aosta
AR = Arezzo
AP = Ascoli Piceno
AT = Asti
BA = Bari
BL = Belluno
BN = Benevento
BG = Bergamo
BI = Biella
BO = Bologna
BZ = Bolzano
BS = Brescia
BR = Brindisi
CA = Cagliari
CL = Caltanisetta
CB = Campobasso
CE = Caserta
CT = Catania
CZ = Catanzaro
CH = Chieti
CO = Como
CS = Cosenza
CR = Cremona
KR = Crotone
CN = Cuneo
EN = Enna

FE = Ferrara
FI = Firenze (Florence)
FG = Foggia
FO = Forli
FR = Frosinone
GE = Genova (Genoa)
GO = Gorizia
GR = Grosseto
IM = Imperia
IS = Isernia
AQ = l'Aquila
SP = la Spezia
LT = Latina
LE = Lecce
LC = Lecco
LI = Livorno
LO = Lodi
LU = Lucca
MC = Macerata
MN = Mantova
MS = Massa Carrara
MT = Matera
ME = Messina
MI = Milano
MO = Modena
NA = Napoli (Naples)
NO = Novara
NU = Nuoro
OR = Oristano
PD = Padova (Padua)

PA	= Palermo	SS	= Sassari
PR	= Parma	SV	= Savona
PV	= Pavia	SI	= Siena
PG	= Perugia	SR	= Siracusa
PS	= Pesaro & Urbino	SO	= Sondrio
PE	= Pescara	TA	= Taranto
PC	= Piacenza	TE	= Teramo
PI	= Pisa	TR	= Terni
PT	= Pistoia	TO	= Torino (Turin)
PN	= Pordenone	TP	= Trapani
PZ	= Potenza	TN	= Trento
PO	= Prato	TV	= Treviso
RA	= Ragusa	TS	= Trieste
RV	= Ravenna	UD	= Udine
RC	= Reggio Calabria	VA	= Varese
RE	= Reggio Emilia	VE	= Venezia (Venice)
RI	= Rieti	VB	= Verbania-Cusio-Ossola
RN	= Rimini	VC	= Vercelli
ROMA (Rome)		VV	= Vibo Valentia
RO	= Rovigo	VI	= Vicenza
SA	= Salerno	VT	= Viterbo

Seven new provinces have been created since the last edition of this book. They are Lodi and Lecco in Lombardy, Vibo Valentia and Crotone in Calabria (where they ran out of suitable 'C's so have used the letters KR), the conurbation of Verbania-Cusio-Ossolo extracted from Novara province and Biella (both in Piemonte), and Prato in Tuscany. The cities of Rome and Milan each count as a separate province, each having a further surrounding province.

Appendix K
Spelling

Sometimes when spelling out your name to Italians you are simply not understood. Below is a recognized Italian 'alphabet' which can prove invaluable when spelling out a name like Strachan or Woodward.

A	Ancona
B	Bologna
C	Como
D	Domodossola
E	Empoli
F	Firenze
G	Genova
H	Hotel (pronounced: *Otell*)
I	Imola
J	Jesolo (pronounced: Ee-*ess*-olo)
K	Kursaal
L	Livorno
M	Milano
N	Napoli
O	Otranto
P	Palermo
Q	Quarto
R	Roma
S	Savona
T	Torino
U	Udine (pronounced: Ooh-*di*-nay)
V	Venezia
W	Washington
X	Icks (pronounced ee-cks)
Y	York (or ipsilon)
Z	Zara

Thus the name Woodward is spelt out Washington – Otranto – Otranto – Domodossola – Washington – Ancona – Roma – Domodossola and pronounced in Italian Voodvord. But the Italians are very amenable to learning the proper (and foreign to them) pronunciation of foreign names.

Appendix L
Writing a Cheque

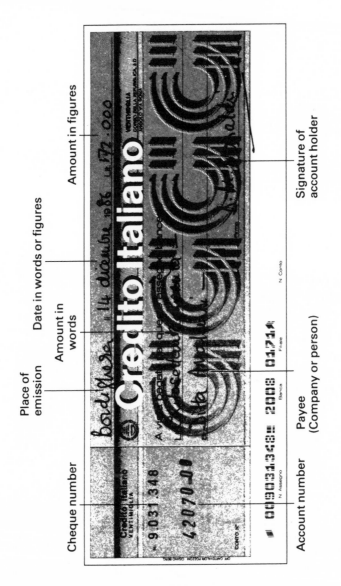

Cheque number

Place of emission

Amount in words

Date in words or figures

Amount in figures

Payee (Company or person)

Account number

Signature of account holder

228

Living in Italy

Filling Out a Paying-in Slip

Amount of cash and in what denomination

A/c number

A/c holder

Cheque – where drawn and at what bank

Total coin

Total cash

Cheques, money orders etc

Date

Signature of payee

Amount paid in

This part is receipt from Cashier of the Bank

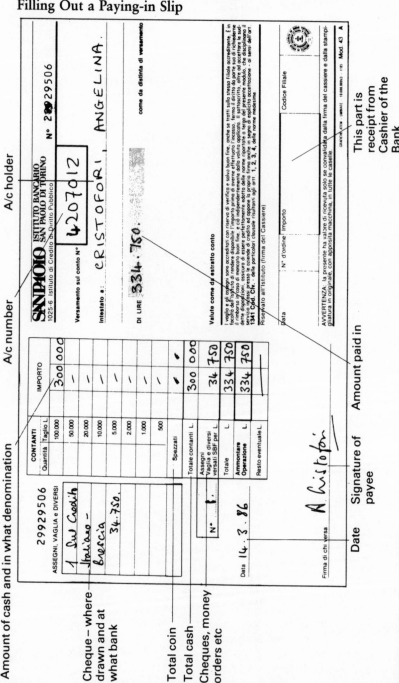

Appendix M
Principal Airports

The following list shows the principal airports with their method of transport to and distance from the town centre and the area served by each airport.

Alghero-Sassari (Fertilia): Bus. 13 km. North and central Sardinia.

Ancona (Falconara): Bus. 18 km. Provinces of Ancona, Macerata, Ascoli Piceno, Pesaro and the Republic of San Marino.

Bari (Palese): Bus. 12 km. Provinces of Bari and Taranto. Also small airport at Brindisi.

Bergamo (Orio Al Serio): Bus. 5 km. Provinces of Bergamo, Brescia and the Valtellina.

Bologna (G. Marconi): Bus. 6 km. Emilia Romagna, Ferrara etc.

Cagliari (Elmas): Bus. 7 km. Southern Sardinia.

Catania (Fontanarossa): Town bus. 7 km. Eastern Sicily.

Genoa/Genova (Cristoforo Colombo): Town bus. 7 km. Provinces of Genoa, Savona, Imperia, Italian Riviera to La Spezia and southern Piemonte.

Lamezia Terme (S. Eufemia): Taxi. 40 km. Calabria, Cozenza and coastal resorts to Reggio Calabria.

Lampedusa: Taxi. 1 km. Lampedusa.

Milan/Milano (Linate): Bus. 10 km.

Milan/Milano (Malapensa): Bus. 46 km.

These two airports serve the Provinces of Milano, Varese, Como, Novara, Vercelli, Piacenza, Parma, Pavia, Bergamo and the Lakes.

Naples/Napoli (Capodichino): Town bus. 7 km. The coast from Terracina to Salerno. Provinces of Napoli, Avellino, Potenza, Salerno, Ischia.

Olbia (Costa Smeralda): Taxi. 6 km. Costa Smeralda and north-eastern Sardinia.

Palermo (Punta Raisi): Bus. 32 km. North and west Sicily.

Pantelleria: Bus. 4 km. Pantelleria.

Pescara (Liberi): Taxi. 6 km. Provinces of Pescara, Chieti, L'Aquila and Ascoli Piceno.

Pisa (G. Galilei): Bus to Pisa (2 km). Train and bus to Florence (82
  km). Provinces of Pisa, Firenze, Siena, Pistoia, Lucca, Livorno
  and Elba.

Reggio Calabria (Tito Minniti): Taxi 5 km. Southern Calabria and
  toe of Italy.

Rimini (Miramare): Town bus. 6 km. Provinces of Rimini, Forlì,
  Urbino and Republic of San Marino.

Rome/Roma (L. da Vinci): Bus. 35 km. Rome and Provinces of
  Latina, Frosinone, Viterbo, Terni, Rieti etc.

Trapani (Sen. V. Florio): Bus. 16 km. West Sicily.

Trieste (Ronchi dei Legionari): Bus. 32 km. Extreme east of Italy.
  Region of Friuli-Venezia-Giulia.

Turin/Torino: Bus. 18 km. Provinces of Torino, Aosta, Vercelli,
  Novara, Asti, Alessandria and Cuneo.

Venice/Venezia (Marco Polo): Bus and water bus. 13 km. Provinces
  of Venezia, Vicenza, Verona, Treviso, Padova, Rovigo and the
  Julian and Carnic Alps, the Dolomites.

Appendix N

Useful Information for Newcomers to Italy

Government and Provincial Offices Most are closed in the afternoon and are normally open from 8 or 8.30 in the morning to the curious hour of 1.20 although there are exceptions. ACI keep to these hours but in the larger towns are also open in the afternoon after 3 p.m. At frontiers they are usually open from 8 a.m. to 8 p.m. Their number is 116 if you have a breakdown and are covered by them. In any event, even if you are not covered by them they or the *carabinieri* will steer you in the right direction. Their local office numbers appear in the relevant directory.

Public Holidays Remember that every town celebrates its own particular patron saint (such as Saint Ambrose in Milan) and all the banks and public offices, including the post office, are closed on its saint's day. Otherwise the main public holidays are:

1st January – New Year's Day
6th January – Epiphany or, for Italian children, *la Befana* who
    brings them presents.
Easter Monday, but *not* Good Friday.
1st May – as a sop to the Italian left.
15th August – *Ferragosta* the opening of the holiday season; also,
    the Assumption of the Virgin Mary.
1st November – All Saints' Day or *Ogni Santi* and everyone goes to
    the cemetery. Many Italians travel hundreds of miles to be with
    their family, both living and dead.
8th December – The Immaculate Conception of the Virgin Mary.
25th December – Christmas Day.
26th December – Saint Stephen's Day.

Post Offices Depending where you are they are either open all day from around 8 or 8.30 a.m. until 6 or 6.30 in the larger towns. In the country they close at 1.20 (and sometimes at noon) and at 11.30 a.m. on Saturdays.

Italian post offices run current accounts for their customers and this is amongst the cheapest banking available in Italy. Many bills are paid through these accounts and each transaction costs around 1,500 lire.

Money Apart from running a 'normal' bank account you can have a credit card which will allow you to get money out of a machine at the weekend, as will your British or foreign credit card. Do be careful, however, since not all cash dispensers accept international cards but seem to swallow anything they are doubtful about. Therefore, check carefully that the cash dispenser you are thinking of using with your British card is an international one.

Banks open from 8.30 or 9 a.m. until around 1 or 1.20 p.m. They open again in the afternoon for one or one and a half hours. This varies from town to town, province to province but occurs between 2.30 and 4 p.m. In high summer many banks are open on a Saturday morning, but this stops around October and does not begin again until May or early June. The computers are not usually linked up with the head office so transactions are limited to paying in and taking out cash.

Museums and Churches Opening times vary from province to province but most museums are closed on Mondays even in the holiday season. Usually they open from 10 a.m. until 12.30 or 1 p.m. There is a long lull in the afternoon and they re-open from around 3 or 4 until 6 or 7 p.m. The further south you get the more the siesta is recognized. Rather like Paris, some of the larger northern cities such as Genoa, Milan and even Venice shut their museums in August. The local tourist office should know which museums are closed and the opening hours of those which are not. Always ring before you go since it is irritating to travel a long distance only to find the place closed. Few museums are free and you should count on paying an entrance fee although, in theory, European Union citizens are entitled to free entrance to most museums, as are bona fide Italian residents whatever their nationality. An Italian Identity Card is the proof. Always ask about purchasing a block of tickets (*biglietti cumulativi*) which can cut the cost if you do have to pay. There are very few, if any, museums in Italy where photography is allowed due to the damaging effect of the flash.

Churches These are a prime target for thieves and a great deal of church 'swag' is illegally exported every year, so most are closed and the key needs to be sought from the sacristan or church offices. Large cathedrals are usually open from around 10 a.m. until lunchtime and then again in the afternoon from around 3 until last evening prayers. Unless you are attending a service you will frequently have to pay for entry. In any event, you will need to feed the light machines in order to see many of the statues and paintings. If you pretend you are attending a service, at least be sure there is one and that you arrive at the right time. You will be watched like a hawk throughout in order to make sure that you are not 'telling a lie in the House of God', as I once heard.

If visiting Ravenna, which is to be highly recommended for those with an interest in history going back to Byzantine times and in the finest mosaics anywhere, it is as well to remember that the famous Pinetum is closed in the summer 'fire' season. Usually it is open from October to March.

Weights and Measures There are differences, although with clothing the various international sizes, particularly American and French are nearly always marked. It is with household items that one gets muddled. Wood, for instance, is sold by the *quintale*, which despite its appearance is 100 kilos. An *etto* is 100 grammes (plural *etti*), and this measurement is much used. Ten of these *etti* make a kilo, spelt *chilo* in Italian. When making calculations for heating purposes this is done in cubic metres arrived at by multiplying the metric area of the room by its height. More sensible really, since ceiling heights can vary greatly.

In plumbing, the Italians use the British or American inch (*pollice*) for diameters, taps etc. Old habits die hard.

Finally, foreigners find that the Italians change place names to such an extent that they are scarcely recognizable to the native. For instance Munich is Monaco in Baviera to differentiate it from the principality of Monaco. Marseilles becomes Marsiglia and Nice Nizza (though it was Italian in the last century). Some are not so obvious, Anversa for Antwerp, Basilea for Basle, Digione for Dijon, Ginevra for Geneva, Lipsia for Leipzig, Norimbergo for Nuremburg, Salisburgo for both Salisbury in England and Salzburg in Austria, Stoccarda for Stuttgart, Tolosa for Toulouse, Treviri for

Trier, Zagabria for Zagreb to name but a few. On the other hand, the English-speaking countries have managed to change the following Italian names: Florence, Genoa, Leghorn, Mantua, Milan, Naples, Padua, Sienna, Syracuse, Turin and Venice, so we should not complain!

Appendix O

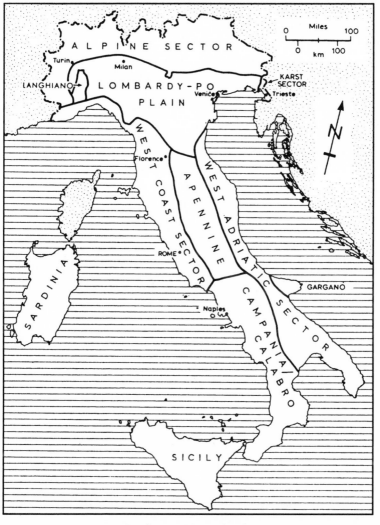

Gardening Map of Italy

Index

Jewish communities, 20, 41, 201
Jewellery, 75, 111, 161

Kilometric ticket, 47
Kingdom of Italy, 17
Kingdom of the Two Sicilies, 17

Land Registry, 83–7, 186
Language, Italian, 25
Lawns, 133
Lega Nord, 22, 23
Legittime, 73
Leichmaniosis, 30
Libretto di Famiglia, 59
Licenza (building permit), 186,
Life tenancy, 84
Lightning, 177
Location of property, 88
Lotteries, 56
Lycées, French 164

Maastricht, Treaty of, 7
Mafia, 22, 39, 53, 55, 56
Maiden name, 64, 98
Maintenance payments, 67
Mani pulite, 22, 185
Marble, 160
Marches, the, 39
Maremma, 33
Marriage
 annulment, 62, 67
 certificate, 84
 regimes, 65
Mediterranean Gardener, The, 139
Mediterranean Gardening, 139
Mentalità borbonica, 184
Metric equivalents, 214
Mildew, 185, 190
Milk, 142
Modena, 41
Monuments, 9
Moray eel, 206
Mortgages, 61–82, 108, 194
Mosquitoes, 203
Motor-rail, 48–9
Motorway tolls, 50–1
Museums, 232

Mushrooms, 142, 151
Mussolini, Alessandra, 121
Mussolini, Benito, 19, 20, 33, 46, 55, 138
Myrtle (herb), 152

Name change, 64
Napoleon III, 16–18
Nationality, 61, 198
'Ndrangheta, 53–6
Newspapers, 30, 221
Notaio, 8, 74–5, 77, 83
 fees, 84
Nurseries, list of, 139–40
Nurses, 121

Offences, driving, 102
Office hours, 235
Olive oil, 152–3
Omertà, 55–6
Operations, cost of, 121
Orient Express, 45

Padania, 23
Paints, 194
Papal States, 16, 19
Parliament, members of, 13
Parco Burcino, 135
Pasta, 144
Patente di guida, 98
Penalty clauses, 183
Pension fund contribution, 187
Pensioners, 122
Pensions, 123
Piedmont, 40
Pinetum (near Ravenna), 233
Plague, the Great, 16
Planning permission, 186–7
Polenta, 145
Post Office, 232
Power of Attorney, 83
Pratiche auto agent, 96
Private patients' plan, 122
Probate, 74
Proceeds of sale, 84
Promessi di vendità, 83
Property
 letting, 128

location, 34
prices (official and unofficial), 35, 82
purchase, documents for, 83
sale of, 84–5
Prosciutto crudo, 142, 147, 148
Provinces, list of, 13, 223
Proxy
 appointing, 92
 Italian form of, 92
Pubblicazioni Matrimoniali, 63

Quarantine, 29

Rab-dovante, 180
Rabies, 29
Radiators, 182
Rail, 21, 45–7
Red Cross, 17
Regime, marriage, 65
Regions and provinces, map of, 42
Registered letters, 93
Repatriation, 122
Rice (*riso arborio*), 142, 145
Right of way, 80
Roads, type of, 51
Risotto, 145
Rogito, 83
Romanesque architecture, 41
Roses, 131
Rubbish disposal, 85, 177
Rugosas (in Tuscany), 137

Salami, 149
Sardinia, 157
Savoy, House of, 17
Scandal, international, 164
Schools
 Roman Catholic, 163
 State, 163
 types of, 163, 165, 166
 UK, 166
Scorpions, 204
Season tickets, 47
Seat belts, 102